The Muvipix.com Guide to CyberLink PowerDirector 14 Ultimate

Steve Grisetti

The fun, easy, powerful way to make great-looking movies on your personal computer.

About Muvipix.com

Muvipix.com was created to offer support and community to amateur and semi-professional videomakers. Registration is free, and that gets you access to the world's friendliest, most helpful forum and lots of ad-free space for displaying your work. On the products page, you'll find dozens of free tips, tutorials, motion backgrounds, DVD templates, sound effects, royalty-free music and stock video clips. For a small annual subscription fee that we use to keep the site running, you'll have unlimited downloads from the ever-growing library of support materials and media.

We invite you to drop by and visit our thriving community. It costs absolutely nothing – and we'd love to have you join the neighborhood!

http://Muvipix.com

About the author

Steve Grisetti holds a master's degree in Telecommunications from Ohio University and spent several years working in the motion picture and television industry in Los Angeles. A veteran user of several video editing programs and systems, Steve is the co-founder of Muvipix.com, a help and support site for amateur and semi-professional videomakers. A professional graphic designer and video freelancer, he has taught classes in Photoshop, lectured on design and even created classes for lynda.com. He lives in suburban Milwaukee.

Other books by Steve Grisetti

Adobe Premiere Elements 2.0 In a Snap (with Chuck Engels)
The Muvipix.com Guides to Adobe Premiere Elements 7, 8, 9, 10, 11, 12 and 13
The Muvipix.com Guides to Photoshop Elements & Premiere Elements 7, 8, 9, 10, 11, 12 and 13
Cool Tricks & Hot Tips for Adobe Premiere Elements
The Muvipix.com Guide to DVD Architect Studio 5
The Muvipix.com Guides to Vegas Movie Studio HD 10 and 11
The Muvipix.com Guide to Sony Movie Studio 12 and 13
The Muvipix.com Guide to CyberLink PowerDirector 12 and 13

An Introduction

CyberLink has included a bundle of exciting new features in its latest version of PowerDirector Ultimate, including some very nice performance enhancements that should make rendering and working with higher-definition video smoother than ever.

Included in version 14 is a new Action Camera Center, ostensibly designed as a one-stop shop for correcting video and adding effects to video from sportcams, like the ever-more-popular GoPro and its imitators – but it's also full of cool new tools for working with more traditional video.

And the brand-new Video Speed Designer not only lets you speed up, slow down and freeze your video clips, it also gives you the option to create several Time Zones on a single clip so that your videos can shift into fast or slow motion or even a freeze frame, then return to normal playback like some stylish action movie.

There are also some noteworthy enhancements to the Title Designer, including an easy-to-use animations library for adding cool starting and ending actions to your text.

A new tool I'm especially impressed with is the Screen Recorder, a tool for recording editable video tutorials or software or game demonstrations. I don't know that this type of tool is found in any other general purpose video editor and, like many of PowerDirector's tools, it's got some pretty amazing capabilities for a tool you might not even notice (if it weren't for a book like this). ;)

In short, whether you're new to PowerDirector or you're upgrading from a previous version, I think you'll find that the folks at CyberLink have packed a lot of great features into this amazing little program.

Our goal with this book, of course, is to introduce you to each of those features and workspaces. To take you step-by-step through all of its processes. And, along the way, to offer you some tips and tricks for helping make your video editing work flow a little more smoothly.

We also hope you'll check out our web site, Muvipix.com, where we offer free basic training, an ever-growing library of tutorials and lots of royalty-free music, video backgrounds and graphics.

Andh it's a great place to make new friends and ask questions.

Muvipix.com was created in 2006 as a community and a learning center for videomakers at a variety of levels. Our community includes everyone from amateurs and hobbyists to semi-pros, professionals and even people with broadcast experience. You won't find more knowledgeable, helpful people anywhere else on the Web. I very much encourage you to drop by our forums and say hello. At the very least, you'll make some new friends. And it's rare that there's a question posted there that isn't quickly, and enthusiastically, answered.

Our learning center consists of video tutorials, tips and, of course, books. But we also offer a wealth of support in the form of custom-created DVD and BluRay disc menus, motion background videos, licensed music and even stock footage. Much of it is absolutely free – and there's even more available for those who purchase one of our affordable site subscriptions.

Our goal has always been to help people get up to speed making great videos and, once they're there, provide them with the inspiration and means to get better and better at doing so.

Why? Because we know making movies and taking great pictures is a heck of a lot of fun – and we want to share that fun with everyone!

Our books, then, are a manifestation of that goal. And my hope for you is that this book helps *you* get up to speed. I think you'll find that, once you learn the basics, making movies on your home computer is a lot more fun than you ever imagined! And you may even amaze yourself with the results in the process.

Thanks for supporting Muvipix.com, and happy moviemaking!

Steve
http://Muvipix.com

The Muvipix.com Guide to CyberLink PowerDirector 14 Ultimate

Section 1: PowerDirector Basics

Section 2: Easy Editing Modes

Section 3: Full Feature Editing

Section 4: Output Your Finished Movie

Section 1

PowerDirector Basics

Get to Know the PowerDirector Workspaces

Basic Video Editing Moves

What's New in Version 14?

Chapter 1

Get to Know PowerDirector 14

What's what and what it does

There's a lot to love about CyberLink PowerDirector.

It's a remarkably accessible program, even if you've never edited video on your computer before. But it's also surprisingly deep, with features usually reserved for professional editing software.

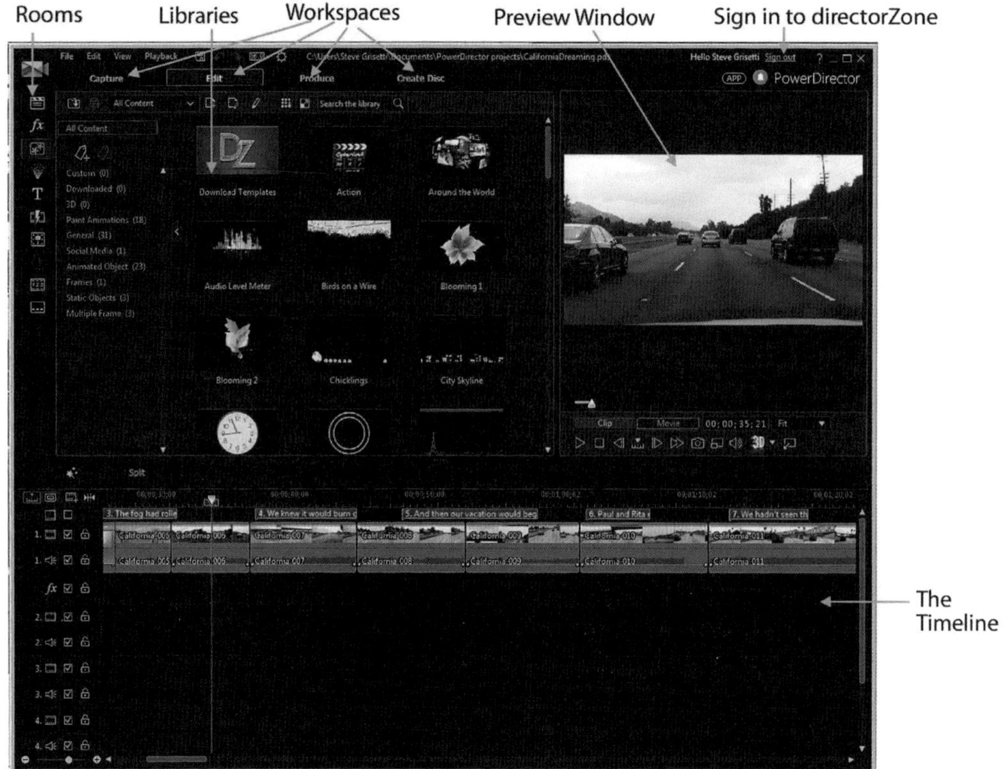

Welcome to easy yet powerful moviemaking!

CyberLink's PowerDirector is one of the most user-friendly video editors on the market. Even if you've never edited video before, you should find yourself very quickly finding your way around.

Yet it's also surprisingly deep, including a few features usually only found in professional editing software. The Multicam Designer itself makes this program a cut above the competition.

PowerDirector is designed to keep your workspace as uncluttered and as easy to navigate as possible. Major workspaces are launched by clicking buttons and tabs, and libraries of media and effects are accessed through various "rooms".

In this chapter, we'll explore these various rooms as well as look at the program's interface (and how to customize it). Then we'll walk you through the basics of video editing in PowerDirector. It's sort of the broad strokes, before we go into the details in subsequent chapters.

Along the way, we'll also look at PowerDirector's three semi-automatic tools – the **Easy Editor**, for making very cool looking movies by combining a batch of your clips with a simple movie theme, the **Slideshow Creator**, for creating great-looking videos from your still photos and images, and the all-new **Express Project** moviemaker, which provides sequence templates for you to drop your footage into.

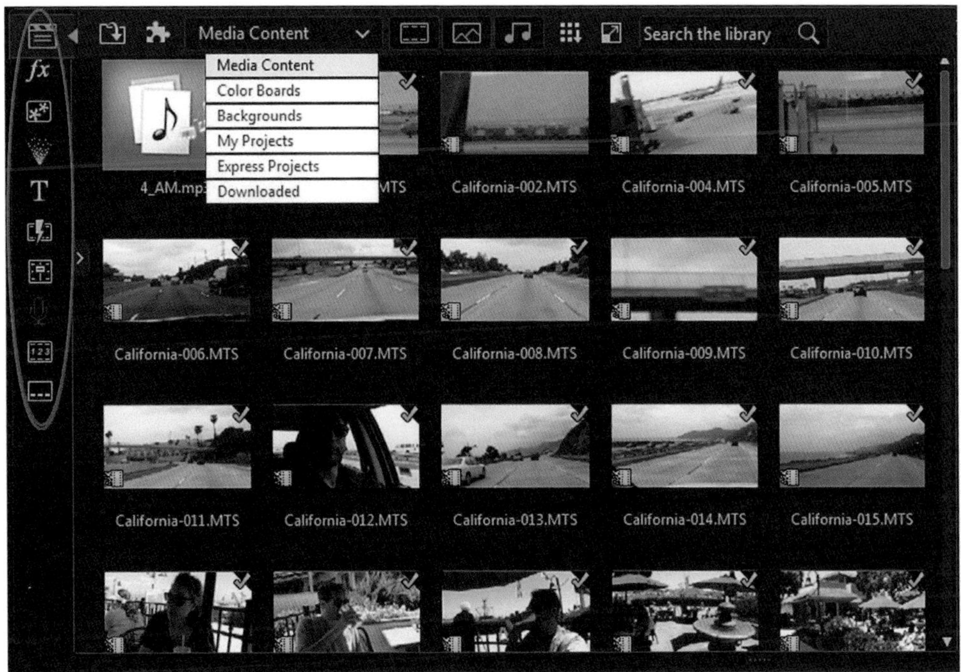

PowerDirector Rooms

The various "**Rooms**" in PowerDirector are accessed by clicking the icons or tabs that run along the upper left side of the interface. Each of these **Rooms** includes a library or a set of tools for working on a particular aspect of your movie.

The Media Room

The **Media Room** is where you gather the video, audio, still photos, graphics and music that you will use to create your movie.

Media is added to this room when you capture video from your camcorder or when you import media files into your project that is already on your hard drive.

An important thing to note about adding media to your project is that the media must remain accessible to PowerDirector throughout your project. In other words, if you have your video, stills or music on an external hard drive or even still on your camcorder when you add it to your project, this device must remain attached to your computer while you are editing your project (or your media must be copied to your hard drive). The media added to your project is merely linked to the original media files.

We'll show you how to gather media files into your **Media Room** in **Chapter 5, Start a PowerDirector Project**.

Included in this room are tools for editing multicamera video (see **Chapter 7**) as well as a tools for prepping your video using the **Content Aware Editor** (page 57) or for breaking a longer clip into shorter clips based on content (page 56).

The FX Room

The **FX Room** includes a library of special effects which you can add to your video.

PowerDirector includes dozens of visual effects, all of which can be modified and customized for your particular need. For more information on the **FX Room**, see page 91.

The PiP Objects Room

This room includes a number of cool graphics – many of them animated – which can be overlayed or added to your movie project. (For more information, see page 143.)

The **Room** also includes tools for creating your own artwork from an existing graphic or by creating animation from scratch using the **Paint Designer** workspace (see page 144).

The Particle Room

Particles are very high level special effects, including light and lens flares, falling snow and rain, pixie dust, animated objects and cool science fiction and outer space effects – a number of which will appear as three-dimensional when used in a 3D project.

As we show you on page 103, adding these dazzling animated effects to your movie is as simple as dragging them to an empty spot on your timeline (or on an upper video track so that they overlay your video).

The Title Room

The **Title Room** includes nearly 100 customizable templates for creating titles and adding text to your movie. We'll discuss this **Room** in much more detail in **Chapter 12**.

Media Room views

The video, still photos, music and other audio files in your **Media Room** can be viewed in a number of ways.

You'll find the options to display your media as **Details** (a list view) or **Icons** (Large, Medium or Small) under the **Library Menu** in the top center of the **Room**.

For more information on importing and managing media in the **Media Room**, see **Chapter 5**.

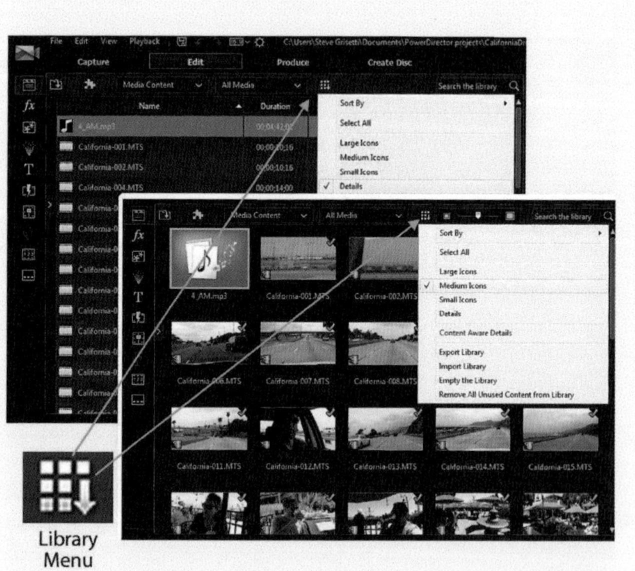

The DirectorZone

The **DirectorZone** is your link to a free online community of CyberLink users. It's also a link to an amazing library of PowerDirector extras.

Once you've created your account and signed in through your program, you'll have access to a huge, ever-growing library of **PiP Objects, Particles, Title templates, DVD Menus, Magic Styles, Sounds Clips** and **Color Presets.**

For more information on joining, downloading from and uploading to the **DirectorZone**, see page 200 in the **Appendix**.

The Transition Room

The **Transition Room** gives you access to a huge library of video transitions, including transitions which will look three-dimensional when added to a 3D project.

We'll look into this room and how to use its transitions in more detail in **Chapter 13**.

The Audio Mixing Room

The **Audio Mixing Room** includes tools for mixing the levels of your various audio tracks and for controlling your various audio levels at precise points.

We'll look at how to use the controls in this room, as well as look at alternative ways to control and mix your audio level sources, in **Chapter 10**.

The Voice-Over Recording Room

As you'd expect, this is where you'll find the tools for recording narration into your movie. We'll look at how to use this tool in more detail on page 124**.**

The Chapter Room

The **Chapter Room** includes tools for adding scenes or chapters to your movie. Once these chapters have been added to your movie, the program will be able to use them to set up links on your DVD and BluRay menus that will allow your viewer to jump to specific spots in your movie.

We'll show you how to use the tools in this room to create chapters, and we'll look at the whole disc authoring processing, in **Chapter 16**.

The Subtitle Room

Among the many high-level features available in PowerDirector is the ability to add optional subtitles to your movie, subtitles that can be turned on and off at the viewer's discretion.

We'll look at this process in much greater depth in **Chapter 14.**

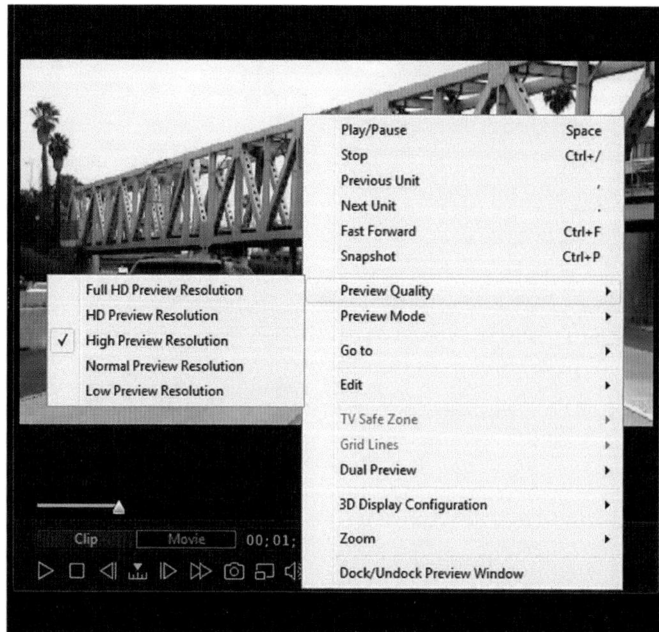

Your preview panel can be set to various quality levels by selecting the option from the right-click menu. Lower quality settings (which are for preview only and do not affect the quality of your finished movie) allow your computer to divert more of its power to your audio and video effects and timeline playback.

The Preview Window

The **Preview** window displays a playback of the clips or movie on your timeline.

Also, when a clip is selected in the **Media Room**, this panel will show you a preview of it.

Among the many features of this panel is an option for setting the quality level of your video playback. This feature can be accessed by **right-clicking** on the preview itself or by clicking on the **Preview Quality** button, as illustrated above.

Higher quality playback demands more power. If your system is struggling to play your video, lowering the **Preview** quality can often smooth your video's playback.

In the event your project is still lugging your machine (i.e., if you're using several tracks of video or you've applied several video effects), you can set your playback to **Non Real-time Preview.** In **Non Real-time Preview**, the audio is muted and your video will play slower than normal. However, your playback will show every frame of your video at full quality.

The toggle on your playback controls can be set to play either a single, looping **Clip** on your timeline or to play your entire **Movie**.

Grab a Snapshot/Freeze Frame

Clicking the camera icon on the playback controls will grab a **Snapshot** of the frame from your movie displayed in the **Preview** window. This **Snapshot** can then be used as a freeze frame in your movie or saved for use in another program or medium. For more details on using this tool, see **How do I grab a Freeze Frame or Snapshot of my video?** on page 201.

Playback controls

The buttons along the bottom of the **Preview** window control the playback of your timeline or selected clip.

While the clip is playing, the **Play** button becomes a **Pause** button. Clicking the **Pause** stops your movie's playback at the point of the playhead. Clicking the **Stop** button stops playback and resets it back to the beginning of your movie.

You can also play and pause your movie using the spacebar on your keyboard.

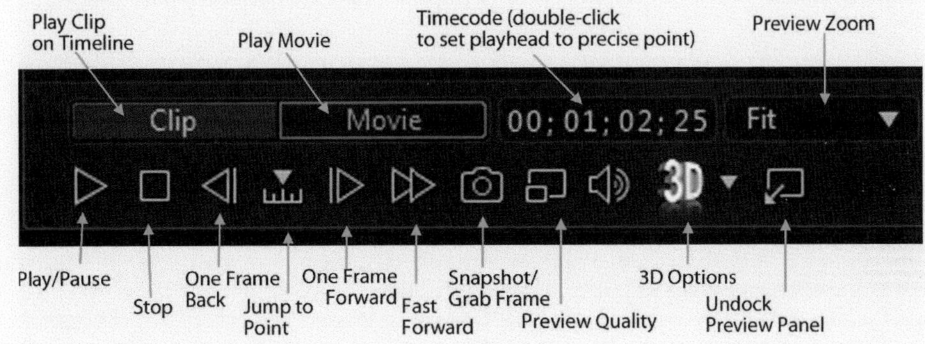

Configure your Preview for 3D Editing

If you are editing 3D video in your project, you'll want to set up your **Preview** panel to interpret and display the 3D image.

To toggle the **Preview** window into 3D mode, click on the **3D** button, as illustrated in the sidebar above. A number of 3D editing **Preview** modes will be displayed.

The most basic setting for 3D editing is **Auto Detect 3D** mode. In this mode, the program will automatically recognize the 3D footage in your project and display it accordingly.

The easiest mode for editing 3D – if you want to see the imagery in 3D as you work – is the **Anaglyph/Red-Cyan** mode. In **Anaglyph** the right-eye and left-eye video channels are displayed as red and cyan-tinted video. If you wear red/blue 3D glasses as you work, you'll actually see the 3D video displayed as three-dimensional.

The beauty of **Anaglyph** 3D is that it requires no special TV or video equipment to display it. All you need is a pair of inexpensive red/blue glasses to view it on any device.

PowerDirector is also capable of working with and outputting more advanced 3D video options.

For more information on editing and outputting 3D video see **Working with 3D** on page 70.

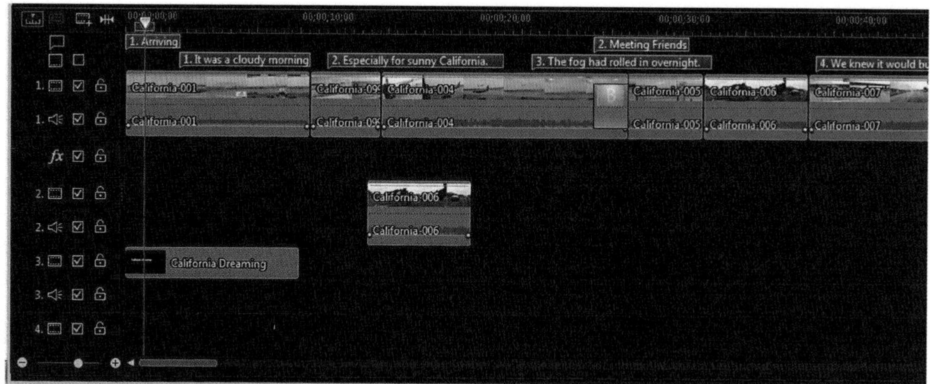

The Timeline

The **Timeline** is where your media files become a movie. The PowerDirector **Timeline** includes tracks for adding video, audio, narration, titles, effects, subtitles and disc chapter markers.

One thing worth noting about the PowerDirector timeline is that it's "upside-down," compared to more traditional video editing timelines. In other words, you layer video from the top track down rather than from the bottom track up. Video on **Video 2** will appear overlayed on top of the video on **Video 1**, despite that fact that is *underneath* it on **Timeline** itself.

The PowerDirector **Timeline** is made up of several tracks, some of which can be optionally displayed.

- A Chapter track (optional), for adding DVD and BluRay chapters to your movie, as discussed in **Chapter 16**.
- A Subtitle track (optional), for adding subtitles to your movie, as discussed in **Chapter 14**.
- A Music Beat track (optional), for pacing your movie to music, as discussed in **Chapter 10**.
- Video tracks, on which you can place video, still photos, graphics or titles.
- Audio tracks, on which you can place music or other audio.
- An FX track, on which video effects can be added to your movie. (In PowerDirector, video effects can be added directly to a clip on your timeline or to this separate track, in which case it works as an adjustment layer, applying the effect to every video paired with it on **Video 1**.)
- A Title track (although titles can also be added to any video track) as discussed in **Chapter 12.**
- A Voice-over track, to which any voice-overs are recorded into your project.
- A Music track (although any audio can be added to this track, and music can be added to any audio track).

Additional video and audio tracks can be added to your timeline as needed – up to 100 additional video and 98 additional audio tracks. (See **Tell stories with multiple video tracks** on page 140.)

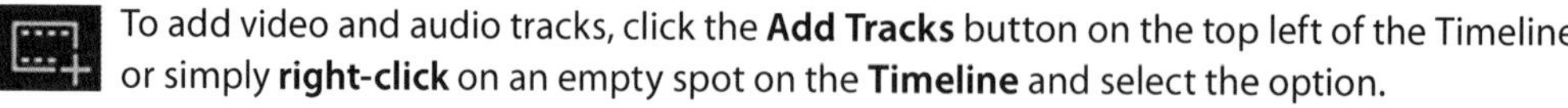
To add video and audio tracks, click the **Add Tracks** button on the top left of the Timeline or simply **right-click** on an empty spot on the **Timeline** and select the option.

Tracks can be locked into place by clicking the **Padlock** icon on the track header, to the left of the timeline.

Tracks can also be temporarily disabled (made invisible or muted) by unchecking the checkbox on the track header.

Custom name your Timeline tracks

Your PowerDirector **Timeline** tracks have, by default, generic names. (If you can't see these track names, drag the seam between the track header and the main timeline to widen the track header.)

To custom name a track, simply click on the generic track name and type over it.

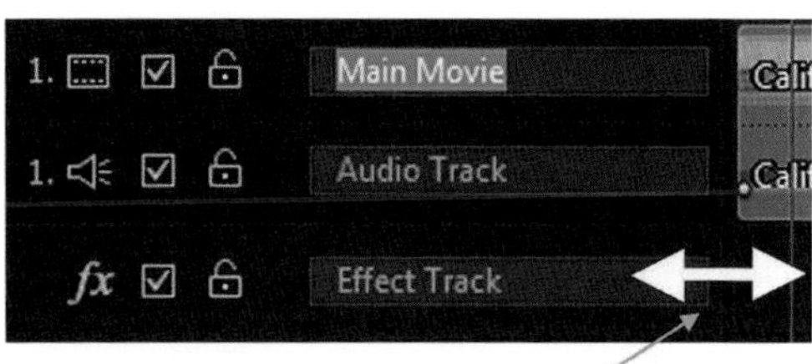

Drag on seam to widen Track Header and display track names.

Re-order your Timeline tracks

Your video tracks are displayed as a stack, with the higher-numbered tracks (which appear lower on the **Timeline**) appearing "on top of" the lower-numbered tracks in your movie.

To change the stacking order of your tracks, click on the track header and drag it above or below other tracks. (The track numbering will automatically update.)

Zoom in and out of your timeline

Sometimes you want to step back and see much or all of your movie at once. Other times you want to zoom in on a single clip or individual frame.

To zoom in or out, adjust the slider in the lower left of the **Timeline** or click its **+** or **-** buttons – or click and drag left or right over the ticker along the top of the **Timeline**.

Alternatively, you can zoom out or in by pressing the **-** key or the **+** keys **(Shift+=)** on your keyboard.

Widen or narrow your timeline

If you're working on a high-level video, with lots of effects and video and audio tracks, you may find that the **Timeline** gets pretty crowded pretty quickly.

There are a couple of things you can do to streamline this workspace.

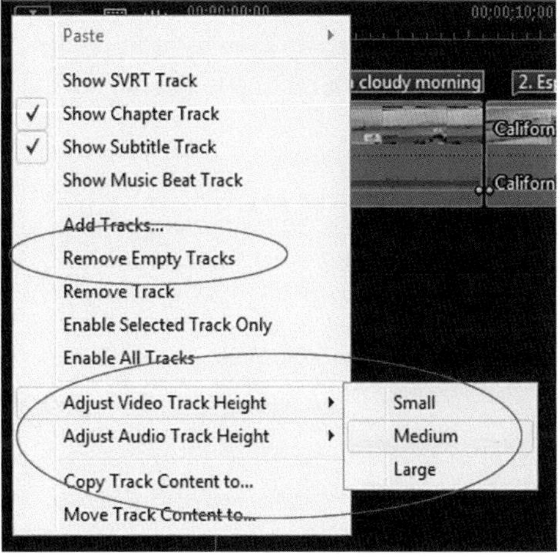

Remove empty tracks. Right-click anywhere on your timeline and you'll find the option to **Remove Empty Tracks.** This strips your timeline view down to only the tracks that you're actually using.

Adjust your tracks' heights. Right-click on any track on your timeline and you'll find the option to change your track's height. The track heights can be displayed as Small, Medium or Large.

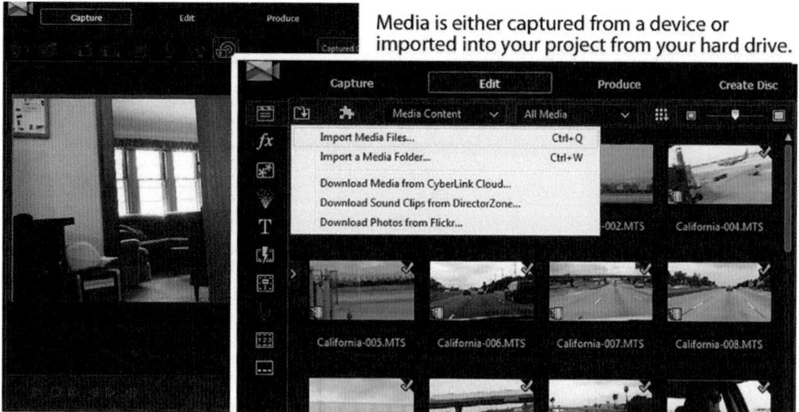

Media is either captured from a device or imported into your project from your hard drive.

Basic editing moves

No matter what you plan to do with your video and no matter how creatively you plan to do it, the video editing process itself will still fit the same basic structure.

Here's a brief walkthrough of the basic steps you'll take creating a video project in PowerDirector.

1 Gather your media

The assets, or media, you gather to create your movie can come from a variety of sources. It can be video, audio, music, photos or graphics. It can be captured from a tape-based HDV or miniDV camcorder or web cam, from a hard drive or storage camcorder (such as an AVCHD camcorder), smartphone or other recording device, from a live TV signal or ripped from a DVD or CD.

To get your media from a camcorder, recording device or disc, click the **Capture** tab along the top of the program's interface.

In the **Capture** workspace, you'll find options for interfacing with these devices. Once you've selected the appropriate tool, set the location the media will be captured to and properly configure your connection to the device, stream the video or other media and select the segment you want to capture. Your media file will be saved to your hard drive and automatically added to your project's **Media Room**.

If your video, still photos, music or other audio is already on your hard drive, you merely need to import it into your project's **Media Room**.

To import media into your project, click the **Import Media** button at the top of the **Media Room** and browse to the media files you'd like to add to your project.

For more information on starting a PowerDirector project and gathering media, see **Chapter 5, Start a PowerDirector Project**.

Trim your clips to remove video from the beginning or end.
Split clips to slice through your clips at the position of the playhead.

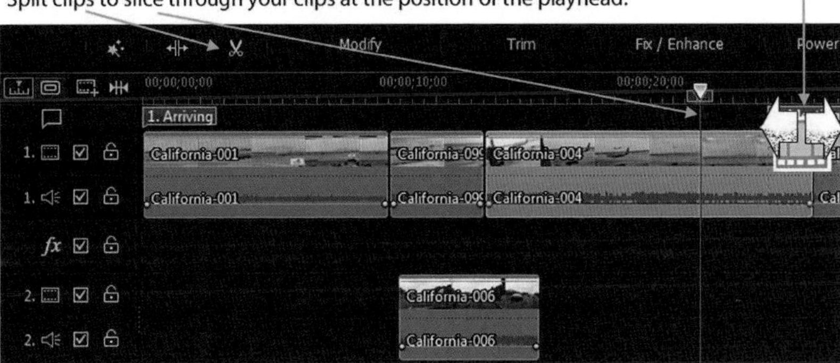

2 Assemble the clips on your timeline

Once you've imported your media clips into a project, you can begin the process of assembling your movie.

PowerDirector offers two views for your timeline: The more traditional **Timeline** view and the quick-assembly **Storyboard** view. You can switch between these views by clicking the buttons on the upper left of the Timeline. We'll look at assembling your movie in either view in **Chapter 6, Gather Media on the Timeline**.

Clips are added to your timeline by dragging them from the **Media Room** to a position on the **Timeline**.

When a clip is dragged onto or will overlap an existing clip on your timeline, a pop-up menu will offer you the option of overlaying the existing clip or splitting it and inserting the new clip into your movie, rippling the rest of the timeline aside to accommodate it.

Once your video or audio clips are added to your timeline, you can begin the process of actually editing your movie clips:

Trim your clips. Trimming means removing footage from either the beginning or the end of a clip. To trim a clip, click to select the clip on your timeline and then drag in either the beginning or end to shorten it, as in the illustration above.

Split your clips. Splitting means slicing through your clips so that you can remove footage from the middle or delete one sliced-off segment completely. To split a clip, position the playhead over your clip where you'd like the split to happen, then click the **Split** button along the top of the **Timeline**.

Place your clip on upper video or audio track. The use of multiple tracks of video is the key to the creation of many of the more advanced video effects, including **Chroma Key** (see page 95) and **Picture-in-Picture** effects (see **Chapter 11**).

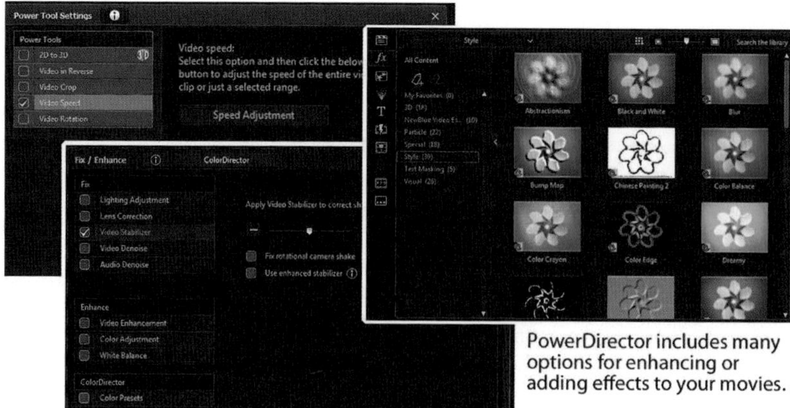

PowerDirector includes many options for enhancing or adding effects to your movies.

3 Add and adjust effects

CyberLink PowerDirector comes loaded with a library of professional effects for adding magic to your movies – everything from fixes, like color adjustments and video stabilizers, to cool visual effects for stylizing the look of your movie, to Particle tools for creating snow and rain effects.

Adding and customizing effects for your movie is fun and easy, as we show you in **Chapter 9, Video Effects and Fixes.**

When a clip is selected on your timeline, a number of **Function Buttons** will appear along the top of the Timeline.

Modify gives you access to tools for creating a **Chroma Key** effect, for adding **Fade Ins** and **Fade Outs**, rotating, sizing and positioning the clip and for using a **Mask** to cut your video into any of dozens of shapes.

Fix/Enhance gives you access to tools for correcting your video clip's lighting or color as well as for stabilizing, or taking the shake out of your videos. Additionally, the library of **Color Effects** tools available in this panel allows you to change to mood or color tone of a sequence with a single click (as we show you on page 82).

The FX Room includes a library of tools for creating unusual video effects, like making your video look like a beat-up old home movie or a pencil-sketched cartoon.

The Particle Room includes a number of high-level tools for adding snowflakes, rain, clouds or even outer-space effects to your movie.

Every effect is easily customized to fit your unique need or vision.

All of these effects can be added overall to your movie or to an individual clip or sequence – or they can be **keyframed** to vary their intensity or create a motion or animation with the effect. (See page 109.)

Among the unique effects available in PowerDirector is the ability to make your 2D video into a 3D movie (see page 71). And it's remarkably effective!

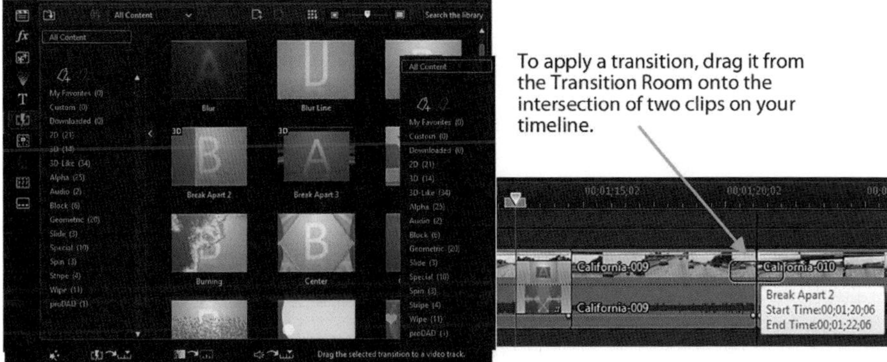

4 Add and adjust transitions

Transitions are the effects or animations that take your movie from one clip to another. Some are subtle and nearly invisible – others are showy and draw attention to themselves. Most transitions are added to your timeline and adjusted similarly to effects:

1 **Select the Transition Room from the tabs that run along the left side of the interface.**

2 **Apply a transition.**

Apply a transition by dragging it from the **Transition Room** onto the intersection of two clips on your timeline.

We'll discuss transitions and how to work with them in greater detail in **Chapter 13.**

5 Add titles

Titles are text, and sometimes graphics, placed over your clips to provide additional visual information for your video story. You can choose an existing template, or create a custom title in the **Title Designer.**

1 **Select the Title Room from the tabs that run along the left side of the interface.**

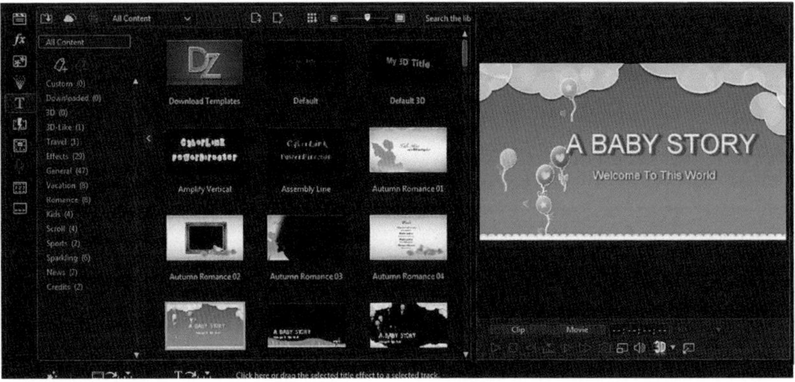

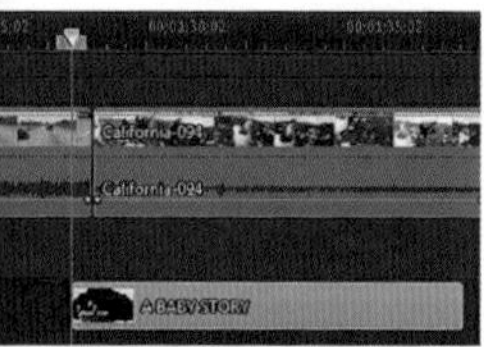

Once a title is added to your timeline, you can customize it in the Title Designer.

2 **Add the title to your timeline.**

Drag a selected title template to your timeline, on a track below the video you'd like it to appear over.

3 **Customize your title's look.**

Double-click the title on your timeline. This will open the **Title Designer**, in which you set your text's color, font and style as well as select a **Motion** animation.

We'll show you how to create and customize your titles in **Chapter 12**.

Produce your movie

When you're happy with the video project you've created, you'll find a number of options for publishing and sharing it, as we discuss in **Section 4** of this book. We'll show you how to publish it as a:

- **Computer file.** Create an AVI, MPEG, AVC, WMV, MP4, MOV or MKV in standard or 3D format!
- **Device file.** Create a video for your smartphone, Apple, Sony or Microsoft device, or send it back to your camcorder for archiving.
- **Web file.** Load your finished video directly to Facebook, YouTube, Daily Motion, Vimeo, Niconico or Youku.
- **Disc.** PowerDirector includes tools for adding chapter markers, creating disc menus and authoring your DVD or BluRay disc.

And that's basically it!

You gather your assets; you assemble them on your timeline; you add effects, transitions and titles; then you share your masterpiece with the world.

But between the lines of this simplicity are the countless variations that can elevate your movie project from the realm of a basic structure to something truly amazing!

And that's, of course, what this book is all about.

What's new in CyberLink PowerDirector 14?

CyberLink has included a wealth of exciting new tools in its latest version of PowerDirector Ultimate.

They've also tuned up the **TrueVelocity** engine (now at version 5), improving your performance even when you're working with ultra high-definition video.

The other cool, new features include:

The Screen Recorder

You may not even notice this tool unless you go poking around the **Capture** workspace – but it's a real bonus, and something rarely included with a typical video editor bundle.

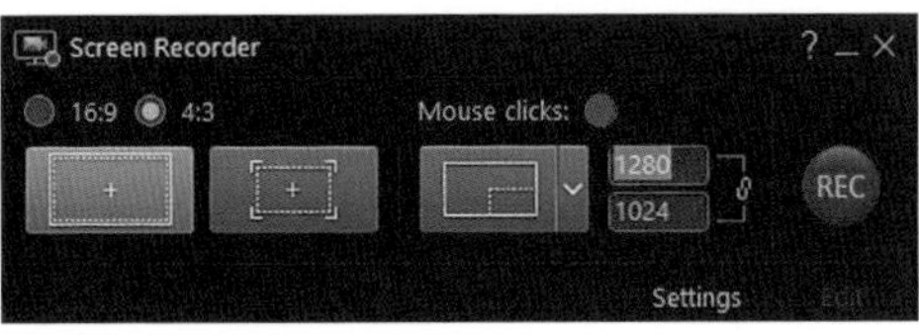

On par with TechSmith's Camtasia and Adobe's Cam Studio, the **Screen Recorder** will record a window, a designated area of your desktop or even your entire computer screen, allowing you to create tutorials and record software demonstrations. Best of all, the tool interfaces perfectly with PowerDirector, which makes editing any video you record a simple part of your workflow.

We show you how to use this cool tool on page 50.

The Action Camera Center

Ostensibly designed as a one-stop shop for correcting and enhancing video from sportcams, like the ever-more-popular GoPros, the **Action Camera Center's** tools are also great for correcting and enhancing traditional video.

The tools in the **Action Camera Center** include a **Lens Corrector**, for removing distortion sometimes caused by extremely wide angle lenses, a **Video Stabilizer** and a **White Balance** tool. Additionally this workspace includes a library of color grading **Presets** and tools for creating repeating loops in fast motion, slow motion and reverse.

We show you around this cool tool on page 100.

The Video Speed Designer

Speaking of shifting playback speed, the new **Video Speed Designer** is a sophisticated workspace for adding fast motion, slow motion and freeze frame effects to your video clips.

These speed effects can be added to your entire clip or to selected **Time Shift** segments, with additional tools for easing in and out of the effects.

We'll show you how to create your own cool time shifts on page 66.

The Motion Tracker

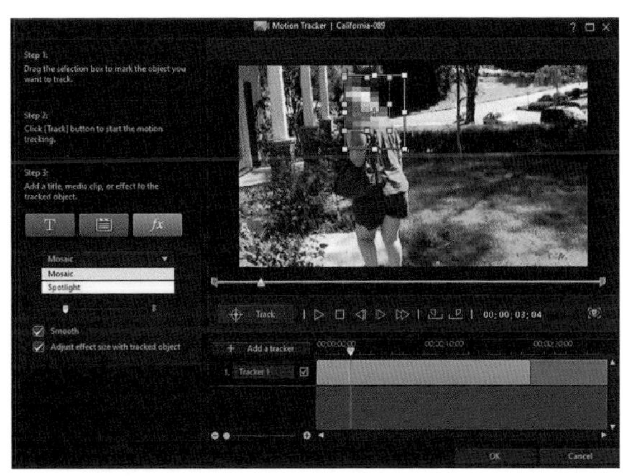

With the **Motion Tracker**, you can track the movements of people or objects in your videos and then attach titles, clips or effects to them so that these clips or effects follow your tracked object's movements across your video frame. This makes locking a mask, a spotlight or an animated graphic to a moving object or a person's face easy and virtually automatic.

We show you how to use this cool tool on page 98.

Title Designer and Menu Designer enhancements

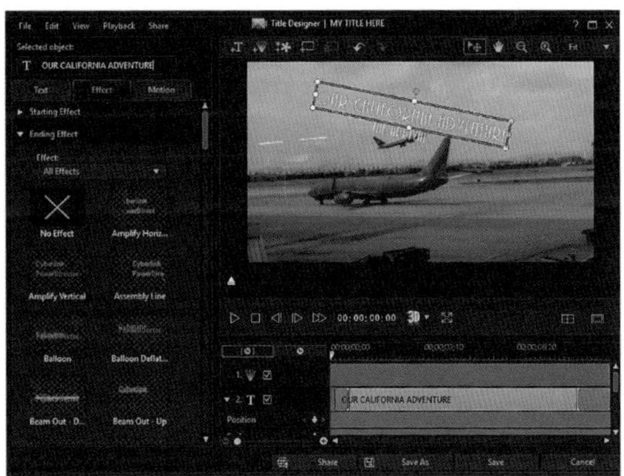

The **Title Designer** and the **Menu Designer** have both been given a boost with a sophisticated library of starting and ending effects for making your text appear over and disappear from your titles and menus.

These libraries include over 75 starting and ending animations that add style and excitement to your titles with only a click or two.

We'll show you how to use them in our discussion of the **Title Designer**, on page 148, and the **Menu Designer**, on page 191.

Search the Library

To quickly locate a design, media clip or effect, you can take advantage of the **Search the Library** box at the top right of many of PowerDirector's **Rooms.** (If you don't see this box, you may need to widen the **Room** panel.)

As you type the name of media clip, production element or effect into this box, the program will do a real-time search of that particular **Room's** library.

You'll find the option to **Search the Library** at the top right of the **Media, Effect, PiP, Particle, Title** and **Transition Rooms**.

Section 2

Easy Editing Modes

The Movie Magic Wizard

Easy Editor Styles

Adjustments and Editing

The Theme Designer

Chapter 2

Make Simple Movies with the Easy Editor

Instant Moviemaking

The Easy Editor in CyberLink PowerDirector is a quick and easy way to produce movies from your video clips.

Easy Editor's Magic Movie Wizard automatically adds the effects, titles, music and fun!

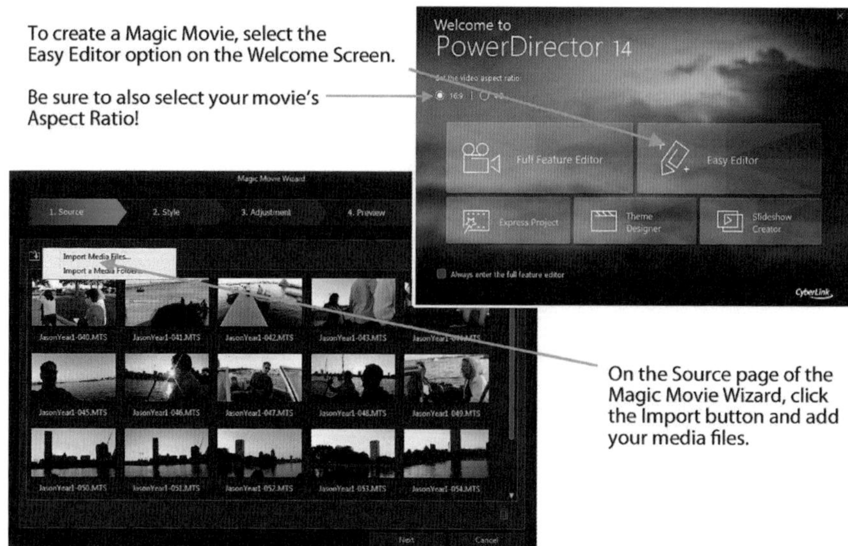

The **Easy Editor** is a semi-automatic workspace for making your movies.

You supply the raw footage or photos; you pick the style of movie; you customize its look and feel – and the **Magic Movie Wizard** does the rest!

It's a fun, easy way to make movies.

1. **Select the Easy Editor**

   At the program's **Welcome Screen**, set the **Aspect Ratio** to either 4:3 or widescreen 16:9 and click the **Easy Editor** button.

   The **Magic Movie Wizard** will open.

2. **Import your media**

   On the **Source** page of the **Magic Movie Wizard**, click the **Import Your Videos and Photos** button.

   You have the option of importing individual photos or video clips or importing an entire folder of media files.

   Click **Next**.

3. **Select a Magic Style**

   Select a **Style** for your movie.

   Note that some styles are indicated as 3D. These styles should be used if you're editing a 3D movie.

   If you're signed in to the **DirectorZone** (see page 200), you can download additional **Magic Styles** by clicking the **DZ** button.

   Click **Next**.

4 Make final adjustments

On the **Magic Adjustment** page, (illustrated below) click the music button to add **Background Music** to your movie.

Use the **Audio Level** slider to adjust if the background music or video sound dominates your movie – or slide it all the way to the right to include only music in your movie.

By default, your movie will be as long as your music or video files (whichever is longer). However, you can select the option to make your movie only as long as your music or set it to a custom duration by using the controls under **Specify the Movie Duration.**

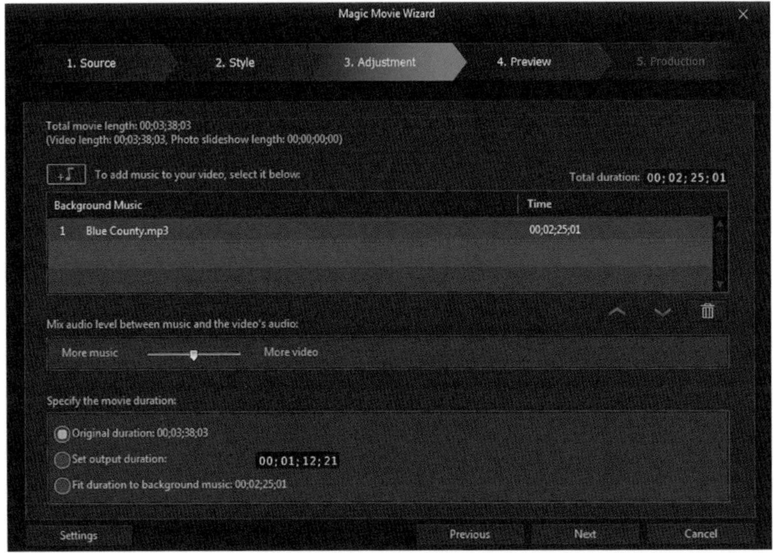

5 **Adjust your Criteria Settings**

Click the **Settings** button at the bottom of the **Magic Movie Wizard** to customize how the Wizard uses your video or photos.

Click **OK** to close the **Criteria Settings**, then click **Next**.

The Wizard will analyze your clips and create a **Preview** of your movie.

6 **Preview and tweak your movie**

Once the Wizard has created a **Preview of** your movie, you can tweak it.

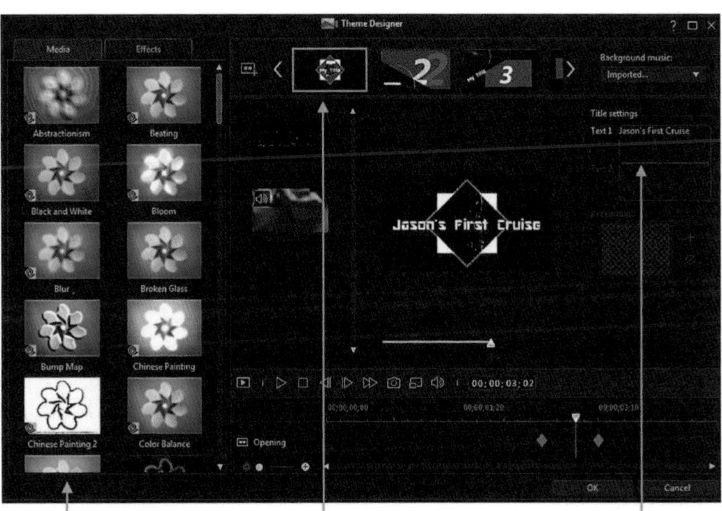

Add Media or Effects. Select Visual Template. Customize title(s).

7 Edit your Theme

To further customize your movie, click the **Edit In The Theme** button along the bottom of the **Preview** page.

A **Theme Designer** will open in which you can add or modify your effects, add titles over individual sequences, change the music and even mute individual clips.

Type in a custom **Title**.

8 Finish your movie

Once you're satisfied with your adjustments, click **OK** to close the **Theme Designer**, then click **Next** at the bottom of the **Preview** page.

You'll be taken to the **Production** page, from which you can output your movie as a video file, upload it to a Web site, create a DVD or BluRay disc or send the file to **Full Feature Editing** for further tweaking.

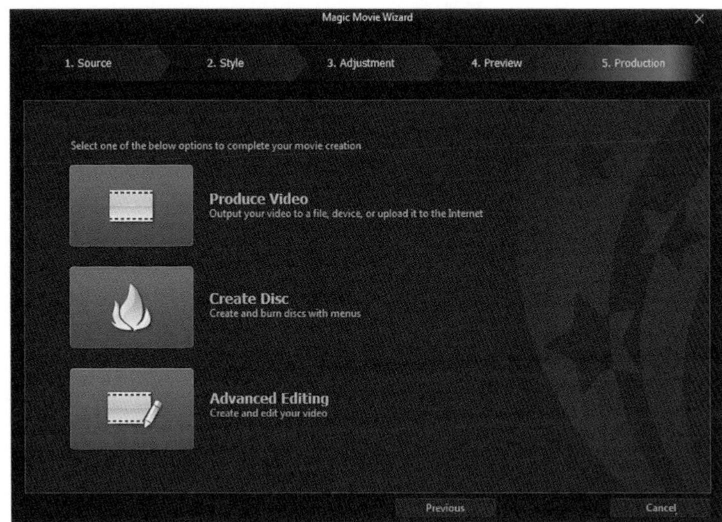

Create your own "instant movie" theme

In addition to the **Magic Styles** in the **Easy Editor**, PowerDirector includes a huge library of **Theme Templates** for making cool "instant movies."

To access the **Theme Designer**, open the **Full Feature Editor** and go to the **Media Room**. Click the puzzle piece icon at the top of the panel and select **Theme Designer**.

A panel will open from which you can select **Themes** and layout **Templates**. Select the theme and layout template you want your movie to use and then click **OK**.

In the **Theme Designer**, drag video clips that have been imported into your project to the scene placeholders. You also have the option of adding new media from your computer's hard drive.

Add custom titles, select layout templates and either leave the default music or import your own.

Click the **Play** button to preview your movie and, if you like it, click **OK**.

Your "instant movie" will be added to your timeline at the position of the playhead.

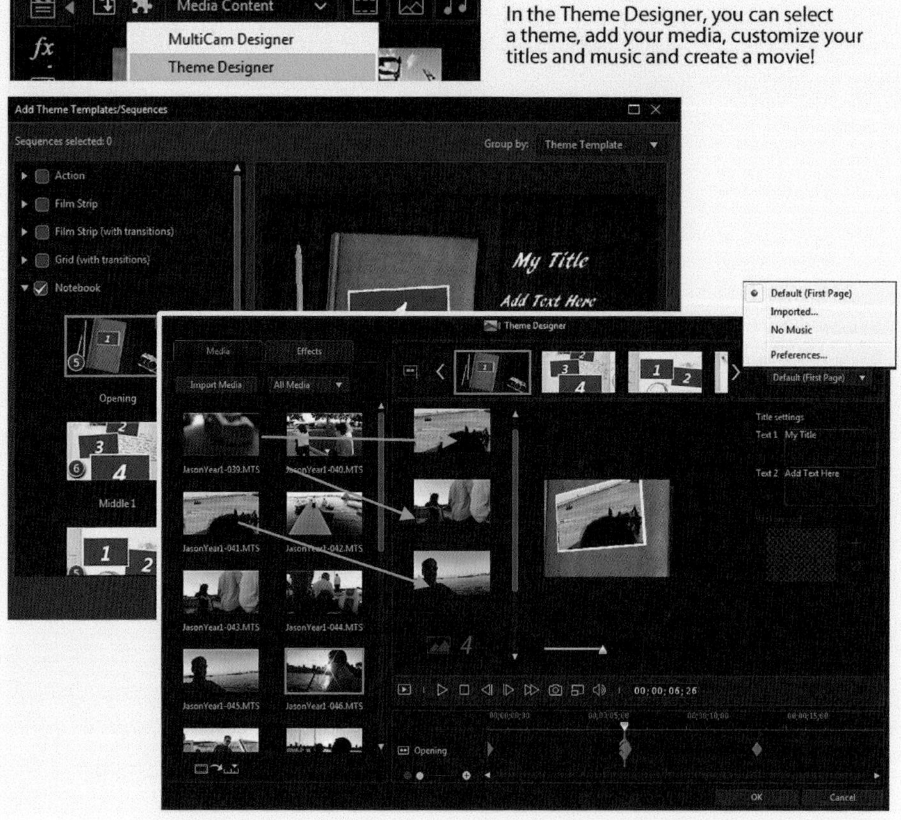

In the Theme Designer, you can select a theme, add your media, customize your titles and music and create a movie!

The Slideshow Creator

Styles & Music

Customizing Your Slideshow

Chapter 3

Create Slideshows with the Slideshow Creator

Giving Life to Your Still Photos

A good slideshow can give life to your still photos. It adds movement, adds focus and piques the viewer's interest in a way a mere photo can not.

PowerDirector includes great semi-automatic ways for building and sharing your slideshows.

Although you can build your slideshows in the **Full Featured Editor**, simply by dragging your photos to the project's timeline, PowerDirector includes an easy-to-use tool for creating great-looking slideshows practically automatically.

1. **Select the Slideshow Creator**

   At the program's **Welcome Screen**, set the **Aspect Ratio** to either 4:3 or widescreen 16:9.

   Click the **Slideshow Creator** button.

   The **Slideshow Creator** Wizard will open.

2. **Import your media**

   On the **Source** page of the **Slideshow Creator**, click the **Import Your Photos** button.

   You'll have the option of importing individual image files or importing an entire folder of image files at once.

   Click **Next**.

3. **Select a Style & Music**

   Select a **Style** for your movie.

   Note that some styles are indicated as 3D. These styles should be used if you're editing a stereoscopic 3D movie.

   If you're signed in to the **DirectorZone** (see page 200), you can download additional **Styles** by clicking the **DZ** button.

    Click the **Select Background Music** button to add music to your slideshow.

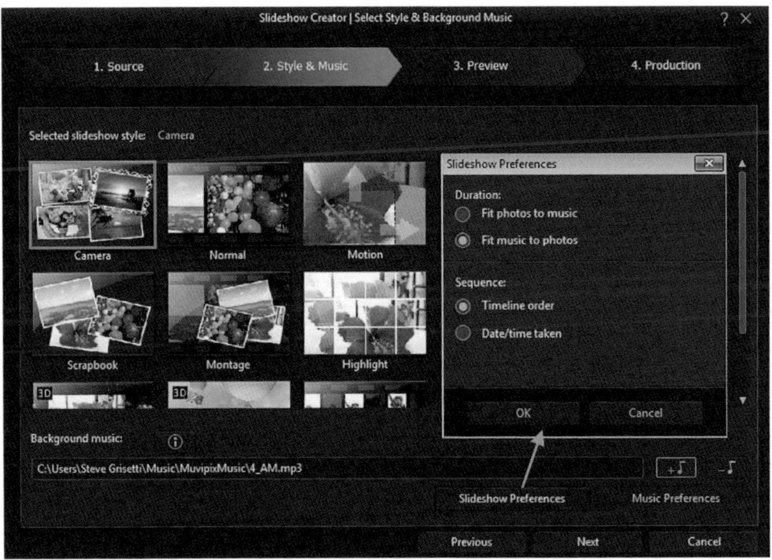

Click the **Slideshow Preferences** button to set whether the slideshow duration is set by your music or photo length.

Click the **Music Preferences** button to trim your music's in and out points and to add a fade in or fade out to your music.

Click **OK** to close the window, then click **Next**.

The **Slideshow Creator** will build a **Preview** of your slideshow.

4 Preview your movie

5 Tweak your Slideshow

Click the **Customize** button at the bottom left of the **Preview** page to open the **Slideshow Designer.**

In the **Slideshow Designer,** you can set the maximum number of photos you'd like to appear on each slide.

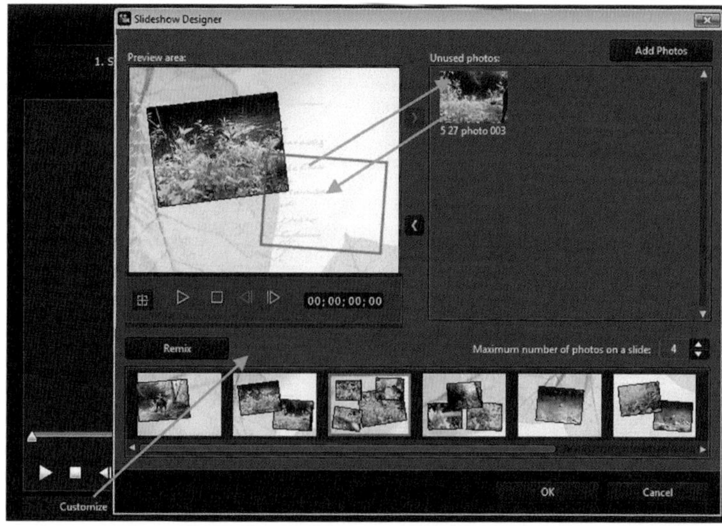

You can also drag unwanted photos from their frames and, if you select **Add Photos**, you can replace photos with photos not previously included in your slideshow.

Click **OK** to close the window, then click **Next.**

6 Finish your movie

You'll be taken to the **Production** page, from which you can output your movie as a video file, upload it to a Web site, create a DVD or BluRay disc or send the file to **Full Feature Editing** for further tweaking.

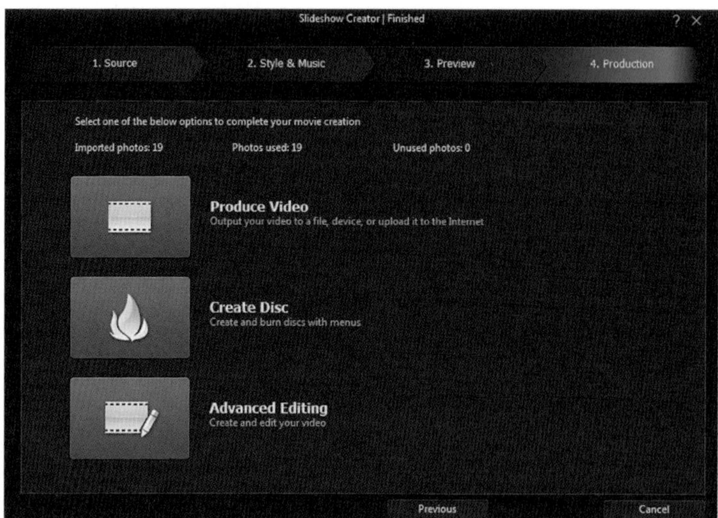

Cool Slideshow Styles

The PowerDirector **Slideshow Creator** also includes a number of very cool styles. Here are a couple of my personal favorites.

Frozen Space creates a slideshow in which your photos seem to float around in space.

Motion automatically adds pans and zooms and transitions to your slideshow.

Time-Lapse Slideshow. This cool style creates a slideshow in which you can designate the length of each slide's duration – making it ideal for creating time-lapse videos in which, say, a camera snaps a picture every five seconds. Clicking the **Customize** button on the **Preview** page opens the option panel for setting your slides' durations.

Balloon and **Outer Space styles** create your slideshows as very cool stereoscopic 3D movies.

Frozen Space

Stereoscopic 3D Outer Space

Time-Lapse with option screen

Using Express Project Templates

Replacing Placeholders with Video

Customizing Your Titles

Chapter 4

Make an Express Project

Building your movies from templates

New to version 14, PowerDirector Express Project is a library of templates that you can use to build exciting movie sequences – complete with titles, transitions and effects – by simply dragging your video clips into timeline placeholders.

It's a bit more hands-on than the Easy Editor, and with more customizable features.

PowerDirector's **Express Project** feature helps you build exciting sequences for your movies by providing pre-designed templates for openings, middles and endings, complete with effects, transitions and cool animated titles.

Express Project library templates are a function of the **Full Feature Editor**, and so the library of templates can be accessed either by selecting the **Express Project** option on the **Welcome Screen** (which will open the **Full Feature Editor**) or by selecting the **Express Project** option under the **Puzzle Piece** at the top of the Full Feature editing **Media Room**.

1 **Select an Express Project template**

The **Media Room** will display the library of **Express Project** templates.

The **Express Project** library can be set to display only templates for creating opening, middle or ending sequences or can be set to display the templates by category (including **Sports, Travel** and **Weddings**). To display only specific sequences or a category of templates, click on the **Content** drop-down menu at the top of the **Room**, as illustrated at the top of the facing page.

2 **Add a template to your timeline**

Drag a template from the **Media Room** to **Video Track 1** on your timeline.

Because templates usually include effects and titles, the template will spread over a number of video and effects tracks. The template is composed of are placeholders which will eventually be replaced by your own video.

You can preview your **Express Project** template or your movie-in-progress at any time simply by playing your movie.

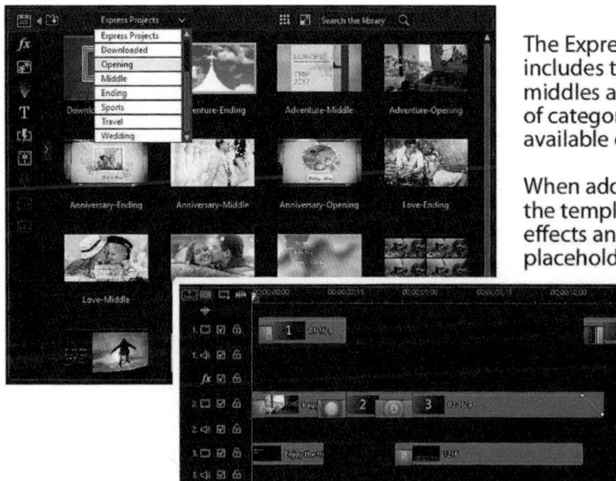

The Express Project library includes templates for openings, middles and endings in a number of categories (even more are available on the Director Zone).

When added to your timeline, the template will add transitions, effects and titles and video clip placeholders.

3 Add media to your project

To replace the template placeholders with your video clips, first reset the **Media Room** to display your project's media by clicking on the **Content** drop-down menu and selecting **Media Content**, as illustrated below. (You may need to scroll up the list on this menu to see this option.)

If you haven't yet gathered the video you plan to use in your project, import your media into your project (as described in **Chapter 5**).

4 Replace the Express Project placeholders

Your **Express Project** video clip placeholders will appear on your timeline as black clips with the numbers 1, 2,3, etc., on them.

To replace a placeholder with a video clip, drag a video clip from the **Media Room** directly onto the placeholder. (If a menu appears offering to overlay your video over the placeholder, you haven't dragged your clip directly *onto* the placeholder.)

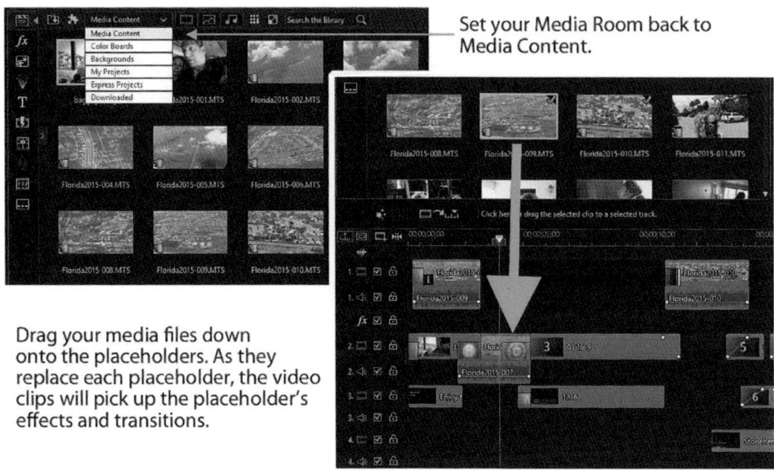

Set your Media Room back to Media Content.

Drag your media files down onto the placeholders. As they replace each placeholder, the video clips will pick up the placeholder's effects and transitions.

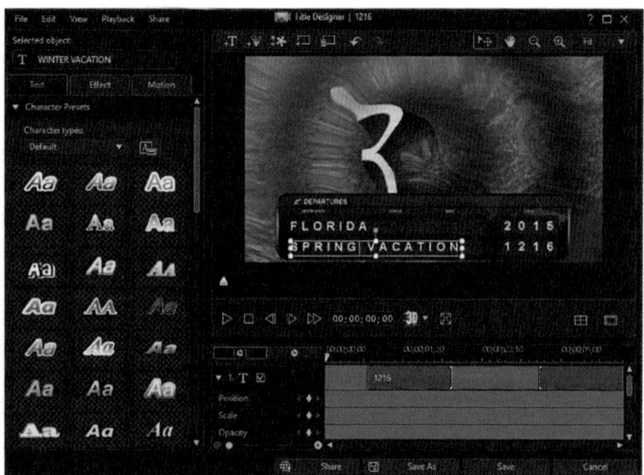

Double-click any template titles to open them in the Title Designer so that you can customize the text and, if you'd like, effects and transitions.

The video clip will replace the placeholder and any effects or transitions that were applied to the placeholder will appear on the clip.

5 **Customize your titles**

Locate any **Express Project** titles on your timeline.

To customize the text on a title, **double-click** on it. The title will open in the **Title Designer.**

Select and overwrite any text blocks in the title. (For more information on the **Title Designer**, see **Chapter 12, Add Titles**.)

Express Project templates are a simple way to build exciting effects and animated titles into your movie.

The effects and titles can be used as is or you can customize the individual elements any way you'd like using the tools in the **Full Feature Editor.**

You, of course, are not limited the templates included with the program. As with a number of effects and templates in PowerDirector, you'll find an ever-growing library of free **Express Project** templates online at the **DirectorZone**, reachable by clicking the **DZ** button at the top left of the **Express Project** library. For more information on the **DirectorZone**, see page 200.

Section 3

Full Feature Editing

The Welcome Screen

Capturing Video from a Tape-based Camcorder

Getting Video from an AVCHD Camcorder or Device

Ripping Media from Discs

Recording Your Computer Screen

Importing Media into Your Project

Chapter 5

Start a New Project

Smart beginnings

No matter how great the journey ahead, it all begins with a few key steps in the right direction.

And, no matter how simple or how complicated your movie project is, a good start can go a long way toward ensuring a successful editing experience.

PowerDirector does a great job of analyzing your source video and setting up its project to match your video's specs.

About all you need to do is indicate whether you want a 4:3 or 16:9 widescreen video frame.

The program will even utilize **shadow files** (see page 202) to make your high-def editing experience as efficient as possible.

Start a new project

There are three ways to start a new project in CyberLink PowerDirector:

- Select an **Editing** mode from the **Welcome Screen**.

  From this **Welcome Screen**, you will find the option to open the **Full Feature Editor**, the **Easy Editor** (see **Chapter 2**), the **Slideshow Creator** (**Chapter 3**) or an **Express Project** (**Chapter 4**).

- Select the **New Project** option under the program's **File** menu.
- In the **Full Feature Editor**, press **Ctrl+n** on your keyboard.

Note that you can select the option to skip the **Welcome Screen** and go directly into a **Full Feature Editing** project by checking the box in the lower left of this screen.

Open into a project in progress?

By default, PowerDirector will open into a new, blank project.

If you'd rather the program open into your most recent work in progress, you can set this option on the **Project** page of your **Preferences**, launched by clicking the **Cog** icon at the top of the interface.

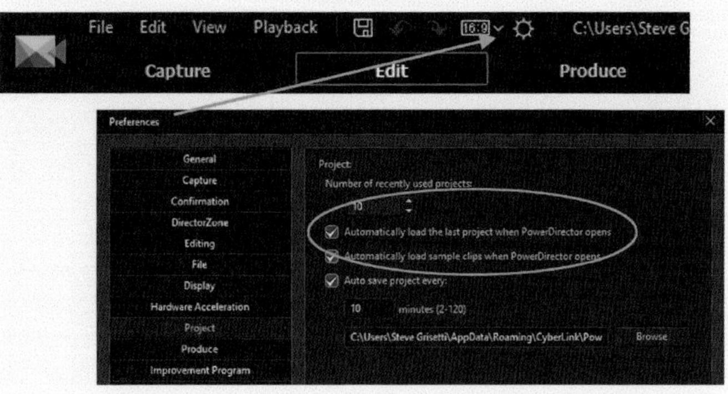

Add media to your project

CyberLink PowerDirector Ultimate will work with a large number of media formats.

Video: 3GPP2, AVI, DAT, DV-AVI, DVR-MS, FLV, M2T and MTS, MKV, MOD, MOV, MP4, MPEG (standard and high-definition), MTS, TOD, MP4 (including MP4s using the new HEVC/H.265 codec), VOB (DVD video), WMV and (new to version 13) XAVC-S 4K video. Additionally, PowerDirector can edit the dual-stream AVI, MVC and MKV 3D video formats.

Still Photos: BMP, GIF, JPEG, PNG, TIFF, Animated GIF and 3D JPS and MPO.

Audio: ALAC, M4A, MP3, OGG, WAV and WMA.

How your media is added to your project depends on where the files are located – and if they need to be captured or downloaded from a camcorder or other recording device. **All media files used in your projects must be stored on your computer's hard drive and always accessible to the program.** If you disconnect a device on which your media files are stored, the program will no longer be able to use its link to these video or audio files to edit and create your project. In other words, you need to copy your video from your camcorder to your computer.

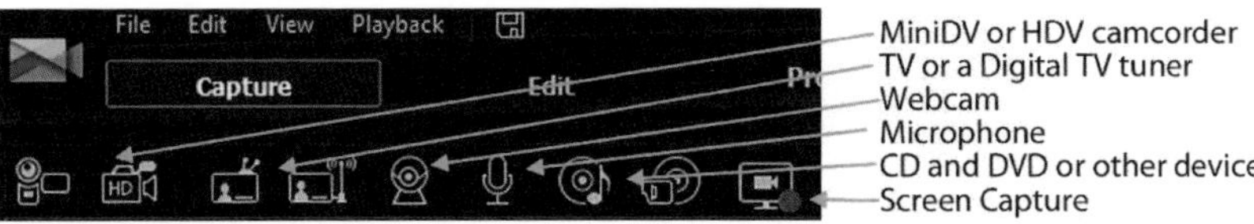

Capture video from a miniDV or HDV camcorder

Capturing video means gathering your video from a device in real time. Real-time capture means that you essentially record the digital video stream as your camcorder plays it or it streams in live.

Devices that PowerDirector can capture streams of video from include:

A **miniDV** or **HDV** (high-definition) tape-based camcorder.
A **live TV** or **Digital TV s**ignal or a **Webcam** or a **microphone** (see page 49 for more details).

To capture tape-based or live video:

1 **Open the Capture workspace**

Click the **Capture** button at the top of the program's interface.

The **Capture** workspace will open and, if your camcorder is connected by an IEEE-1394 (FireWire) connection or your TV signal or Webcam is receiving a signal, its corresponding **Capture** tab will be highlighted.

2 **Select your device**

Your video will be displayed in the **Capture Preview** window.

Click PowerDirector's playback controls to play and cue up your tape.

3 **Select your Capture Profile and location**

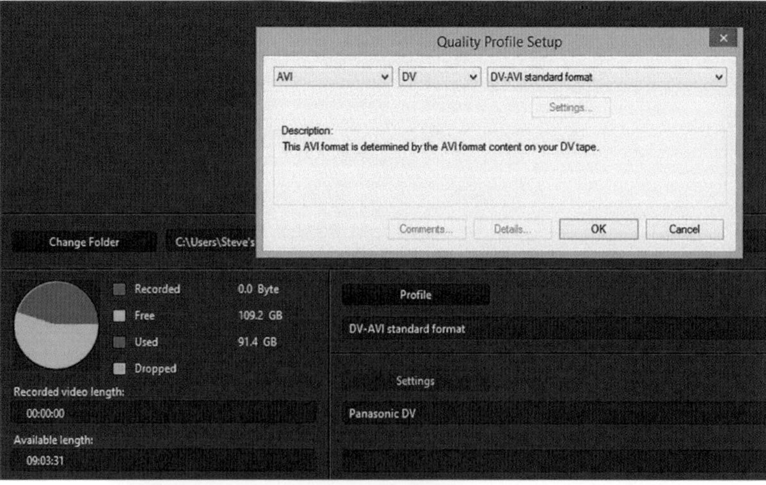

Click the **Profile** button in the lower right of the **Capture** workspace.

If you are capturing video from a miniDV camcorder, select the **AVI/ DV** format.

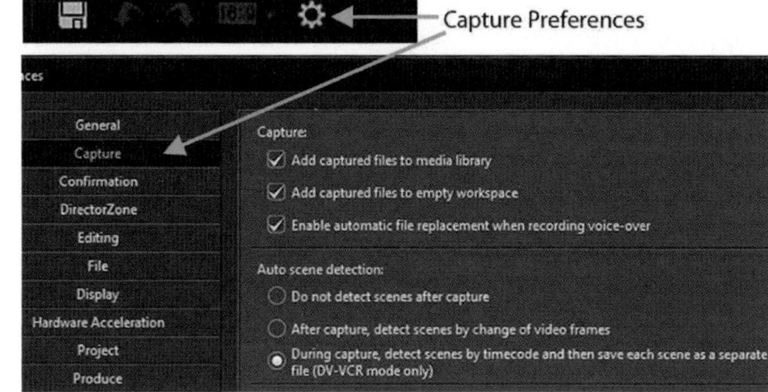

If you are capturing high-definition or HDV video, you should select the **MPEG2** or **H.264** format – although, for some devices, the program will make this selection for you.

Click the **Change Folder** button (illustrated at the top of this page) to select where on your computer your captured video will saved.

4 **Set Capture Preferences**

Click the **Cog** at the top of the interface to open **Preferences** and go to **Capture**.

On this page you can opt to have the program break your captured video by scenes, based on your camcorder's timecode.

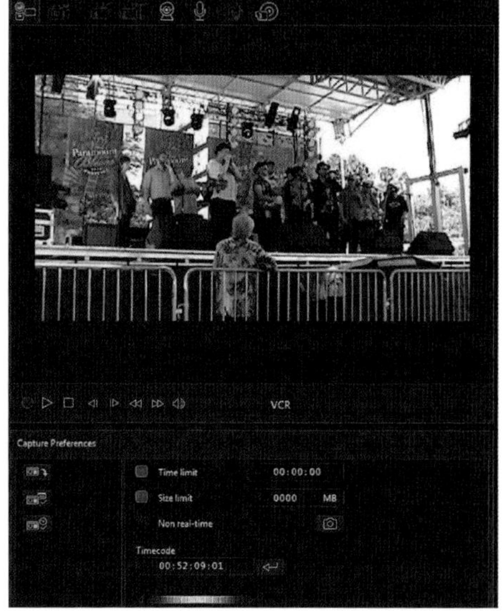

5 **Begin your capture**

To begin capture, cue your tape (if you're capturing from a camcorder) to the spot you'd like capture to begin, and click the **Capture** (red dot) button.

The video will be recorded to your computer's hard drive as the video data is streamed in and displayed in the **Preview** window.

To end your capture, click **Pause** or **Stop**.

Batch Capture your tape-based video

The biggest challenge to capturing tape-based video in real time is that you have to pretty much sit next to your computer and wait for the video to stream in.

PowerDirector includes two **Batch Capture** modes that the program can use to do the actual capturing automatically, based on parameters you've set.

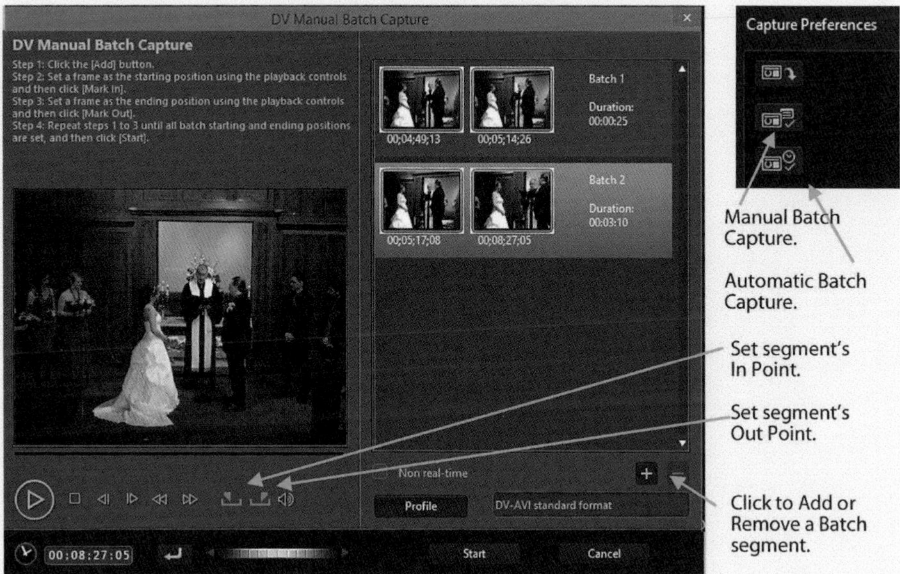

Manual Batch Capture

When you select **Manual Batch Capture,** the program will open up into a workspace in which you can set where on your tape you'd like your video captures to begin and end. You can set up several of these segments (which is why it's called "batch" capture).

To add a batch capture segment, click the **+** button in the lower right of the panel.

To set a beginning for a segment, use the playback controls to cue your tape, then click the **In Point** button. To set where you'd like your capture to end, re-cue your tape and click the **Out Point** button. Use **+** to add as many **In** and **Out Points** as you'd like.

When you've set all of your **In** and **Out Points,** click the **Start** button – then go grab a cup of coffee while the program does the actual capturing for you.

Automatic Batch Capture

When you select **Automatic Batch Capture,** the program will ask you to rewind your camcorder to the beginning of your tape. When you click the **Start** button, the program will capture your tape, breaking your captured video into scenes, based on the tape's timecode, wherever you've paused or stopped your camcorder's recording.

Import video from AVCHD camcorders, smartphones and other video recording devices

In order to use your video or other media in a PowerDirector project, this media must ultimately be on your computer's hard drive or on an external drive that is permanently connected to your computer. This is because your PowerDirector project will link to these media files, and they must be available to the program whenever you edit your movie.

In short, your first step in gathering your video and audio assets for a project is to get this media from your camcorder or other device to your computer.

There are actually a couple of ways to get video from camcorders (including smartphones, iPads, etc.) that store video on an internal hard drive or SD card.

The most common way to get your video or audio from an external device is to simply copy the video and/or audio files to your computer using your computer's operating system and then importing this media into your project, as discussed in **Import video and audio already on your hard drive** on page 52.

To copy your video files from a camcorder or other recording device to your computer, connect your camcorder to your computer with a USB cable and open Windows Explorer. (In fact, often, when you connect a device to your computer, Windows will probably offer to open Explorer for you.)

Your camcorder will need to be turned on and in **Play** mode. Many camcorders will also require you to have your camcorder plugged into an AC outlet and some may need some additional configuration in order to interface with your computer.

1 **Browse to the camcorder's video storage**

In Windows Explorer, your device will be displayed under **Computer** as either a **Hard Disk Drive** or **Portable Device. Double-click** on the device listing.

As illustrated on the facing page, you'll likely need to browse down through a number of folders to find the video files, which are usually in the form of .mts, .mp4 or sometimes .mov files.

2 **Copy your files**

Select the files you want to copy by clicking while holding down the **Shift** key (to select several in a sequence) or the **Ctrl** key (to select several individually).

Right-click on the selected files and select **Cut** or **Copy.**

3 **Paste to your computer**

Browse to the location on your computer's drive you'd like to add your files to, **right-click** and select **Paste.** The files will be copied or transferred to this location.

4 **Import the files into your project**

In PowerDirector's **Edit** workspace, click the **Import** button at the top of the **Media Room** (or along the top of the **Timeline**) and select **Import Media Files** – then browse to and select your video files. Click **Open.**

The files will be added to your project's **Media Room** library.

Rip video files from your AVCHD camcorder or device

An alternative way to move the video files from your camcorder to your computer is to "rip" them from the camcorder using tools in the program's **Capture** workspace.

Your camcorder will need to be turned on and in **VTR/Play** mode. Most camcorders will require you to have your camcorder plugged into an AC outlet and some may need additional configuration in order to interface with your computer.

1 **Open the Capture workspace**

Click the **Capture** button at the top left of the interface.

The **Capture from External or Optical Device** tab should be highlighted along the top of the **Capture Preview** window.

Capture from an External or Optical Device.

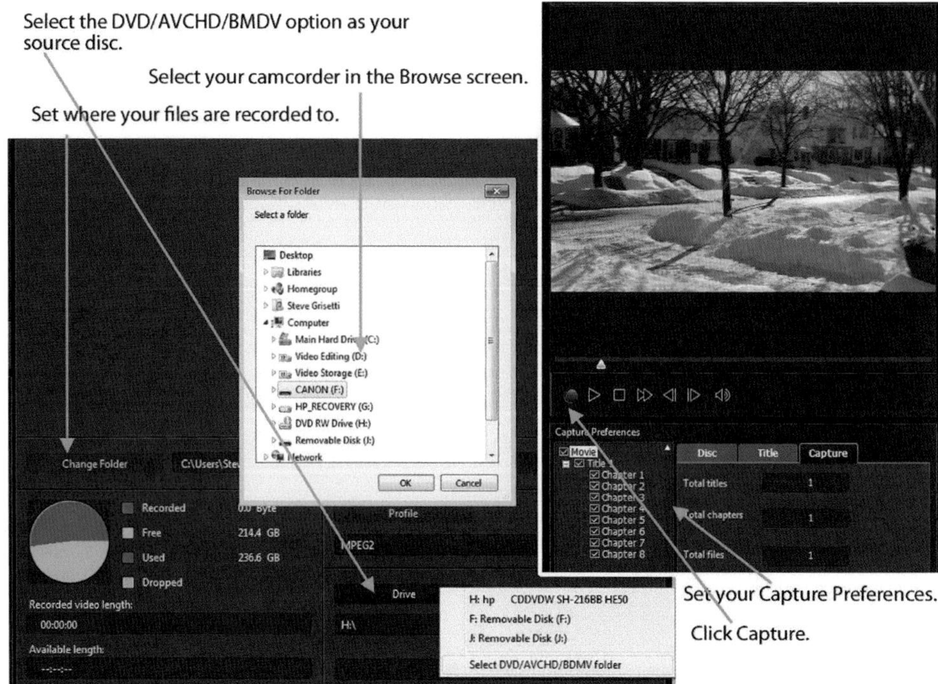

2 **Set your camcorder up for Capture**

When you select this tab, your video should be visible in the **Capture Preview** window.

If it is not, click on the **Disk** button in the lower right of the **Capture** workspace and set it to **Select DVD/AVCHD/BDMV Folder**, as illustrated above.

In the option panel that opens, select your camcorder, listed under **Computer**.

To set where your captured video files are saved, click the **Change Folder** button.

3 **Set your Capture Preferences**

In the box below the **Capture Preview** window, check which of the clips on your camcorder you'd like to capture.

You can preview the clips using the playback buttons on the **Capture Preview** window.

Note that each time you capture using this method, your video clips will come in as a single file – even if the file is actually several individual clips in the camcorder.

4 **Click Capture**

When you click the red **Capture** button, your selected video files will be copied to your computer and added to your PowerDirector project.

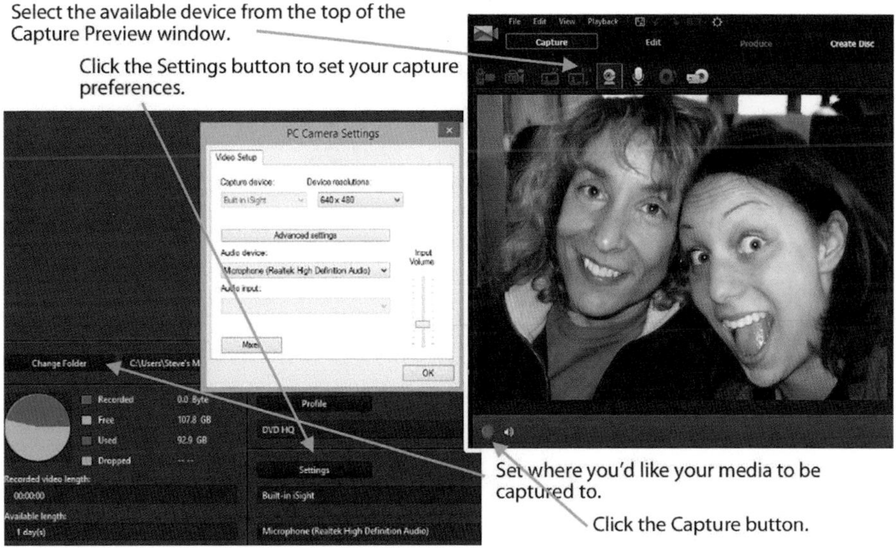

Capture video from a live Webcam, microphone or TV tuner

If your computer includes a TV Tuner card or Webcam or you have a microphone plugged into your computer, you can capture the audio and/or video live from this device.

1 **Select your device**

In the **Capture** workspace, select your device or tuner card from the options highlighted along the top of the **Capture** window, illustrated on page 39.

2 **Set Capture Preferences**

Click the **Settings** button in the lower right of the **Capture** workspace. Set your capture's resolution and parameters, as illustrated above.

To set where your captured video files are saved, click the **Change Folder** button.

3 **Click Capture**

When you click the red **Capture** button, your live feed will be recorded to your computer and added to your PowerDirector project.

Rip video or audio from a CD, DVD or BluRay disc

To copy video from a disc, place the CD, DVD or BluRay disc in your computer's disk drive and use the method described in **Rip Video Files from Your AVCHD Camcorder or Device** on page 47.

Note that most *commercial* DVDs and BluRays include copy protection software that will block you from copying these discs.

If your disc is from a DVD camcorder, ensure that the disc is **finalized** before placing it in your computer's disk drive.

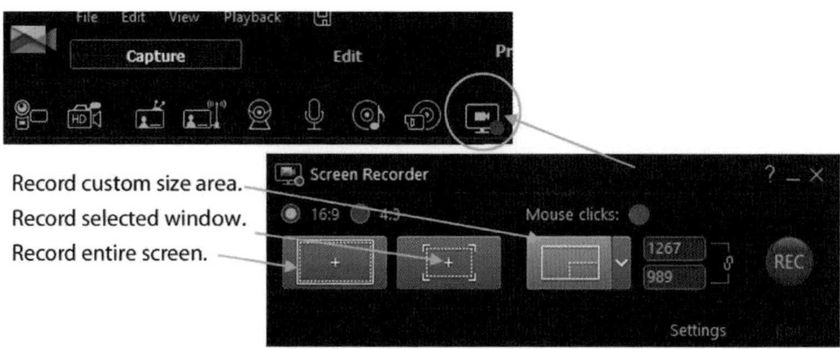

Record your computer screen

New to version 14 is a tool for recording your computer's screen.

Video as well audio are recorded from your computer (including your own voiceover, if you've got a microphone attached) and it is saved in a fully editable format – or, if you'd prefer, in a format you can upload directly to a social media site like YouTube. This is a great tool for, say, recording tutorials or recording demonstrations of software, games or web browsing.

1 **Open the Screen Recorder**

   In the **Capture** workspace, click the **Record from Screen** button.

   The **Screen Recorder** will open, as illustrated above.

2 **Select your video dimensions**

   Select whether you'd like your recording to appear as 16:9 or 4:3.

   If the window or area of your screen recording is not the same shape as your video capture dimensions, your recording will float within a black background in your final recording.

3 **Optionally indicate mouse clicks**

   When you record your screen, any mouse clicks you make will be indicated with a small, color animation. If you click the dot right of the **Mouse Clicks** option, you will be able to select the color of this indicator – or select the option to not indicate mouse clicks at all.

4 **Select the area you'd like to record**

   You can set the **Screen Recorder** to record your entire screen, a selected window or any custom dimension (measured in pixels).

If you are recording a 16:9 movie, your custom button will include presets for 1280x720 and 720x480 screen areas. If you are recording a 4:3 movie, your custom button will include presets for 640x480 or 960x720 areas.

Screen Recorder settings

Clicking on the **Settings** link button on the **Screen Recorder** will open up the tool's preferences. They include:

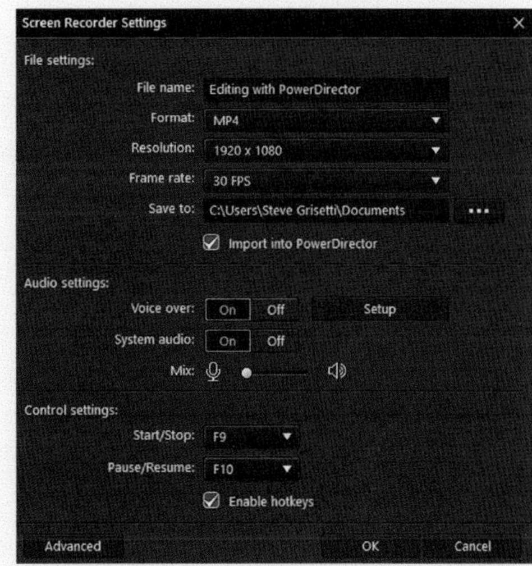

File Name and **Save To** – Name your recording and set the directory into which you'd like your recording saved.

Format – You may record your video as a MP4 or WMV. If you plan to edit your video in PowerDirector, MP4 is probably the preferred choice.

Resolution – If you'll be recording at 16:9, you can save your recording as 1920x1080, 1280x720 or 720x480. If you'll be recording at 4:3, you can save your recording as 1440x1080, 960x720 or 640x480.

Frame Rate – You may record at 30, 25 or 15 fps. Most tutorials are recorded at 15 fps.

Audio Settings – You may record your computer's **System Audio**, your microphone **Voice Over Audio** or mix the two. If you select the option to record your **Voice Over**, click the **Setup** button to ensure your microphone is properly configured.

The **Advanced** button will open a screen for selecting whether you'll be recording from your **Primary** or **Secondary Monitor** and if you'll use the **Hardware Video Encoder**.

If you select the custom option, the recorded area will appear as a highlighted area on your computer screen. By dragging the corner handles on this highlight, you can resize this area and, by dragging on the center crosshair, you can position it over whatever area of your computer screen you'd like to record.

5 Record your screen

Click the red **Record** button or press **F9** to begin recording. A countdown will appear before your recording begins.

6 Pause or stop your recording

To pause you recording, press **F10**. Press **F10** again to resume your recording.

To finish and save your recording, press **F9**. Windows Explorer will open, displaying your recorded video. You may then preview it, use it as is or import it into your PowerDirector project for editing.

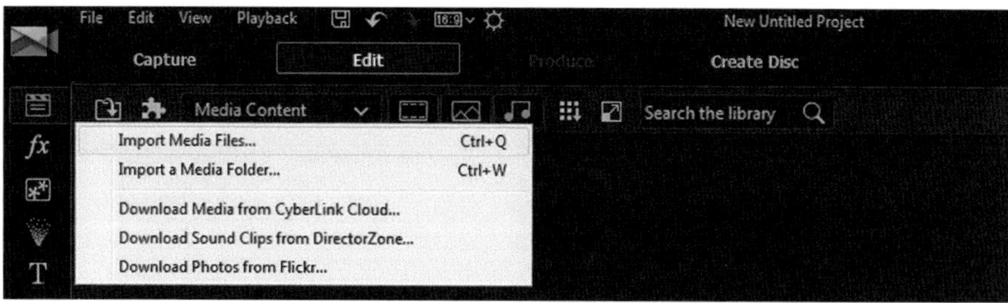

Import video and audio already on your hard drive

To add video, photos, music and other audio files that are already on your computer to your project, you will need to import them into your project.

In the **Edit** workspace, click the **Import** button at the top of the **Media Room** (illustrated above), select the option to either **Import Media Files** or **Import a Media Folder** and browse to and select your media files. Then click **Open**.

The imported media will appear in your **Media Room**.

As you can see in the illustration above, you also have options for downloading media from your online **Flickr** or **CyberLink Cloud** (see page 204) account.

You can also download free video and audio clips from the CyberLink **DirectorZone**, as discussed on page 200.

Indicating 3D video

PowerDirector does a great job of automatically assimilating and interpreting whatever video you add to it. However, it's a good idea to "advise" the program when you've added a 3D clip (even if you plan to use it in a 2D project).

To set these preferences, **right-click** on the clip in your **Media Room** (or on the **Timeline**) and select the option to **Set 3D Source Format**.

On the option panel that opens, select the 2D or 3D format of your video – or simply click the **Auto Detect** button at the top of the panel.

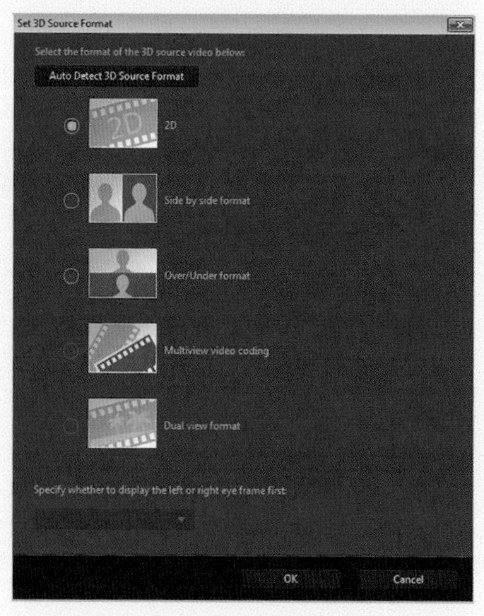

Prepping Video in the Media Room

Adding, Trimming and Splitting Clips

Powerful Tools Available Through the Function Buttons

The Video Speed Designer

Working in 3D

Chapter 6

Edit on the Timeline

Turning clips into movies

The Timeline is where your media files become a movie.

It's where you remove what you don't want, enhance what you do and arrange the whole thing into something that tells a story.

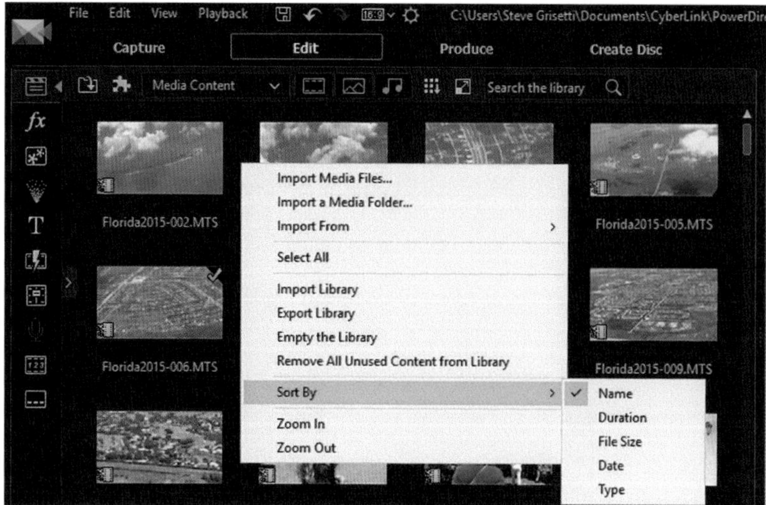

Once you've gathered your media into your project, as described in **Chapter 5,** they become your library of assets – video, still photos, music and other audio – that you will use to tell your story.

This library of assets resides in a panel that CyberLink calls the **Media Room**, opened by clicking the tab along the upper left of the program.

A **Search the Library** box in the upper right of the **Room** allows you to real-time search for a specific file (see the sidebar on page 19).

Media Room views

There are a number of ways to view your media files in the **Media Room**. Some of these views make your media files easier to identify, while others make more efficient use of the panel's space or allow you to sort or filter your media files to make it easier to find a specific clip.

Filter your media views

To display only the video, audio or still images in your project, or any combination, toggle the media filters at the top center of the **Media Room**.

Sort your media files

To change the order that your media files are displayed, click the **Library Menu** button at the top of **Media Room**.

A drop down menu will appear. Select the **Sort** sub-menu and you will find options to arrange your media files by **Name, Duration, File Size, Date** or **Type**.

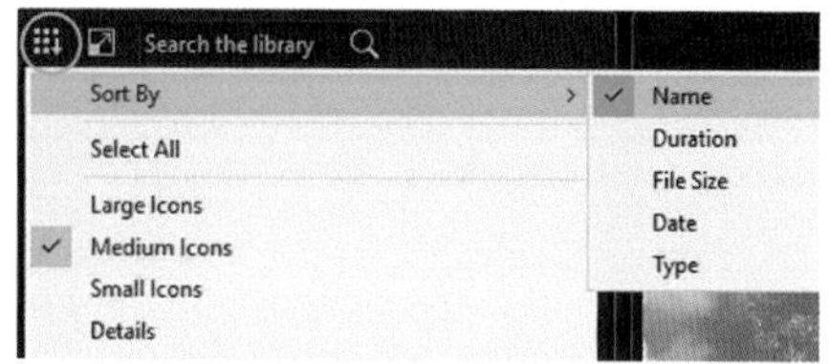

Change how your media files are displayed

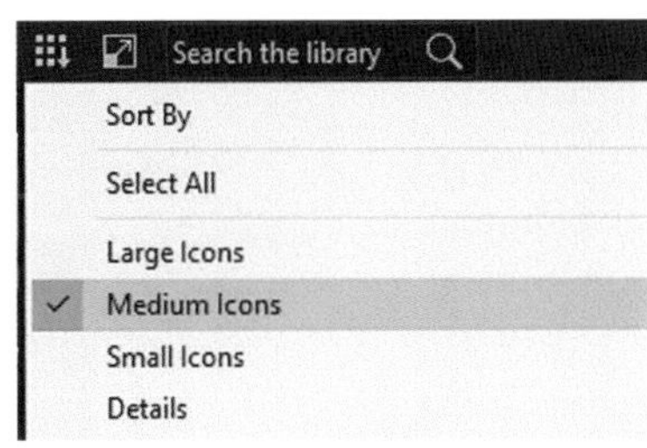

To change how your media files are displayed in this panel, click the **Library Menu** at the top of the **Media Room** and set whether your media is displayed as **Large Icons, Medium Icons, Small Icons** or a **Details** list.

You can also control the size of the icons precisely by clicking the **Adjust Thumbnail Size** button just right of the **Library Menu** button.

Create media in the Media Room

The **Media Room** includes access to some additional media content. To access this content, click the **Media Content** button at the top of the panel.

A drop-down menu will offer you a number of options.

Media Content, the default setting, displays your main media library, consisting of the video, still photos, music and other audio files you've added to your project.

Color Boards gives you access to a library of color panels that can be used for backgrounds, foregrounds and other forms of media in your project.

To create a custom color for this library, click the **Create a New Color Board** button at the top center of the **Color Boards** panel.

Backgrounds gives you access to a library of stylish and colorful backgrounds for your video slideshows.

By **right-clicking** on an empty area of this panel, you can import your own custom backgrounds to this library.

My Projects displays your CyberLink PowerDirector 14 projects as thumbnails. As we discuss on page 61, PowerDirector projects can be used as media in other projects.

For information on **Express Projects**, also available through this menu, see **Chapter 4**.

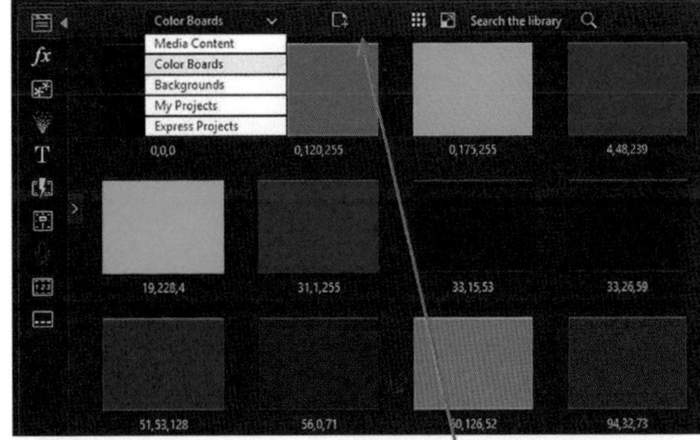

Color Boards

Create a New Color Board

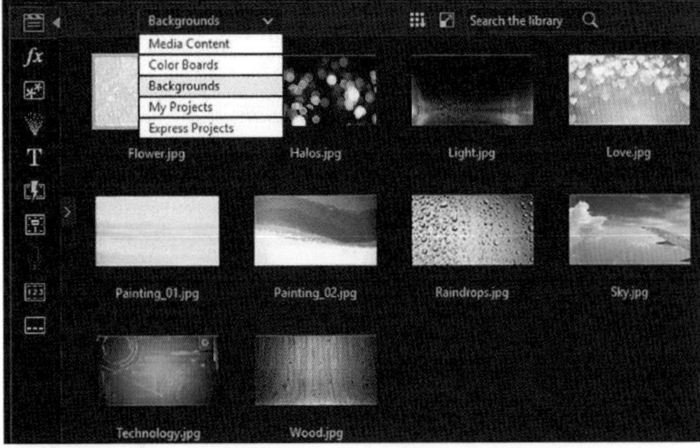

Backgrounds

My Projects

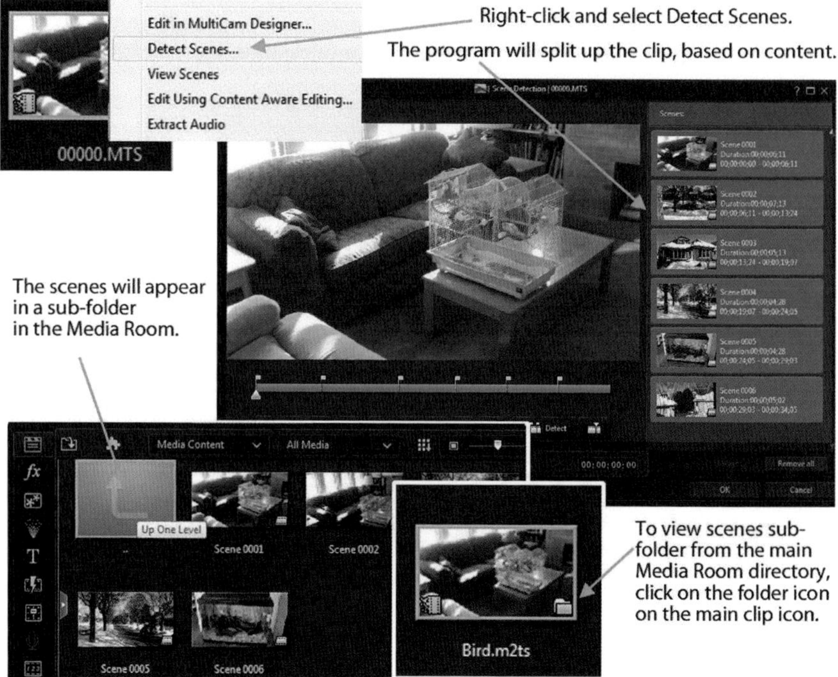

Break a clip into scenes

Once you've added a clip to your **Media Room** library, you can break it into shorter scenes, based on the clip's content.

To break a clip into scenes, **right-click** on the clip in the **Media Room** and select **Detect Scenes...**

The program will analyze the clip and break it into scenes, placing these trimmed clips inside a sub-folder linked to the main media clip.

Content Aware Editing

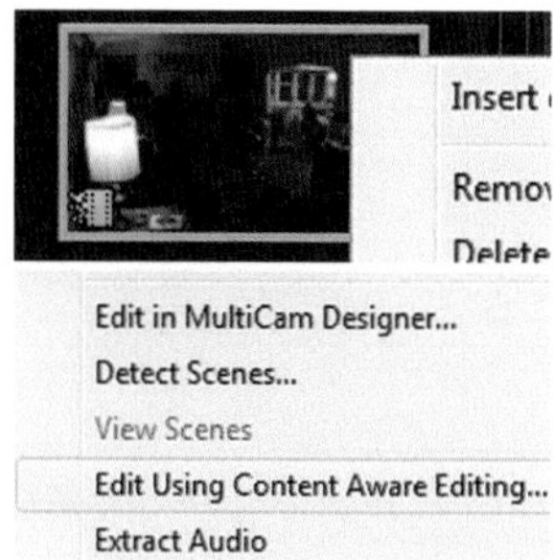

The PowerDirector **Media Room** tool can analyze your video clips for quality issues. To use this tool, **right-click** on the clip in the **Media Room** and select **Edit Using Content Aware Editing**.

The program will analyze your clip and indicate segments of the clip that include **Zooms, Pans, Faces, Speech, Motion, Shaky Video** and **Poor Lighting**.

Based on those characteristics, you then have the option of trimming the clip into one or several shorter clips, as discussed in the sidebar on the facing page.

Trim a longer clip

Often you have a longer clip but you only want to use a short segment – or a couple of segments – from it in your movie.

You may also want to trim around poor quality segments of this clip, as indicated by the **Content Aware Editing** panel, discussed on the previous page.

To open the **Content Aware Editing** trimmer, **right-click** on the clip in the **Media Room** and select **Edit Using Content Aware Editing.** Once the program completes its analysis, a **Timeline** along the bottom of the **Content Aware Editing** panel will indicate content and quality issues in your clip.

To create a shorter segment of your clip, position this **Timeline's** playhead where you'd like your segment to begin and click **Mark In**, as illustrated below. Then position the playhead where you'd like the segment to end and click **Mark Out**. You can adjust the length of this segment by dragging the **In** and **Out** points on this **Timeline.**

Click the **Selected** button. A segment will be created and the tool will offer to automatically fix your quality issues. Your saved segments will be listed on the right side of the panel.

Create as many segments as you'd like.

When you click **OK**, these segments will be added to your project's timeline, at the position of the playhead.

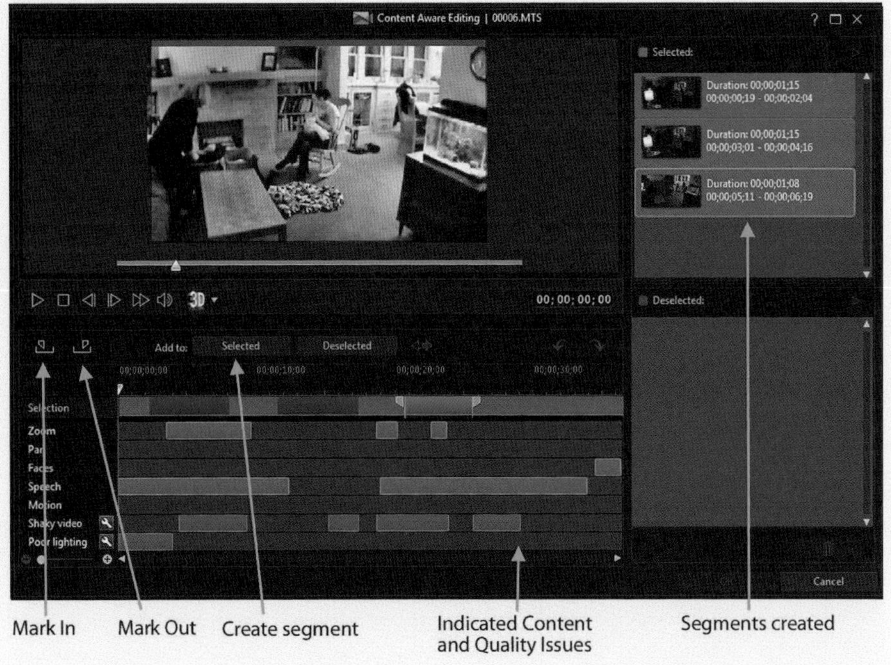

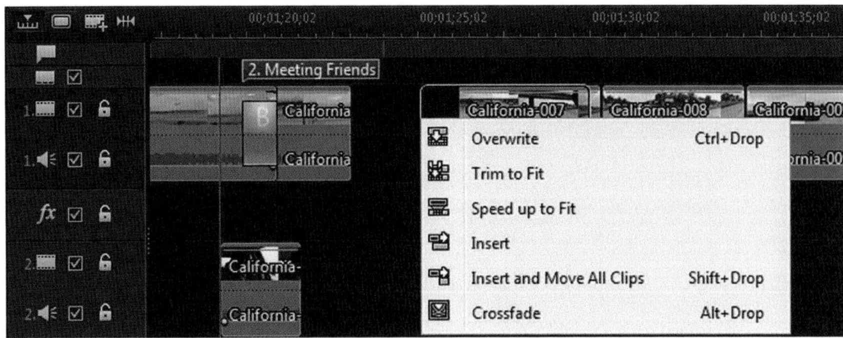

Add media clips to the Timeline

Adding video and audio clips to your timeline is pretty much as simple as dragging the clips from the **Media Room** to a track on the **Timeline**.

However, when you try to insert a clip into an assemblage of clips on your timeline or over an existing clip, the program will prompt you with a number of options.

Depending on how many clips your new clip will overlay or if you are placing your clips between existing clips, PowerDirector may ask you if you would like to:

Overwrite the existing clips on your timeline.

Trim to Fit, if you're placing the clip in an empty spot between two clips.

Speed up to Fit, if you're placing the clip in an empty spot between clips.

Insert to ripple the clips on this video/audio track only to the right.

Insert and Move All clips to ripple the clips on *all* video and audio tracks on your timeline to the right.

Crossfade, or fill the gap and add a crossfade to the clips it will overlay.

Video 1, at the top of the **Timeline,** is the main video track. It will also be the *bottom* video track as you build your movie. In other words, video text and effects you add on **Video tracks 2, 3,** etc. will appear over the video on **Video 1** in your movie, despite being under it on the **Timeline** itself.

You can add up to 100 video and audio tracks to the **Timeline.** For more information on the managing and viewing the timeline, see **The Timeline** on page 10.

Trim a clip on your timeline

Trimming a clip means removing video or audio from the clip's beginning or end.

The most common way to trim a clip on your timeline is to click to select the clip, then hover your mouse over the end of a clip until the **Trim** indicator appears, as in the illustration on the facing page. Click and drag left or right to remove footage or extend the clip. (You can get more precise trims if you zoom into your timeline.)

When you **Trim** a clip, a pop-up menu will ask if you'd like to:

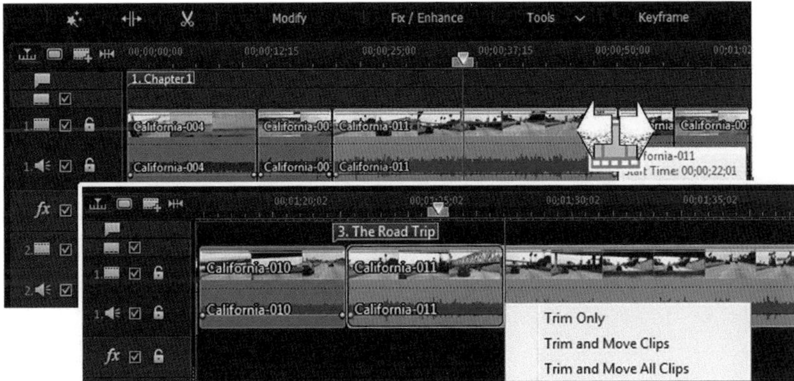

Trim Only, which trims the clips but keeps the rest of your timeline in place, leaving a gap at the point of your trim.

Trim and Move Clips, which moves only clips on that video/audio track left to fill in the gap.

Trim and Move All Clips ripples all tracks left to fill in the gap.

As an alternative, you can select a clip on your timeline and click the **Trim** button (the scissors icon) along the top left of the **Timeline.** This will open a **Trim** panel in which you can set in and out points for your clip. When you click **OK,** the selected clip will be trimmed and all clips on the timeline will ripple left to fill in the gap.

Split a clip on your timeline

Splitting a clip on your timeline means slicing it into two or more pieces so that you can delete a portion of the clip or so that you can apply an effect or an adjustment to only a segment of the clip.

Splitting a clip is as simple as positioning the playhead where you'd like the split to appear and then clicking the **Timeline's Split** button.

If you have several tracks of clips and you have *no clips selected* on your timeline, your split will slice through *every clip* on every track.

If you have a clip selected on your timeline, only that clip will be split.

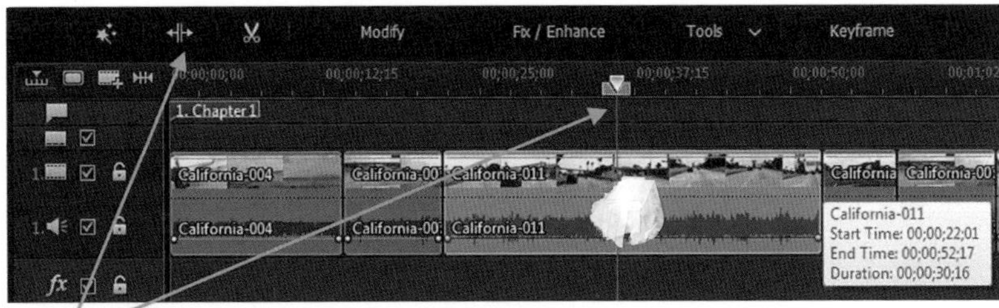

Split clips to slice through your clips at the position of the playhead.

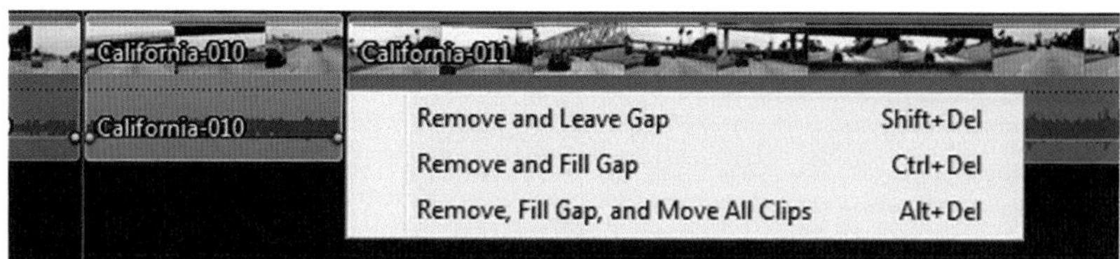

Delete clips from your timeline

To delete a clip from your timeline, select it and press the **Delete** button on your keyboard. The program will ask you if you want to:

Remove and Leave Gap, in which the clip will be removed and no other clips will move, leaving a gap on your timeline.

Remove and Fill Gap, which ripples the clips on this video/audio track only left to fill the gap.

Remove, Fill Gap and Move All Clips, which ripples the clips on all tracks left to fill the gap.

As an alternative, you can skip this pop-up menu and use keyboard combinations to remove your clip in a single move.

Shift+Delete will remove the clip and leave a gap on your timeline.

Ctrl+Delete will remove the clip and ripple the clips on the same track only.

Alt+Delete will remove the clip and ripple the clips on all tracks.

Select, copy and paste clips

To select several clips on your timeline, hold down the **Shift** or **Ctrl** key as you select your clips. You can also select a number of clips by clicking and dragging from a spot on the **Timeline** that has no clips over the clips you want to select.

To **Cut** from your timeline, select a clip or clips and **right-click** or select the **Cut** option from the **Edit** menu. The program will offer three options:

Cut and Leave Gap, in which the clip will be removed and no other clips will move, leaving a gap on your timeline.

Cut and Fill Gap, which ripples the clips on only this video/audio track left to fill the gap.

Cut, Fill Gap and Move All Clips, which ripples the clips on all tracks left to fill the gap.

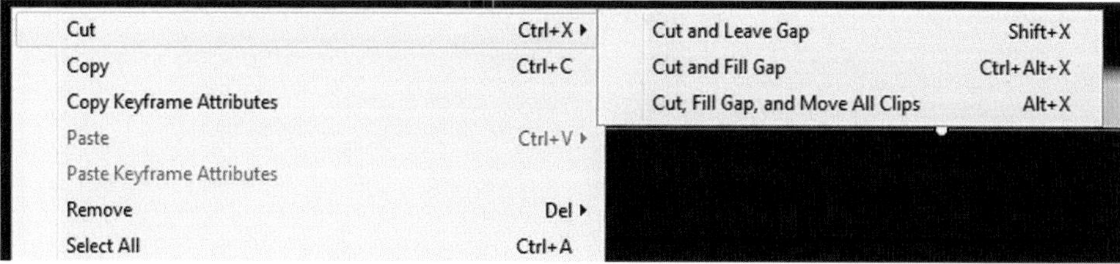

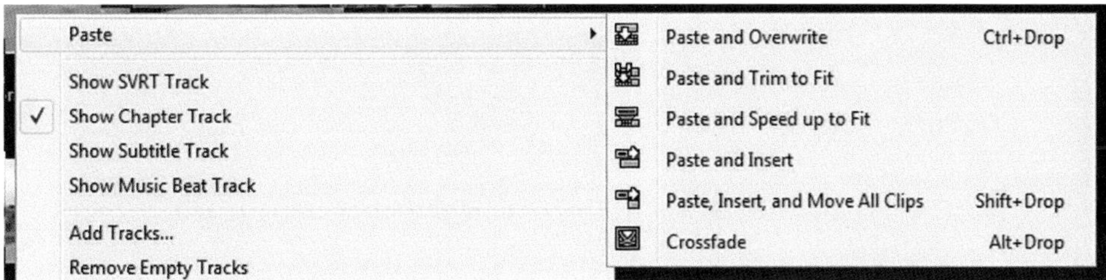

To **Copy** a clip or clips on your timeline, **right-click** or select **Cut** from the **Edit** menu – or use the Windows shortcut **Ctrl+c**. Because copying doesn't affect your timeline, you will see no pop-up options menu.

To **Paste** a clip or clips to your timeline, select the video/audio track on which you'd like the clip to be pasted and position the playhead where you'd like this paste to begin, then **right-click** or select the **Paste** option from the **Edit** menu – or use the Windows shortcut **Ctrl+v.**

If you have the playhead positioned on your timeline at a point where the pasted clip(s) will not fill a gap and will not overlay existing clips, the **Ctrl+v** shortcut simply pastes to the timeline with no pop-up menu options.

If your paste will place your clips into a gap between clips or onto an existing clip on your timeline, the program will offer you a number of options:

Paste and Overwrite the existing clips.

Paste and Trim to Fit, if you're placing the clip in a gap between to clips.

Paste and Speed up to Fit, if you're placing the clip in a gap between clips.

Paste and Insert to ripple the clips on this video/audio track only.

Paste, Insert and Move All Clips to ripple the clips on all tracks on your timeline.

Crossfade, fill the gap and add a crossfade to the clip(s) it will overlay.

Insert one project into another

Unrendered PowerDirector project files can also be used as media in a project.

To insert one project's entire timeline into another project, position the playhead on your timeline to the point at which you'd like this insert to appear.

From the **File** menu, select **Insert Project...** and browse to a project file.

The program will insert all audio and video tracks from the timeline of the selected project into your current timeline.

Add a Fade In or Fade Out

A **Fade In** or **Fade Out** can be added to a clip by opening it in the **Modify/PiP Designer** panel and checking the option, as discussed on the facing page.

Remove audio or video from a clip

To remove the audio or video from a clip on your timeline, **right-click** on it and select **Unlink Audio and Video.** Once the audio and video for the clip are unlinked, you can select either its video or its audio and remove it by pressing the **Delete** button on your keyboard.

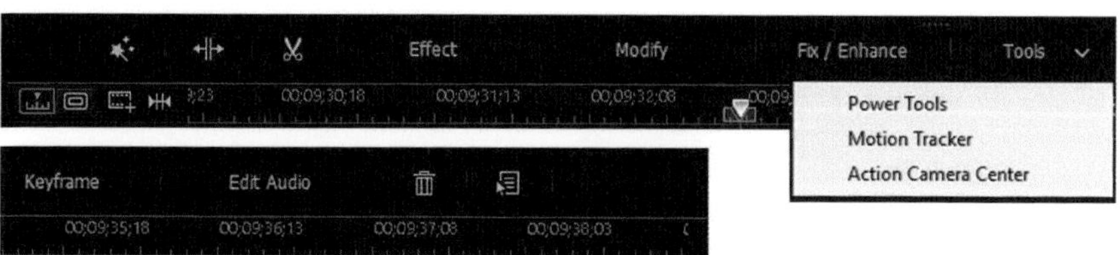

Function buttons

When you've selected a clip on your timeline, the **Function Buttons** along the top of the **Timeline** become active. They include:

Magic Tools (the **Magic Wand** button), a cool set of semi-automatic tools for creating movies, fixing, stylizing and creating music for your movie. We'll discuss these tools in more detail in **Chapter 8.**

Split slices your clips, as discussed on page 59.

Trim opens a panel for precisely trimming your clip, as described in **Trim a Clip** on page 59.

Effect (available only if you have a video effect applied to your clip) opens the clip's **Effects Settings**, in which you can customize your effect (see page 93).

Modify opens the **PiP Designer** for the selected clip (see facing page), in which you can add effects (including **Chroma Key**), scale or rotate your video, add motion paths or use "cookie cutter" masks to cut your video into a number of shapes, as discussed on the facing page.

When an effect on the **FX Track** rather than a clip is selected, the **Modify** button will open the **Effects Settings** panel, as discussed on page 93.

Fix/Enhance (page 64) opens a panel for adjusting your clip's lighting, color and audio.

Tools includes options for opening **Power Tools** (page 65), with which you can crop, change the speed of or reverse playback of your clip or apply the **2D to 3D** effect; **Motion Tracking** (page 98); and the very powerful **Action Camera Center** (page 100).

Keyframe (page 109) opens a panel in which you can create animations or make adjustments and customize effects and have their levels change over time.

Edit Audio launches the **AudioDirector** or **WaveEditor** programs, if you have either installed. We show you how to use the **WaveEditor** on page 128.

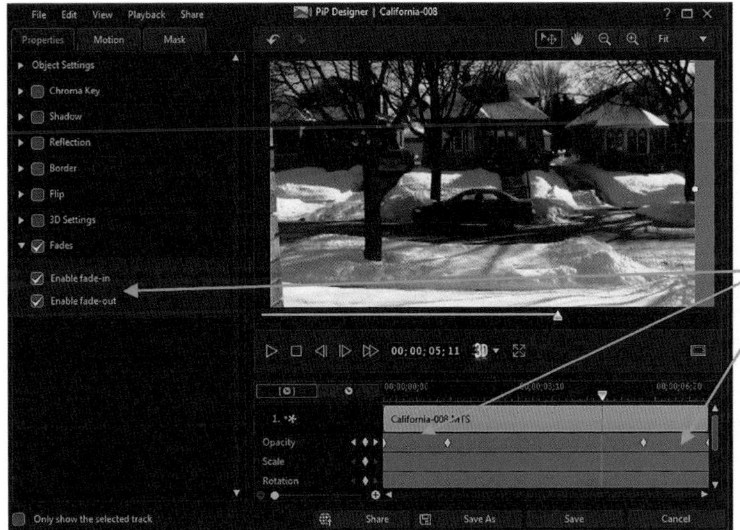

Fade Ins and Fade Outs create Opacity keyframes.

The Modify/PiP Designer function

When you **double-click** a clip on your timeline or select a clip and click the **Modify** function button along the top of the **Timeline**, the **PiP Designer** opens, a powerful workspace for modifying your clip.

Many of the features in this panel are designed for working on video on an upper video track. This is because these features resize or reshape your clip or make areas of it transparent, revealing the video on the video track or tracks below it.

We discuss a number of these features in more detail in **Chapter 11, PiP and Multitrack Video Effects**. We also discuss the **Chroma Key** effect in detail on page 95 of **Chapter 9, Video Effects and Animations**.

To add a **Fade In** or **Fade Out** to a clip, select one of the options under the **Fades** property, on the **Properties** tab. You might note that, when you check either of these options, little yellow diamonds are added to the **PiP Designer's Timeline,** as illustrated above. These diamonds are called **keyframes**, and they represent levels of **Opacity** for the clip. A faded in clip has one keyframe that represents 0% opacity and, a second later, another keyframe that represents 100% opacity. The transition between these two keyframes creates the fade in.

We discuss keyframing in greater detail on page 109 of **Chapter 9**.

An important thing to note about **Fade Ins** and **Fade Outs** is that they are the result of a transition of **Opacity** (the opposite of transparency). So, when you are at zero **Opacity**, you will only see a black screen when the clip is on **Video 1** – because there is nothing on a video track below it.

However, if your clip is on an *upper* video track, 0% **Opacity** (or 100% transparency) will *show the video on the track below it* – and your fade in will actually appear as a dissolve from the lower video clip to the upper.

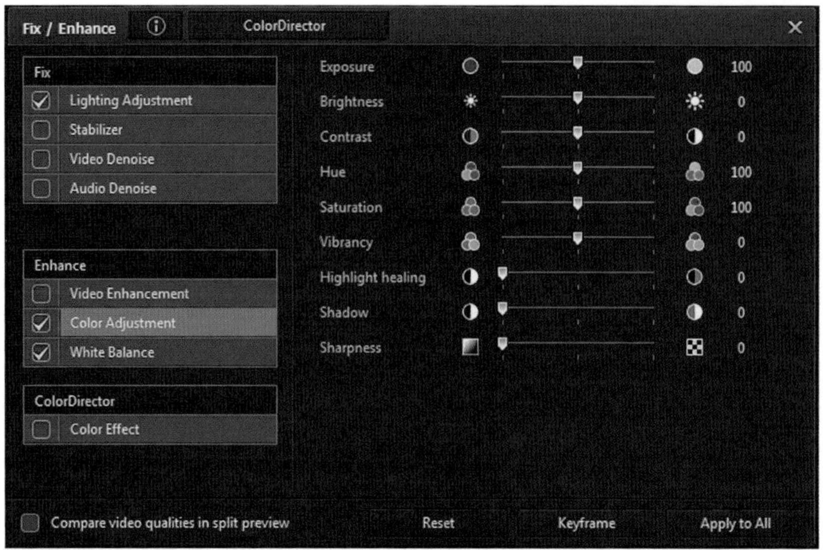

The Fix/Enhance function

When you select a clip on your timeline and click the **Fix/Enhance** function button along the top of the **Timeline**, the **Fix/Enhance** panel opens.

In this panel, you can check and select a number of picture adjusters (including a **Stabilizer**) and set the levels for each using a slider.

The **Color Adjustment** tool, illustrated above, includes a whole arsenal of color adjustments.

One of my favorite tools, the **White Balance** tool, will automatically correct color temperature/tint issues with your video clip. Levels of **Temperature** and **Tint** can be set manually – or, using the eye dropper in the **White Calibration** adjuster, your white balance can be set automatically, based on a white spot or object you sample (click on) in the preview frame of your video.

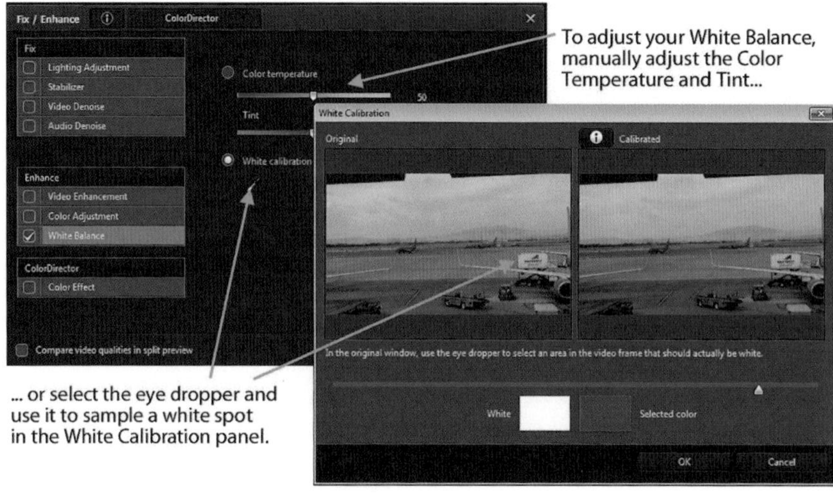

To adjust your White Balance, manually adjust the Color Temperature and Tint...

... or select the eye dropper and use it to sample a white spot in the White Calibration panel.

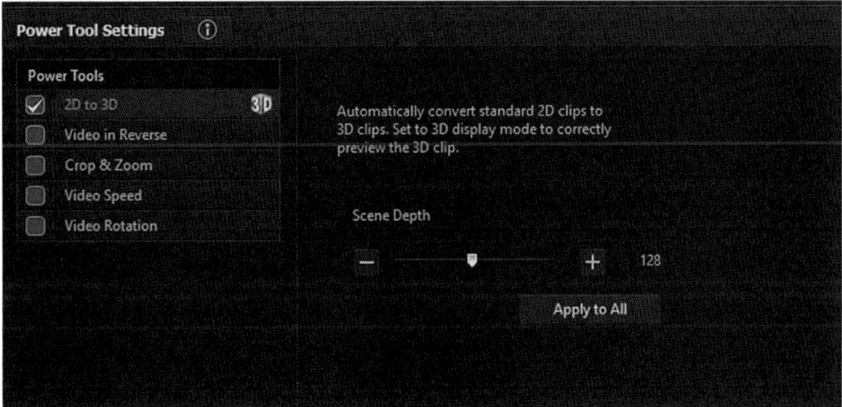

Power Tools

Power Tools are available when you select a clip on your timeline and click the **Tools** function button along the top of the **Timeline** and then select the **Power Tools** option.

Power Tools are tools for rotating your video clip or setting it to play in fast or slow motion or even backward.

This panel also includes an amazing **2D to 3D** effect that creates surprisingly effective 3D video from standard 2D footage (For more information, see **2D to 3D** on page 71) .

The **Crop & Zoom** option gives you access to the **Crop/Zoom** option panel. This tool can be used to keyframe animated **Pans & Zooms** over your videos, as we show you on page 113. (A **Pan & Zoom** over a *photo* is created using a different tool – the **PiP Designer** – as we show you on page 109.)

The **Video Speed** option launches the **Video Speed Designer**, a cool, new tool for controlling your video's playback speed at precise points. We show you how to use its amazing time shifting features on page 66.

The Video Speed Designer

New to PowerDirector 14 is a cool workspace for controlling the playback speed of your video at precise points. With the **Video Speed Designer**, you can not only control how fast and how slow your video plays, but you can also set your video clip to shift from fast or slow to normal speed at precise points in the clip. In fact, you can create several **Time Shift** ranges in a single clip and have it change speed any number of times.

To open the **Video Speed Designer**, select a clip on your timeline and then click the **Tools** Function button along the top of the timeline. From the **Tools** sub-menu, select **Power Tools** – then, on the **Power Tools Settings** panel that opens, select the **Video Speed** option and click the **Speed Adjustment** button.

In the **Video Speed Designer**, you can set the playback speed of the **Entire Clip** or for a **Selected Range** (or ranges). Select the tab for the adjustment you want to make.

Change the speed of your Entire Clip

If you are setting the playback speed for your **Entire Clip**, set your speed by either changing the **New Video Duration** or **Speed Multiplier**. Either option can be set using the adjusters or by simply overwriting the number that represents its setting.

Changing one setting automatically changes the other. In other words, if you change your **New Video Duration** to half its original length, the **Speed Multiplier** will automatically shift to 2x.

Change the speed of a Selected Range

In the **Video Speed Designer**, you also have the option of selecting one or more segments or **Ranges** on your clip and then applying a speed change or **Time Shift** to that segment. Each **Range** can have its own separate **Time Shift** settings applied to it.

continued on next page

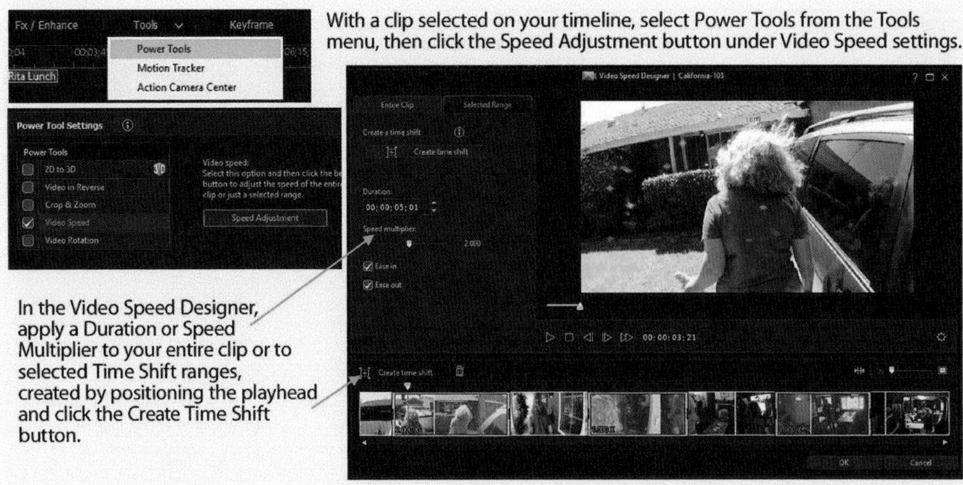

With a clip selected on your timeline, select Power Tools from the Tools menu, then click the Speed Adjustment button under Video Speed settings.

In the Video Speed Designer, apply a Duration or Speed Multiplier to your entire clip or to selected Time Shift ranges, created by positioning the playhead and click the Create Time Shift button.

To create a **Range**, position the playhead where you'd like the **Range** to begin and then click one of the **Create Time Shift** buttons. Both the **Create Time Shift** button on the timeline and the button on the settings panel do the same thing: Create a one second **Range** on your timeline, indicated by a yellow-orange overlay.

By dragging the handles on either end of this **Range**, you can change its length or its location on your clip.

You may create as many **Ranges** as you'd like on a clip. The currently selected **Range** – the one you will be applying your settings to – will be yellow-orange. Unselected **Ranges** will appear as blue.

With a **Range** selected, change either the **Duration** of the segment or set the **Speed Multiplier.** As when you set the speed for your **Entire Clip**, changes one setting automatically changes the other. In other words, changing the **Speed Multiplier** to 2x automatically changes the **Duration** to half of the **Range's** original length.

The **Ease In** and **Ease Out** options are simple interpolations for controlling how abruptly your video goes into and out of its **Time Shifts.** Easing in or out of a **Time Shift**, for instance, ramps up or slows down your video rather abruptly shifting its speed to fast or slow motion.

Remove a **Range** by selecting it on the timeline and clicking on the **Trash Can** icon.

By default, your audio will match the playback speed of your video – which can sometimes produce an unwanted effect. You may or may not want your audio slowing to a crawl as your video slips into slow motion.

Clicking on the **Cog** (preferences) on the upper right of the timeline gives you access to options for controlling the pitch of the audio so that its change in speed isn't quite so jarring as well as the option to remove the audio completely from your time-shifted clip. (Note that the pitch control is really only effective between .5x and 2x playback speed.)

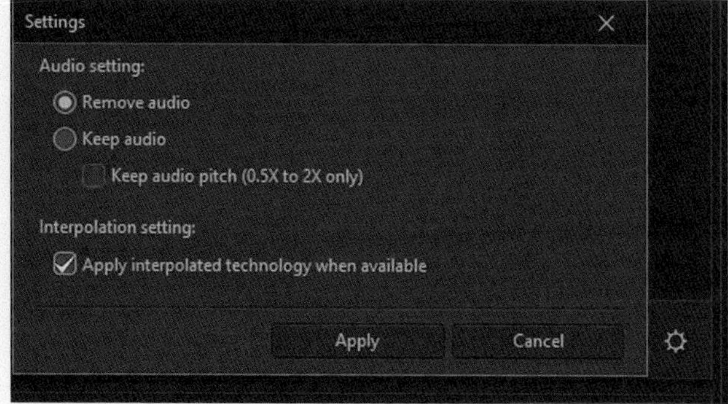

Another option available under **Video Speed Designer** settings is to **Apply Interpolated Technology When Available. Interpolated Technology** blends frames for video that has had a slow motion effect applied to it, and the result can be a much cleaner, smoother slo-mo sequence.

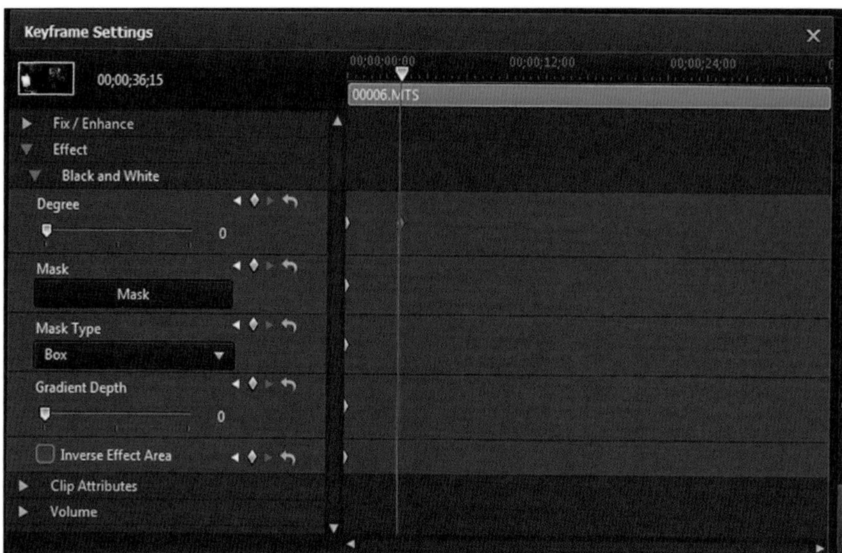

The Keyframe function

Keyframing is a function in which levels of an effect or properties like scale, position and opacity can be set to vary over time. Keyframes can be used to create animations or effects that transition over time.

When you select a clip on your timeline and click the **Keyframe** function button along the top of the **Timeline**, the **Keyframe Settings** panel will open.

The panel will display a list of your clip's properties, many of which can be adjusted by clicking on the corresponding **Function Button**. They are:

Fix/Enhance (as described on page 64), which includes **Lighting, Video Denoise, Audio Denoise, Video Enhancement, Color Adjustment** and **White Balance.**

Clip Attributes (adjusted in the **Modify/Pip Designer**, as described on page 63), including **Opacity, Scale, Rotation, Position/Motion** and **2D to 3D** levels.

Volume level (if your clip includes audio).

Effects, if any have been added to your clip, as discussed in **Chapter 9**.

The **Keyframe Settings** panel is a workspace for creating animations and transitions with any of these properties. As illustrated above, every property is displayed with a timeline representing the duration of your clip. At the head of each timeline is a yellow diamond, a keyframe representing a setting for this property.

To add a second keyframe, move the playhead on this timeline and change a property or effect's setting. A new keyframe representing that setting will automatically be created.

The program will create the animation or transition between these two keyframes. In the illustration above, for instance, the **Degree** of the **Black and White** effect

Storyboard View

Most often you'll likely be working with the traditional **Timeline.** It allows you to layer video and add titles and effects on upper video tracks.

However, the program also offers a simplified **Storyboard View** for quickly assembling your movie. It is accessed by clicking the button along the top of the **Timeline.**

In **Storyboard View,** only one video/audio track is available, and the clips are simply dragged to fill placeholders. The order of your clips can be re-arranged by dragging the clip thumbnails around and between the other clips.

The **Function Buttons** along the top of the **Storyboard Timeline** function the same way as they do in **Timeline View** (see page 62), and you can switch back and forth between **Timeline View** and **Storyboard View** as you edit your movie.

will begin at 200 and, at the second keyframe, will drop to zero. The result will be a transition of the clip from black and white to color.

We discuss keyframing in more detail on page 109 of **Chapter 9, Video Effects and Fixes**.

Select and output a Range of your timeline

When you define a **Range** on your timeline, by spreading the yellow tabs on either side of the playhead, you indicate a segment of your timeline for a specific use.

If you **right-click** on your selected **Range**, you will find options setting this area to **Loop** continuously (so you can focus on it) or to **Produce** it (output a video of this defined area of your movie only rather than your entire movie).

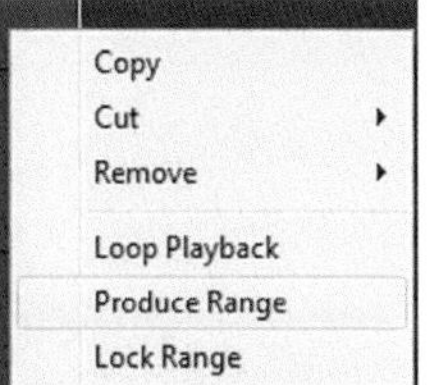

Right-click options for your selected Timeline Range.

Drag Region markers left or right to define a Timeline Region.

Working with 3D

CyberLink includes a wealth of tools for working with 3D video and even creating 3D content.

Creating a 3D video project is easy. Just add your 3D video and PowerDirector will usually auto-detect your 3D content and adjust your project settings accordingly.

3D clips are identified by a little "**3D**" in the upper left corner.

Among the great **Power Tools** in PowerDirector is an amazing tool for creating rather effective 3D-looking video from standard 2D video. We show you how to use it in the sidebar on the facing page.

The program also includes a number of output options for your finished 3D video.

Set your 3D Source Format

In most cases PowerDirector will auto-detect your 3D footage and set up your project accordingly. However, because 3D video comes in a variety of source formats, you may need to designate the clip's format.

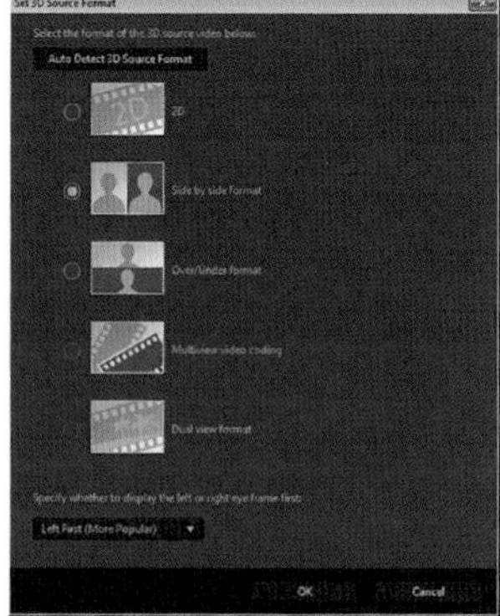

To do so, **right-click** on the clip in your **Media Room** library and select **Set 3D Source Format**. Then select from the following options:

2D advises the program that your clip is actually a 2D video.

Side by Side Format, if your 3D video uses a format which has the right and left images side-by-side, PowerDirector will merge them together to create the 3D image.

Multiview Video Coding if your 3D video is of the high-def MVC format.

Dual View Format if your video uses the dual view AVI format.

Preview window settings for your 3D footage

The **Preview** window includes a number of ways to view your 3D video files. To access them, click the **3D** icon to the right of the playback controls.

When you select **Auto Detect**, your 3D video will usually display as **anaglyphic**.

Anaglyph video displays the right and left channels of your stereoscopic 3D video as shades of red and cyan. The chief advantage to viewing your video in **Anaglyph Red/Cyan** is that you don't need any special equipment to view the 3D image – except for a pair of standard red/blue 3D glasses. This makes it very simple for you to check the effectiveness of your 3D as you work on any computer system.

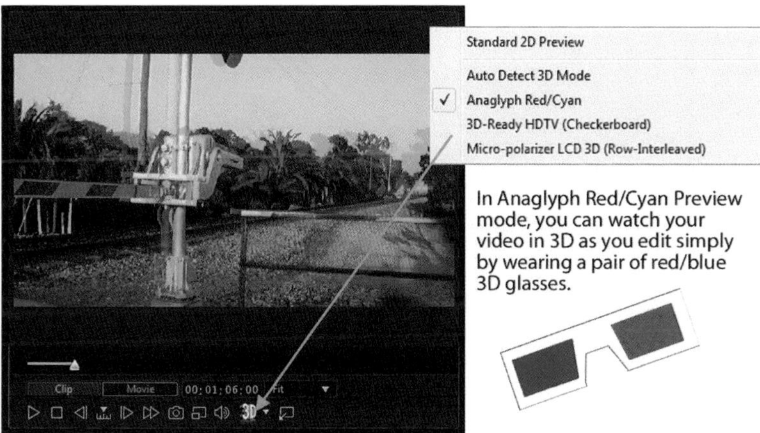

The other 3D preview options are **3D-Ready HDTV** and **Micropolarizer LCD 3D**, which may require specialized equipment to view effectively.

If you'd prefer, you can also set the 3D display to be displayed as **Standard 2D Preview** so that you can focus on editing rather than the 3D.

Your Preview setting does not affect the format of your final output.

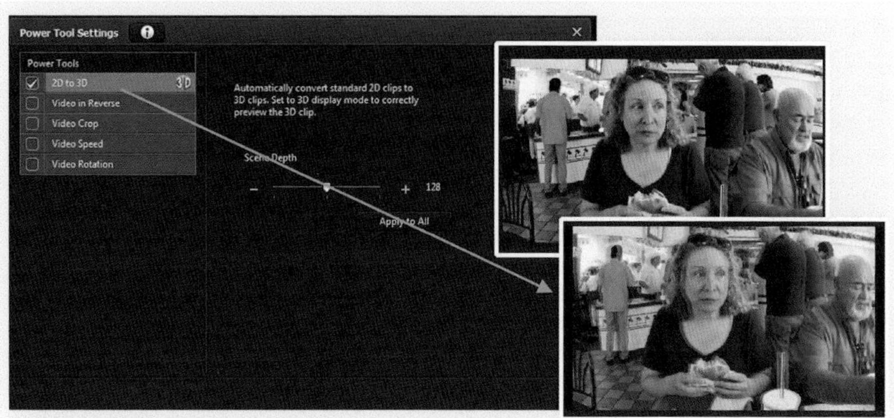

2D to 3D

One of the most amazing tools in PowerDirector is a tool which creates faux 3D content from standard 3D video – and the results are strikingly effective!

To create 3D video from your video, select the video clip on your timeline and click the **Power Tools** function button, as described on page 65.

On the **Power Tools Settings** panel, check the **2D to 3D** option. You may adjust the **Screen Depth** if necessary.

If you click the **Apply All** button, **2D to 3D** will be applied to all clips on your timeline.

Output your 3D video

Editing your 3D video isn't all that much different than editing regular 3D video. And PowerDirector includes a number of great options for outputting your finished piece.

Click the **Produce** button at the top of the interface then, in the **Produce** workspace, click on the **3D** tab.

Select an output format.

Windows Media produces a WMV file. This format includes profiles for 320x180, 640x360, 1280x720 and 1920x1080.

MPEG-2. A format that includes profiles for outputting DVD-ready 720x480, 720x576. 1280x720, 1440x1080 and BluRay-ready 1920x1080.

Quicktime produces an MOV file. This format includes profiles for 160x90, 320x180, 640x360, 960x540, 1280x720 and 1920x1080 at a variety of frame rates.

AVC. An H.264 compressed format that can be used to output an MP4, M2TS or MKV file. These various file formats include profiles for outputting 640x480, 720x480, 720x576, 1280x720, 1440x1080 and 1920x1080 video at a variety of frame rates. MP4s and M2TSs also include the option to output the 3D video in the **MVC (Multi-View Coding)** format.

Additionally, you have the option of creating custom profiles for any format.

All 3D output templates give you the option of outputting **Side-by-Side (L/R)** or **Anaglyph** 3D. **Anaglyph** 3D can be viewed on any device with a pair of red/blue 3D glasses. **Side-by-Side** 3D requires a monitor or TV capable of displaying it.

MVC, or Multi-view Video Coding, is an advanced 3D video encoder that saves visual data from several cameras as a single video stream. **3D BluRay discs use the MVC coded video.** MVC is also backwards compatible, so that it can be viewed as 3D on a 3D enabled device or 2D when played on a standard TV.

BluRay discs can also be output in the **3D-BD f**ormat.

For information creating 3D DVDs and BluRay discs, see page 195.

Using the Multicam Designer

Synchronizing Clips

Selecting Camera Angles

Tweaking Camera Cuts

Editing Multicam Video on the Timeline

Chapter 7

Edit MultiCam Video

Cutting between camera angles

One of my favorite features in PowerDirector is a tool usually seen only in professional video editing software – the ability to cut between video taken from several camera angles of the same event.

As with most of its tools, PowerDirector makes the process intuitive and easy.

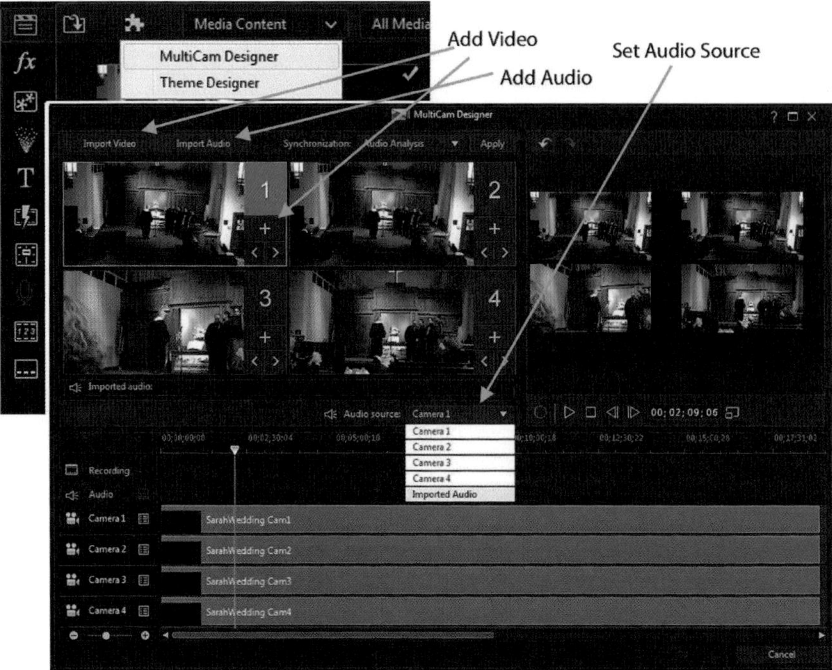

One of the most advanced tools in CyberLink PowerDirector is a tool for editing multi-camera video.

Multicam video is video in which two to four (or more) camcorders shoot the same event simultaneously from different angles.

With PowerDirector's **MultiCam Editing** tool, you can view all of your video sources at once, and then select which video source you want to appear in your movie at any given point.

1 **Open the MultiCam Designer**

To edit your multicam video, click the puzzle piece icon at the top of the **Media Room** and select **MultiCam Designer**, as illustrated above.

A browse screen will open. Gather your multicam video files and click **Open**.

Up to four separate video sources can be displayed in the in the **Source Video** monitors on the panel's upper left.

You can import more video sources or replace video in this workspace by clicking the **Import Video** button at the top left of the panel or by clicking the **+** button on any of the four **Source Video** monitors.

Video can be imported from your hard drive or from the **Media Room**.

2 **Select your Audio Source**

Click the **Audio Source** drop-down menu below the **Source Video** monitors.

You can use the audio from one of your camcorders as your multicam's master audio or import a separate audio file.

3 **Sync your videos and audio**

Since all of your video sources are recordings of the same event, you'll want to synchronize them before you begin cutting between them.

Under the **Synchronization** drop-down menu at the top of the panel, you'll find a number of ways to sync your video sources.

If your camcorders were synchronized with exactly the same timecode or time settings, you can use the **Timecode** or **File Created Time** options. You can also sync to **Markers On Clips** or even **Manually**.

But in our experience, the **Audio Analysis Synchronization** option is very effective. (Assuming, of course, that all of your camcorders were recording audio of the event.)

Once you've selected your **Synchronization** method, click **Apply**.

In order to synchronize the videos, the **Multicam Designer** may add black to the beginnings or ends of some clips.

4 **Select your initial camera angle**

Select your initial camera angle by clicking on its **Source Video** monitor. Once selected, this **Source Monitor** will be outlined in blue and its video will display on the panel's main **Preview** window.

If your playhead is over an area of your timeline in which only one, two or three of your clips are available you'll, naturally, see only that or those **Source Videos** as available.

5 **Record your camera angles**

Play through your video and plan where you'd like your cuts to occur.

When you're ready, click the red dot **Record** button under the **Preview** window and, as the video plays, click to select the camera angle you'd like at that particular moment.

As you switch camera angles, the angles you've chosen will be recorded to the **Recording** track at the top of the timeline.

6 **Tweak your angles**

Once you've finished recording your camera angles, tweaking them is very easy.

To divide one camera angle recording into two, position the playhead over the angle recording you want to divide and then click the **Split** button on the upper left of the timeline.

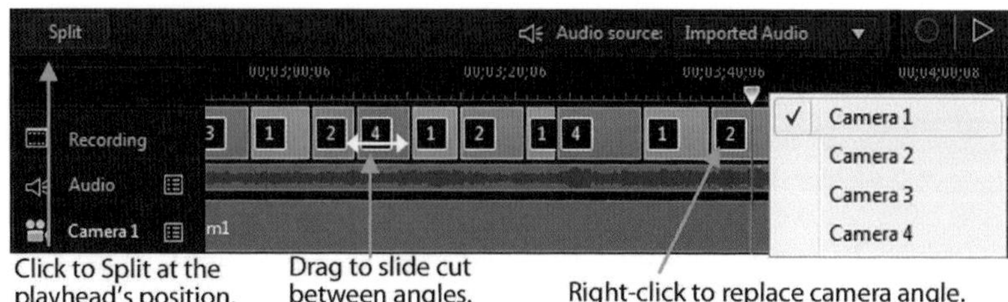

To extend or shorten a camera angle on the **Recording** track, hover your mouse over the intersection of two angle recordings until you see a double-headed white arrow, as illustrated at the bottom of page 68.

Click and drag to slide the cut point between those two camera angles.

You can also replace a camera angle completely by **right-clicking** on the camera angle on the **Recording** track and selecting a different **Video Source**, as illustrated at the bottom of page 76.

When you are happy with your multicam recording, click **OK**.

Your finished video will appear on your timeline as a series of short video cuts, indicated with "**MCx**", and a separate track.

Create a synced video collage with 100 track Multi-Cam Editing

In addition to the dedicated **Multi-Cam Editor** workspace, PowerDirector 14 allows you to sync up to 100 simultaneously shot videos on the timeline and then combine them in your video frame with a variety of effects.

In other words, in PowerDirector 14, you can synchronize video of a concert, wedding or sports event shot from up to 100 different angles and then cut or fade between these clips or even combine several clips into a split screen collage effect.

1 **Place your video on your timeline.**

As an example, I've place the four simultaneously-shot videos of a wedding on my timeline – each video on a separate track.

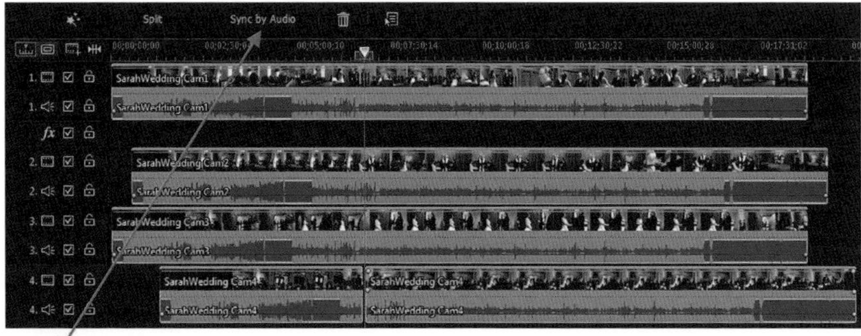

When several simultaneously-shot videos are placed on your timeline, PowerDirector can use their audio to synchronize them.

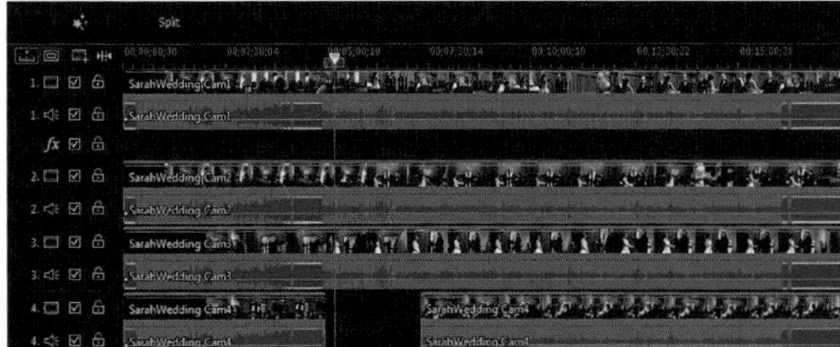

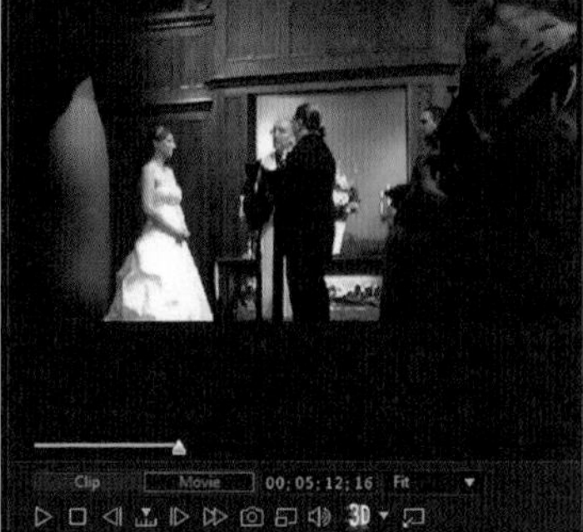

Once your tracks are in sync, your upper tracks can be cut, trimmed, split or have various effects added to them in order to reveal video on the lower tracks.

2 **Select and sync your videos.**

Select the video clips you want to synchronize on your timeline either by dragging across your timeline or, to select all, selecting your **Timeline** and then pressing **Ctrl+a** on your keyboard.

The **Sync by Audio** button will become active on the upper left of the **Timeline**. Click on this button.

The program will analyze the audio from all of the clips on your timeline and then align the clips so that their video and audio is synced.

Because your videos are layered on top of one another and each fills the video frame, only the video on "top" (in my example, the video on the **Video 4** track) will be visible in the **Preview** window. But, by scaling, positioning, changing the opacity and removing video on the upper video tracks, you can reveal one or more of the lower video tracks – sort of like spreading a deck of cards out so that several cards can be seen at once.

3 **Slice and trim your videos.**

The simplest way to reveal videos on lower video tracks is to delete segments from video on upper tracks. You can do this by using the **Split** and **Trim** tools, as described on pages 58 and 59.

When you **Trim** video on one track of a synced project, the remaining segments of the video will remain in sync. When you **Split** and then **Delete** a segment, selecting the option to **Remove and Leave Gap** will keep your clips in sync.

4 **Change a clip's opacity.**

Opacity is the opposite of transparency. When you lower a clip's opacity on the timeline, you make it transparent or semi-transparent, revealing the clip or clips on tracks below it.

To change a clip's transparency, select the clip on your timeline an d click the **Keyframe** button along the top of the timeline. The **Opacity** level can be adjusted under the **Clip Attributes**.

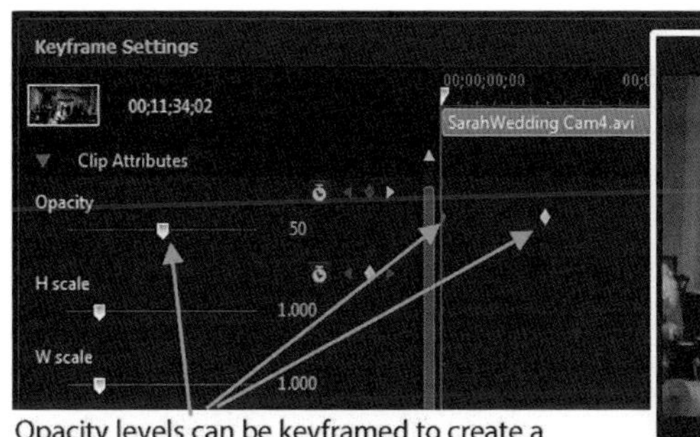

Opacity levels can be keyframed to create a dissolve between camera angles.

By using **Keyframing** (see page 109), you can vary the level of transparency to cross-dissolve between video tracks.

5 **Create a split screen effect.**

Splitting your screen enables you to show two or more video angles at the same time, creating a video collage.

The easiest way to create a video collage of your synchronized videos is to select one track at a time on your timeline (beginning with the uppermost track, since it's the one you'll see in the **Preview** window) and then size and position it using the corner handles and gripper than appear in the **Preview** window, as in the illustration below.

By using **Keyframing** (see page 109), you can animate the clips so that they change size and position within your video frame.

If you select a clip and click the **Modify** button to open the **PiP Designer** (see page 63), you'll find options to apply a **Fade In** and **Fade Out**, add **Masks** (to cut your video clip into various shapes) and add **Motion** paths to create pre-programmed animations of one video over or under the others.

Using Masks in the PiP Designer, you can crop or cookie cutter a clip into a shape or size.

By dragging corner handles or the "grippers" on the clips, you can position them to create a split screen collage.

The Magic Tool Collection

Magic Fix

Magic Cut

Magic Style

Magic Music

Chapter 8

Magic Tools

Easy ways to create cool movies and effects

PowerDirector includes a whole library of Magic Tools – easy-to-use tools for creating effects, generating animation and even creating music.

Magic Tools are so cool, even veteran editors enjoy using them!

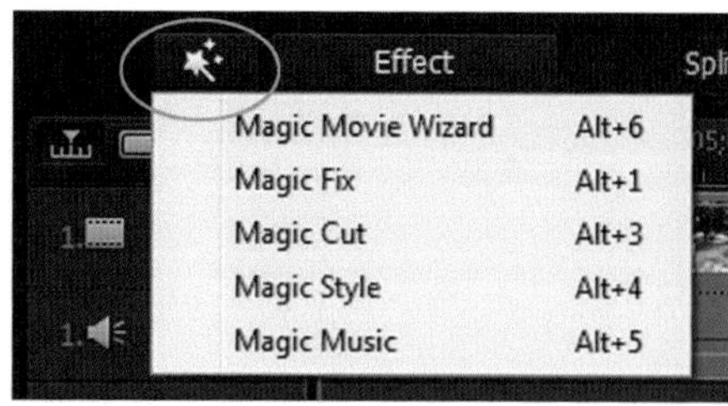

Magic Tools are semi-automatic tools for accomplishing tasks and creating media for your PowerDirector project. You provide the media and set the criteria and the tool does the rest.

Magic Tools are launched by clicking on the magic wand button in the upper left of the **Timeline.**

Which tools are available depends on whether or not you have a clip selected on your timeline. Some tools can be used on more than one clip at once.

Magic Tools include:

The Magic Movie Wizard, a tool for creating a movie based on your media and preferences. We show you how to use it, along with the very cool **Theme Designer**, in **Chapter 2, Make Simple Movies With The Easy Editor**.

Magic Fix automatically stabilizes your video, adjusts its lighting or removes video or audio noise.

Magic Cut automatically trims your clip to remove unwanted characteristics, based on criteria you select.

Magic Style places your selected clip or clips into a selected style template.

Magic Music uses integrated **SmartSound** technology to create a custom music track, at a custom length, based on your criteria.

Magic Fix

The **Magic Fix** tools will automatically fix video and audio problems in your selected clip. To open the **Magic Fix** panel, select a clip on your timeline and select **Magic Fix** from the magic wand menu at the top left of the **Timeline**.

Select the fixes you would like to apply, then click to select a fix and set it to the level you'd like it applied.

Lighting Adjustment corrects the lighting or exposure in your video.

Checking the **Extreme Backlight** option advises the program to correct for a scene in which the subject is not lit as brightly as the background.

Lens Correction removes the image distortion that is sometimes caused by shooting with a very wide-angle lens.

Video Stabilizer zooms in slightly on your video and, adjusting the video's position according to your video frame's content, takes some of the shake out of your handheld video footage.

When you check **Fix Rotational Camera Shake,** the tool will also correct sideways rolls of the camera as much as possible. The **Enhanced Stabilizer** option can improve the quality of your finished, stabilized video.

Video Denoise softens snowy white noise that can creep into low-light video.

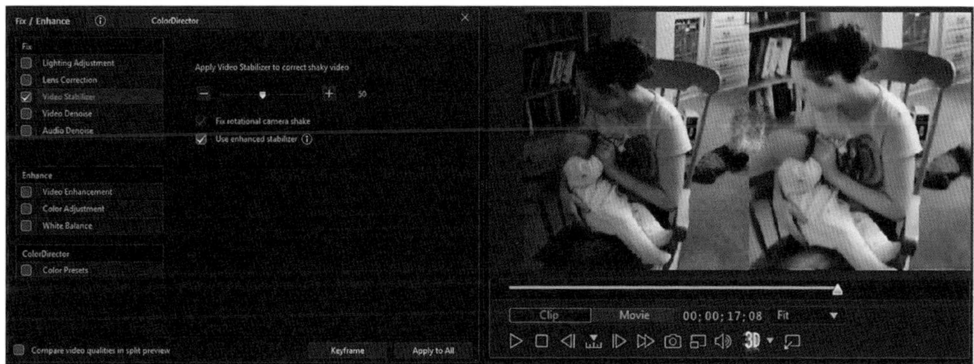

Audio Denoise will reduce background audio noise as much as possible. It can be set to remove **Stationary Noise** (room noise), **Wind Noise** or **Clicking Noise**. This isn't true magic, of course, so there are limits to what it can do – though it does serve as a pretty effective noise gate for most audio!

A checkbox option at the bottom of the panel allows you to compare your video's before and after looks, as illustrated above.

For more advanced color work, you also have the option to launch the clip in **ColorDirector**, if you have it installed, by clicking the button at the top of the panel. (ColorDirector is included with PowerDirector Ultra and Director Suites.)

Magic Cut

The **Magic Cut** tool will analyze your video for quality issues and then automatically remove unwanted segments, based on the levels of each criterium you apply. To open the **Magic Cut** panel, select a clip or clips on your timeline and select **Magic Cut** from the magic wand menu at the top left of the **Timeline**.

By default, the tool will add a fade between each cut, and a music track can be optionally added.

Click **Preview** to preview the cuts and, if you're happy with them, click **Apply**.

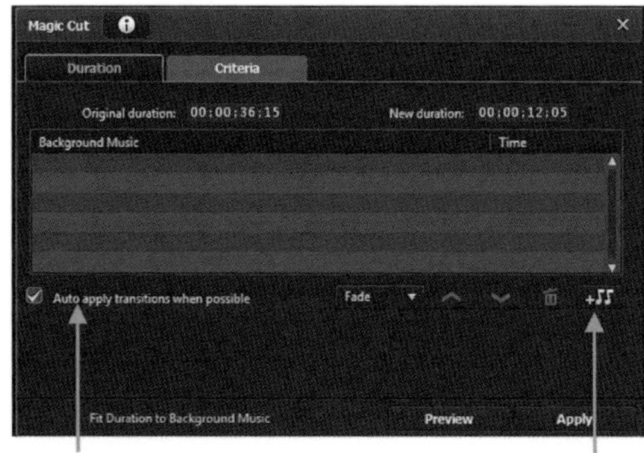

Apply fade between cuts. Add music.

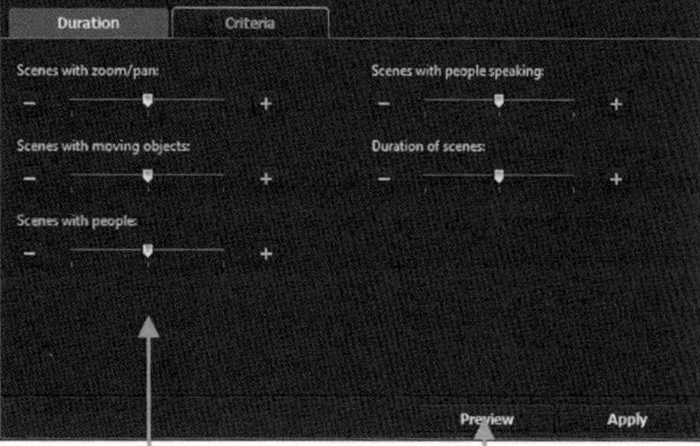

Set criteria levels. Preview results.

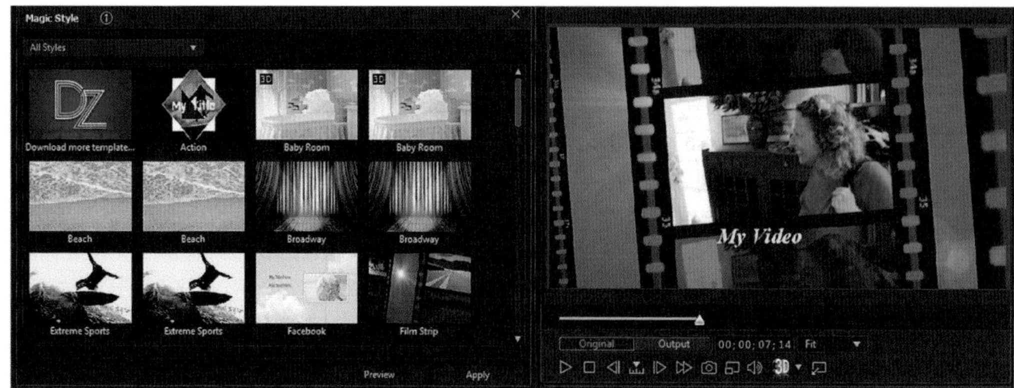

Magic Style

The **Magic Style** tool will edit and arrange your video clips using one of its stylish, animated movie templates – usually with pretty cool results!

Some **Styles** add an animated title to the beginning of your movie. Others place your video clip into an animated background.

Once you've opened the tool, creating one of these highly-styled movies is as simple as selecting one of the **Styles**, clicking **Preview** to test drive it and, if you like it, clicking **Apply**.

The **Styles** in this panel can be viewed all at once or, by clicking the button at the top left of the panel, you can opt to see only certain categories.

You can also download any of thousands of free **Style** templates from the CyberLink **DirectorZone** by clicking on the **DZ** button at the top left of the panel. For more information on the **DirectorZone**, see the discussion on page 200.

Once you've applied a **Style** to your clip or group of clips, the stylized movie will replace the selected video on your timeline.

To customize the titles and tweak the style, **double-click** this movie or select the movie on your timeline and click the **Theme Designer** button along the top of the **Timeline**, as illustrated on the facing page.

A box will appear warning you that, "**Any edits you made to the selected content on the timeline will be reset once you enter the Theme Designer. Do you want to continue**". Click **Yes**.

In the **Theme Designer**, you can customize your titles and opt to import your own custom background music.

You can also choose to add more video clips to your mini-movie from your **Media Room** or import video from your hard drive. To add another video clip to your mini-movie, drag the clip from the media panel into one of the placeholders along the left side of the **Preview** window.

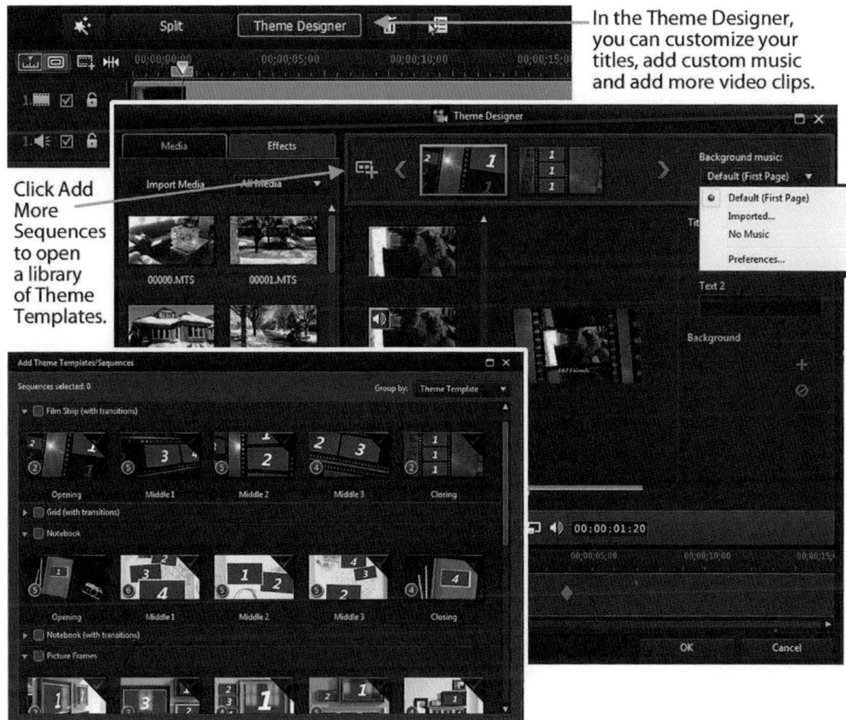

If all of these placeholder spaces are occupied, you'll need to either first remove an existing clip out of a placeholder or click the **Add More Sequences** button.

If you click the **Add More Sequences** button, as illustrated above, the **Theme Templates** panel will open, from which you can opt to add more templates, which will create additional placeholders to drop your video clips into.

Under the **Effects** tab, you'll find a library of effects you can drag onto your clips. (To remove or adjust an effect, **double-click** on the little **FX** icon that appears on the lower right of a clip you've added an effect to.)

Once you've finished editing your movie's **Theme** and **Style**, click **OK**.

If you re-open the **Theme Designer** to further edit your clip, you'll once again be warned that, "**Any edits you made to the selected content on the timeline will be reset once you enter the Theme Designer. Do you want to continue.**"

Click **Yes** to re-edit your theme or style.

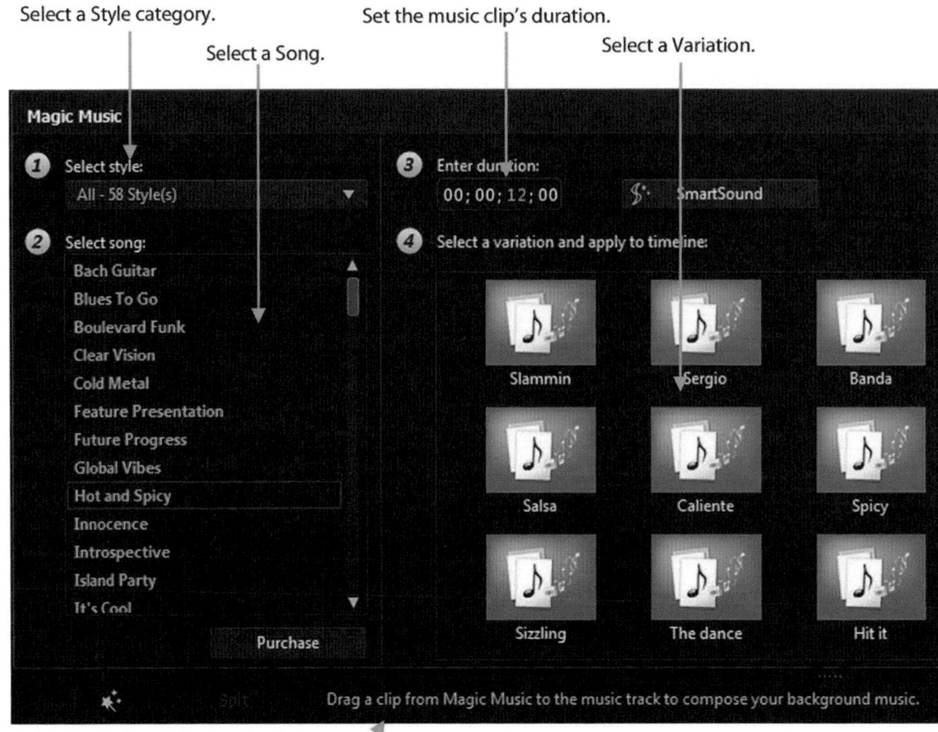

Click the Add Music Track button or drag the Variation to the Music Track on the Timeline.

Magic Music

The **Magic Music** tool uses **SmartSound** technology to create a custom, royalty-free music track for you, created to your specifications – including duration. In other words, if you need a suspenseful musical clip exactly 9 seconds long, the **Magic Music SmartSound** tool will create a suspenseful 9-second music clip for you that includes a natural beginning, middle and end.

To open the **Magic Music/SmartSound** panel, select **Magic Style** from the magic wand menu at the top left of the **Timeline**.

SmartSound is a company that sells music for video and movie producers. Creating a custom music track with **SmartSound** is as easy as following a couple of simple steps.

1 **Select a Musical Style**

The **SmartSound** tool gives you access to 58 different musical styles. Leave it set to **All Styles** to see the entire musical library.

2 **Select a Song**

Although **SmartSound** offers a vast library of musical styles and songs, only the thirty-six songs highlighted in blue are included free with PowerDirector.

If you select a song other than one highlighted in blue, you will be prompted to click the **Purchase** button, which will open an option screen from which you can buy the song or buy an album which includes the song along with similarly-themed music.

Most "songs", by the way, are actually musical themes, usually including several variations, as you'll see in **Step 5.**

3 **Set the Duration**

Type in the **Duration** you'd like your music track to be, with the timecode representing **Hours:Minutes:Seconds:Frames.**

In other words, the **Duration** of a 12-second song would be listed as 00:00:12:00.

4 **Select a Variation**

Most songs include a number of **Variations.** To test drive each, select the **Variation** and click the **Play** button under the **Preview** window.

5 **Generate your music clip**

When you've selected a **Song** and **Variation** and you've set the **Duration**, the **Add to Music Track** button will appear below the **Magic Music** panel, as illustrated on the facing page.

When you click this button, a musical clip, at the exact duration you specified, will be generated and placed on the **Music Track** for your movie. (This track is way down, below all of your video, audio, title and narration tracks, so you may need to scroll way down to see it on the **Timeline** panel.)

Once your **Magic Music** track has been added to your movie, you can move it to any audio track you'd like.

Your Magic Music clip will be added first to the Music Track, at the bottom of the Timeline – after which you can drag it to any other track in your movie.

Adding and Modifying Effects

Using the Chroma Key Effect

Adding and Modifying Particle Effects

Keyframing Motion Paths, Effects and Animations

Chapter 9

Video Effects and Animations

Color tone and special effects

CyberLink PowerDirector includes a wealth of video effects and movie overlays.

Some adjust the look or change the style of your video. Others add elements or special effects to your movie.

There are lots of cool ways to add visual styles and special effects to your movie with CyberLink PowerDirector.

Some of these effects change the tone or mood of your movie. Some allow you to add fantasy elements to your movie. Some are overlays, which allow you to add cool animated elements to your movie.

And with the power of **keyframing**, you can customize their adjustments and behavior precisely at any given point.

Color Presets

Presets are pre-created adjustments to the color temperature, tint and tone of your video. Using **Color Effects**, you can change the entire look and mood of your movie with just a couple of clicks.

To open your library of **Color Effects**, select a clip on your timeline and then click the **Fix/Enhance** function button along the top of the **Timeline.** On the **Fix/Enhance** panel, check and select the **Color Presets** option.

To test drive each effect on your video clip, ensure that the **Timeline's** playhead is over your selected clip and then click on one of the **Color Presets.**

The program comes with 20 presets, although, if you set the panel category to **All Presets** and you are logged into the **DirectorZone**, thousands of additional presets can be downloaded free by clicking the **DZ** button in the upper left of the panel. For more information on the **DirectorZone**, see page 200.

Among these **Color Presets** are effects for making your video look like an old home movie, a low-budget 1970s movie, a surrealistic dream, a Martian landscape or like it was shot on a sun-washed summer day.

To apply an effect to one clip, simply select the preset. To apply this preset to your entire movie, click the **Apply To All** Button. To close the panel, click the **X** in its upper right corner.

To fine tune the look, you can further tweak your clip's **Color Adjustment**, as described in The **Fix/Enhance** function on page 64.

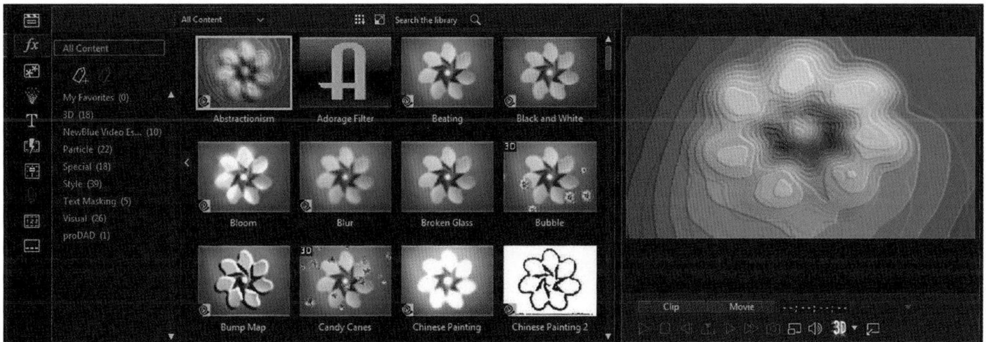

Add Video Effects

PowerDirector's library of video effects is found in the **FX Room**, available by clicking the **FX** tab along the upper left of the program. A **Search the Library** box in the upper right of the **Room** allows you to real-time search for a specific effect (see page 19).

PowerDirector includes over 100 video effects, including a package of effects from **NewBlue**, one of the world's top visual effects companies. The Ultimate and Director Suite versions include additional effects packages, and you can purchase even more effects from **NewBlue** by clicking on the **Download NewBlue Effects** button.

Many of these effects will add elements or particles to your video – like snow, fireworks, a lens flare, fire and smoke, bubbles, fog and rain. And a number of these effects are 3D, which means they'll appear 3-dimensional when used in a stereoscopic 3D project (see page 70).

A number of effects will break up your video image, dividing it into a grid of several images or making it look like an Andy Warhol collage. Others will make your video look like a pen and ink, pencil or crayon drawing or make it appear to be reflected in a rippling pond. The program even includes a **Tilt Shift** effect, which we discuss in the sidebar on page 94.

Finally, there are a couple of **Text Masking** video effects. We'll show you how to use them on page 152 of **Chapter 12, Add Titles**.

You can, of course, preview an effect's look or animation in the **Preview** window by clicking on its thumbnail in the **FX Room**.

Power Tools

In addition to the video effects covered in this chapter, PowerDirector includes **Power Tools** which allow you to crop or create animated pans & zooms, change the speed of or reverse playback of your clip or even to change your 2D video into 3D.

For more information, see **Power Tools** on page 65.

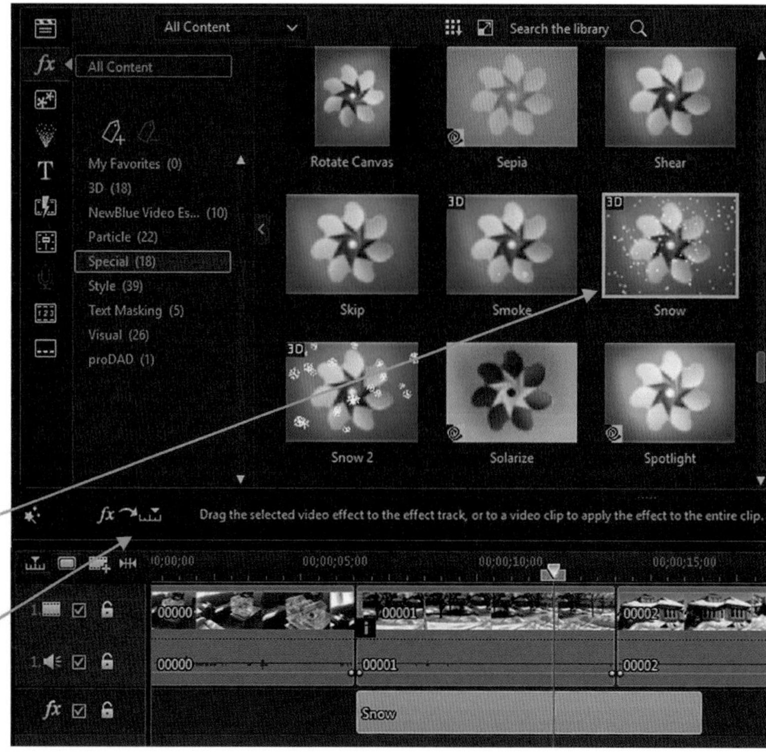

A selected effect can be dragged directly to a clip or added as an adjustment layer to the FX track by clicking on the Add to Effect Track button.

Apply an effect

Effects can be applied directly to a clip or can be used as an "adjustment layer" by adding them to the **FX track** on your timeline.

To add an effect directly to a clip, drag it from the **FX Room** onto a clip on your timeline.

More than one effect can be applied to an individual clip. However, only one effect can be used as an adjustment layer over a given segment of your movie at a time.

To add an effect as an adjustment layer, drag the effect from the **FX Room** to the **FX track** on the **Timeline** – or select the effect and click the **Add to Effect Track** below the **FX Room** panel.

When you add an effect to the **FX Track** as an adjustment layer (as illustrated above), the effect will be visible on every clip on the **Video 1 track** that is covered by the effect.

Once your effect has been added to the **FX track**, you can reposition it on the timeline or extend or shorten it by dragging on its ends.

An effect on the F**X track** can, therefore, be set to apply to only one clip, positioned to apply to a sequence of several clips – or it can be stretched to cover your entire movie.

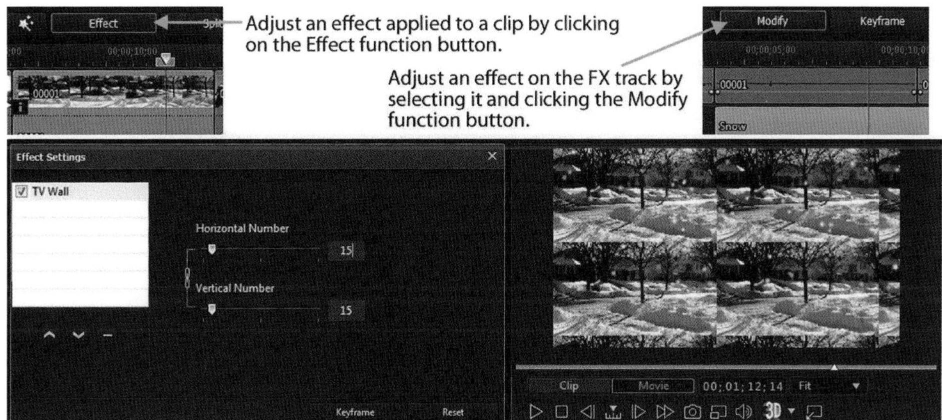

Adjust your video effect

When a video effect has been applied to a clip, a small, yellow icon will appear on the clip.

To adjust or customize a video effect applied to a clip, select the clip and click the **Effect** function button along the top of the **Timeline**.

To adjust or customize an effect on the FX track, double-click on the effect or select the effect and click the **Modify** function button.

In either case, the **Effects Settings** panel will open.

Every effect has settings that can be custom adjusted. If the playhead on the **Timeline** is over a clip to which the effect is applied, you will see the results of your adjustments in the **Preview** window.

A number of effects are animated and their settings change over time. For instance, the **TV Wall** effect, illustrated above, starts with a single image then, as the effect plays, it divides the video frame into more and more images. You should be able to see this by playing the effected clip or by scrubbing (dragging) the playhead across the clip or clips. This animation is created using **keyframes**. And, when you attempt to make an adjustment to an animated effect, a panel will pop up advising you that "**This operation resets all keyframes in this effect. Do you want to continue?**"

In other words, making an adjustment to the effect will remove its preset animation. When you change the **TV Wall** effect to 15 horizontal and vertical squares, for instance, the effect will now display 15 horizontal and vertical squares *throughout the clip's duration*. The animation that zooms back from a single image to a grid of images will have been removed.

You can recreate this animation manually or create a custom animation from scratch for any effect by adding your own **keyframes** for the **Effects Settings**. We show you how to create and modify **keyframed animation** beginning on page 109.

The Effects Mask

Many video effects need not be applied to your entire video frame. Using the **Effects Mask**, you can isolate an area of your video frame and apply the effect to that area only.

We put the **Effects Mask** to work on **How do I blur a face like on TV's COPS** on page 205.

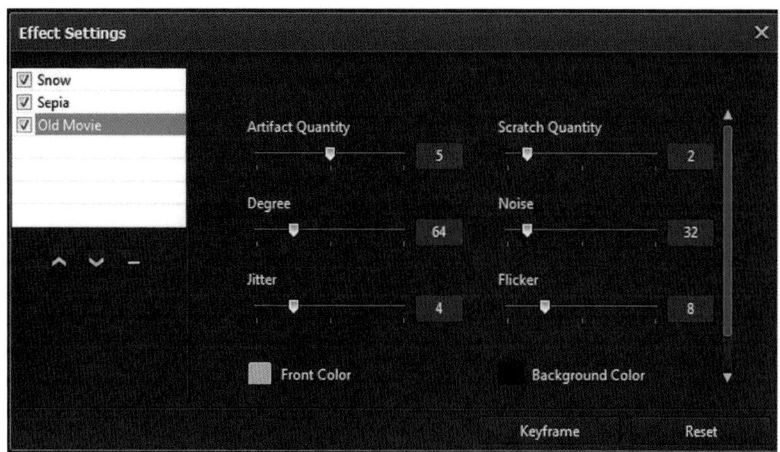

Disable or Remove effects

You can drag any number of effects onto a clip. And, when you select this clip and click the **Effect** function button, the **Effects Settings** panel will display the list of effects applied, as illustrated above.

Select any effect to adjust its specific settings.

Uncheck an effect to temporarily disable that effect.

To remove an effect completely, select it and click the **–** button below the list.

The Tilt/Shift effect

A trendy but still pretty cool visual effect is the **Tilt/Shift**. The **Tilt/Shift** effect applies a blur to the top and bottom thirds of your video. When applied to footage shot from an oblique angle (about 45 degrees above ground level, with a close foreground and distant background), the result is a video that appears to have an extremely short depth of field – which makes your real-life scene look as if it were composed of toys or miniatures!

One of the most effective uses of the **Tilt/Shift** effect I've seen is a clip created from a time-lapse video of Disney World. You can see it at www.youtube.com/watch?v=HyZfIlxwsfI or by searching "Tilt Shift Disney" on YouTube.

Apply Chroma Key

To "key" a clip, in video editing, means to make it transparent. When you key a clip, you replace its current background with a new background.

Chroma Key is the essential effect of fantasy and science fiction films – although it has lots of down to Earth uses too. For instance, on the nightly news, a weather forecaster is often shown in front of a moving weather map. In actuality, that forecaster is standing in front of a green backdrop, and the animation behind him or her is being added – or "keyed in" – electronically.

The **Chroma Key** effect can be used to place an actor, shot in a studio, in front of any real or imagined background in the universe.

The basic principle of **Chroma Key** is that footage of an actor or prop is shot in front of a flat-colored background (usually a green or blue background, since these colors are the opposite of human skin tones). This video is then placed over footage of a new background. When the green or blue background is made transparent, the actor appears to be in front of this new background.

To effectively use the **Chroma Key** effect, you will need two clips:

- A video of someone or some thing standing in front of a smooth, evenly-lit blue or green screen backdrop. We'll call this our **Foreground** video.
- A video or still image of a **Background** scene.

Although you can use a smooth, wrinkle-free sheet, blanket or even a wall as your backdrop, blue and green backdrop screens work best if they are bright and vivid. Bright, professional-style green or blue screens can be found online at sites like Amazon and greenscreensystems.com for surprisingly little cost.

Good lighting is also crucial to creating a good key. Make sure your green or blue screen is well lit and without any shadows or hot spots – and make sure your foreground actor is lit separately and equally well.

Once you've got the parts, the rest comes pretty easy:

1 **Add your background to the Video 1 track**

   Place the video or still image that will serve as your new **Background** on the **Video 1** track, as illustrated on page 96.

   If you're using a video or photo that doesn't fill your video frame because it doesn't have the same aspect ratio, click to select the clip on your timeline and then drag on the corner handles that appear in the **Preview** window to enlarge your video or photo to fill the frame.

2 **Add your Foreground video to an "upper" video track**

Place your **Foreground** video on **Video 2,** aligned with your **Background** clip. Ensure that the videos on both tracks are of equal length. (If you're using a photo as your **Background**, you can drag its end to extend it so that it's the same duration as your foreground video.)

Remember that, in PowerDirector, clips on **Video 2** will appear over clips on **Video 1**, even though **Video 2** is *below* **Video 1** on the **Timeline** itself.

3 **Open the PiP Designer**

Double-click on the **Foreground** clip on **Video 2.** The **PiP Designer** will open with **Video 2** displayed, as illustrated below.

4 **Enable Chroma Key**

Click the triangular toggle under the **Properties** tab to open the **Chroma Key** properties. Check **Enable Chroma Key.**

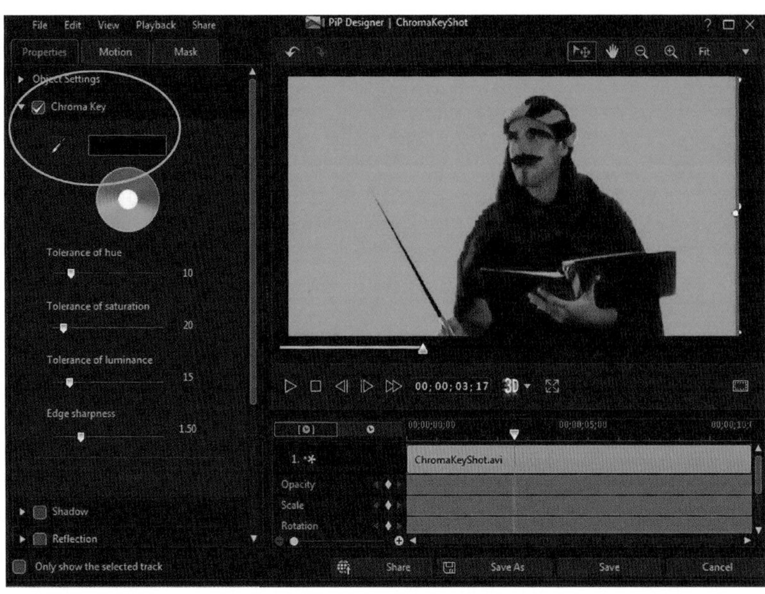

5 **Define the key color**

Click to select the eyedropper next to the color swatch above the color wheel. Hover your mouse over the clip's background and click to sample the background's color.

Most or all of your green or blue background should become transparent, revealing the background clip on **Video 1** behind your actor.

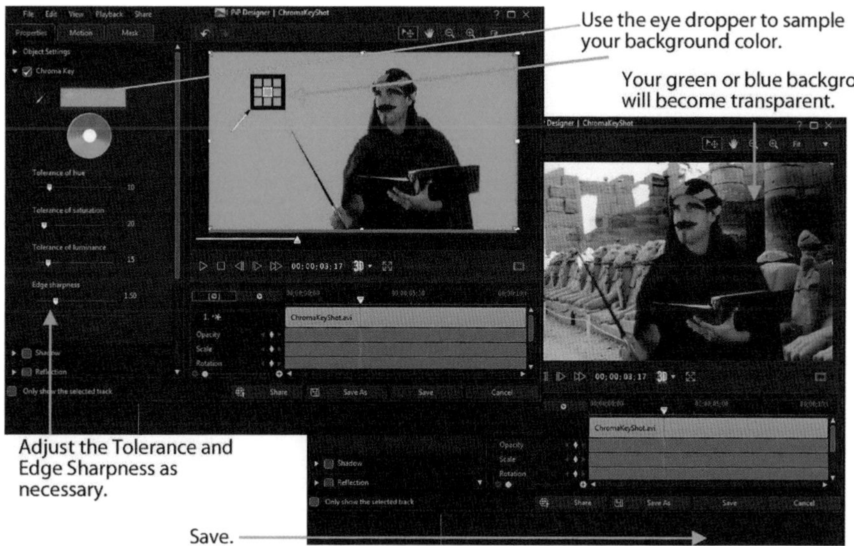

The smoother and more evenly colored this clip's green or blue screen is, the easier it will be to get a good, clean key.

If your green or blue background doesn't disappear completely or the break between the key and your actor needs tweaking, adjust the **Tolerance** levels and **Edge Sharpness**.

When you're satisfied with your key effect, click **Save**.

Masks and Garbage Mattes

Masks cut your video into various shapes by "masking" or making areas outside the selected mask shape transparent.

They can also be used as **"garbage mattes"** to remove areas of **Chroma Key** shot where the edge of the backdrop shows or where the background has a blemish or wrinkle that just won't key properly.

To apply a mask, **double-click** your clip to open it in the **PiP Designer** and click on the **Mask** tab.

Select a **Mask** (a rectangle will do) and then drag on the **Mask's** corner handles in the **Preview** window to size and position it to mask the problem areas in your shot.

It's best to apply a **"garbage matte"** before enabling **Chroma Key.**

Motion Tracking

New to version 14 is the ability to apply **Motion Tracking** – to track the movement of a person or object in a video clip – and then to set a graphic, title or media clip to lock onto and follow that object's movement across your video frame. This tool can often be used, for instance, to lock a **Mosaic** effect to an object or person in order to mask or censor a face or image.

1 Open the Motion Tracker

Open the **Motion Tracker** by selecting a clip on the timeline and, from the **Tools** Function button along the top of the timeline, select **Motion Tracker**.

The **Motion Tracker** panel will open.

To create a **Motion Tracker** effect, first identify a moving object in your video frame. Ideally this object should be distinct from the background and should remain fairly consistent in look and color throughout.

Once you've identified and created a **Tracker** that follows your object, you'll assign an element to it – a graphic or small video clip, a block of text or an effect – and this element will follow the object's movements.

In my sample clip above, I'm tracking the movement of a jet over a runway.

2 Define the object to be tracked

Position the playhead on the panel's timeline to the point you'd at which you'd like your **Motion Track** to begin.

By dragging its corner handles, size and position the white **Selection Box** over the object you want to track. (The **Motion Tracker** assumes the point at which you've defined your object to be the beginning of your **Motion Track**, and it will automatically trim the blue-green **Tracker** overlay on the **Motion Tracker** timeline, as illustrated above.)

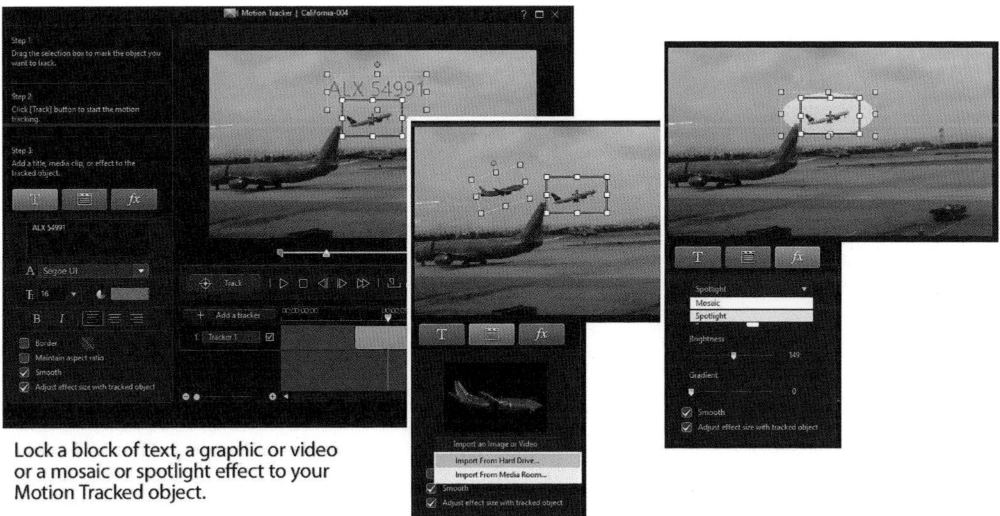

Lock a block of text, a graphic or video or a mosaic or spotlight effect to your Motion Tracked object.

3 **Track your object**

Click the **Track** button, as illustrated on the facing page. The program will track your object and , if it's done so correctly, the **Selection Box** will follow your object across your video frame. The track will continue as long as the object is visible and identifiable in the frame.

4 **Add a tracking element**

Select the option to add either a **Title**, a **Media Clip** or an **Effect**.

A **Title** will follow your object and, if you select the option to **Adjust Effect Size with Tracked Object,** the text will enlarge or shrink as the object tracks nearer or farther away. Once you've created and customized the text, drag it into position on or around the tracked object and it will remain in that position, relative to the object.

A **Media Clip** will appear as a picture-in-picture, which you can size and position relative to the tracked object. This clip can be a video or a still photo – and, if you are using a transparent PNG or even animated GIF file, as I did when I added the second jet, above, the opaque elements in the graphic will be visible and the transparency around the graphic will remain transparent.

You may also choose to lock a **Mosaic** or **Spotlight Effect** to the tracked object so that it either hides or highlights the selected object as it moves around the video frame. (We show you the more traditional method for masking or blurring an area of your video on page 205.)

In my example, I added a **Title** – the (fictional) name of the flight – which follows the jet's flight into the sky. Because I selected the option to **Adjust Effect Size with Tracked Object**, this title disappears into distance the with the jet.

If you click the **Add a Tracker** button, you can create one or more additional **Motion Tracks** on different objects on the same clip – each with its own **Title, Media Clip** or **Effect** added to it.

The Action Camera Center is a one-stop-shop for fixing, stylizing and enhancing video from sport (and other) camcorders. It includes a lens distortion fix and a library of stylish color grades.

The Action Camera Center

The **Action Camera Center** is a new workspace that includes a number of tools for enhancing and correcting your video clips. The main purpose of the **Action Camera Center** is to provide a one-stop shop for working with footage from action cams – video from GoPros and similar sport or heavy duty camcorders – although you can also use it with any standard camcorder footage.

Among the features included in the **Action Camera Center** is a tool for creating repeating **Time Shift** segments and a tool for adding a **Freeze Frames** to your clip.

The **Action Camera Center** is opened by selecting a clip on your timeline and then selecting the **Action Camera Center** option on the **Tools** Function button, as illustrated above at the left.

Fix your clips

Under the **Fix** tab in the **Action Camera Center** are tools for correcting and enhancing the look of your selected video. Many of these same adjustments can also be found on the program's **Fix/Select** panel (see page 64). In fact, if a **Fix** is made on either of these panels, the fix and its settings will be indicated in the settings on both panels.

Fixes in the **Action Camera Center** include:

Lens Correction. A fairly automatic tool that corrects distortion caused by the extreme wide-angle lenses on a number of sport cams, this advanced system includes correction presets for a number of **Makes** and **Models** as well as settings for fine-tuning the effect.

Video Stabilizer is a tool that takes a lot of the shake out of a wobbly shot.

White Balance is set of adjustments for correcting white balance issues in your video. As we show you on page 64, an automatic way to correct white balance is to select the terrific **White Calibration** tool (eyedropper) and the use it to click on, or "sample," a white area in your video.

Color Presets are a library of color grade presets that can be used to add style or a cool look to your video. (These are the same Presets available through the Fix/ Enhance panel, as discussed on page 90.)

The program comes with 20 stylish presets, including presets for making your video look like a 1960s home video or to make it look like it was shot on Mars. In addition to the nearly two dozen stock presets, you can also download many more for free from the **Director Zone** and, if you've got the **ColorDirector** add-on program, you can even create your own.

Create Time Shift effects

The **Action Camera Center** includes three tools for creating time shifts in your video.

The **Time Shift** tool can be used to shift your selected video segments into fast motion or, just as suddenly, pull them back to slow motion and back again. We show you how to use this tool in our discussion of the **Video Speed Power Tool** on page 66.

The **Replay** and/or **Reverse** tool sets a selected **Time Zone** segment of your clip to suddenly replay or reverse, as we discuss below.

The **Freeze Frame** tool briefly freezes your video's playback.

To Replay and/or Reverse a segment of your video.

1 **Create a Time Shift segment**

Position your playhead to the point on your timeline you'd like your **Replay/ Reverse** to begin, then click the **Create Time Shift** button at the top left of the timeline or on the **Effect** panel. (Either button will work.)

2 **Select the option to Replay/Reverse**

Check the **Apply Replay and Reverse** option and set the number of times your selected segment will **Repeat**.

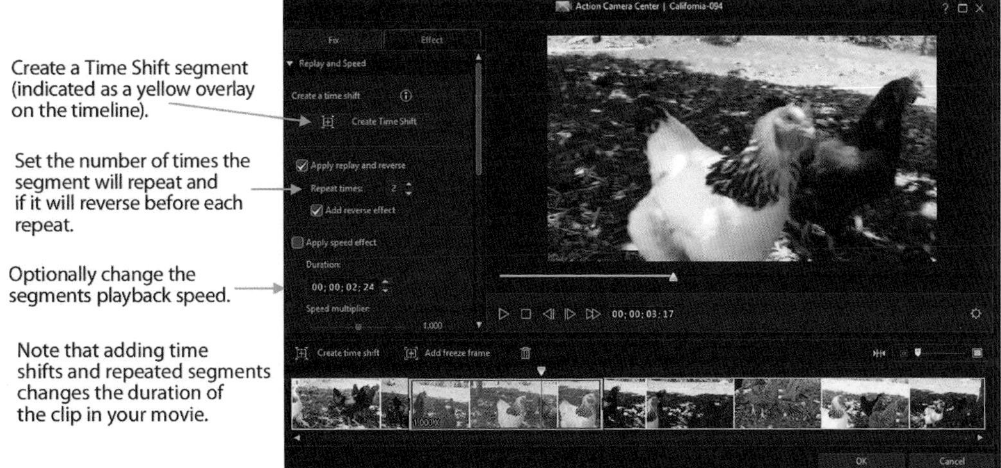

If you select the **Add Reverse Effect** option, the selected video segment will play, then reverse, then replay up to the number of **Repeat Times** you've set.

If you do not select the **Add Reverse Effect** option, your video will play, repeat the segment as set, then continue.

Speed Effects can also be added to your **Replay/Reverse** segment. See page 66 for more information on applying a **Speed Effect**.

To add a Freeze Frame to your video clip.

1 **Select the frame you want to freeze on**

Position the playhead on the frame in your video you'd like to freeze. Click the **Add Freeze Frame** button at the top left of the timeline or on the **Effects** panel. (Either button will work.)

A small marker along the top of the timeline will indicate the frame you've chosen to freeze. This marker is yellow when selected.

2 **Set your Freeze Frame attributes**

You may need to scroll down the Action Camera Center's **Effects** panel to see the **Freeze Frame** options.

Set a **Duration** for your **Freeze Frame**.

Optionally, toggle on the **Zoom Effect**. This effect adds a bit of interest to your **Freeze Frame** by suddenly zooming in and out of the area of the frame you indicate.

Note that adding a **Freeze Frame**, like adding a **Time Shift**, will change the overall length of your video. In other words, adding a 2-second freeze frame will make your clip 2 seconds longer than it was before. This means that, if the clip you're adding the **Freeze Frame** to is part of a movie on your timeline, the rest of the movie will ripple right to allow for the now longer the clip.

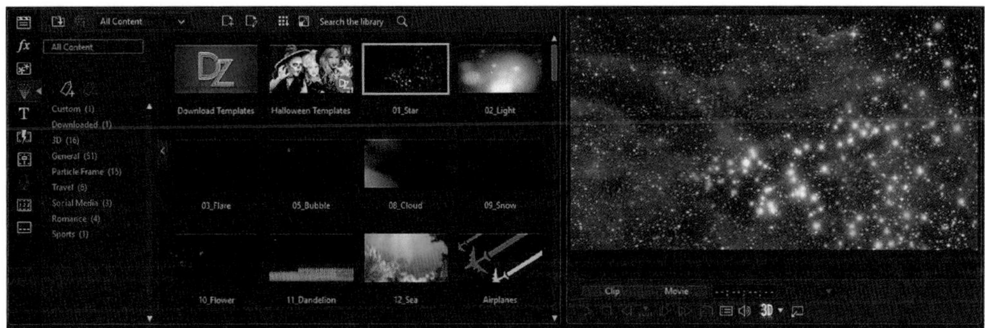

Particles can add animated effects like snow, fireworks, lens flares and shooting stars to your movies.

Add a Particle effect

PowerDirector's library of **Particle** effects is found in the **Particle Room**, available by clicking the **Particle** tab along the upper left of the program.

Particles are very cool special effects overlays that can add new elements to your movie scenes. Among the **Particle** effects available are clouds, bubbles, flares, shooting stars and pixie dust, fire, fireworks, snow and lots of interesting waves and trails. A **Search the Library** box in the upper right of the **Room** allows you to real-time search for a specific effect (see page 19).

Most particles include transparency so that you can use them to add special animated effects over your videos!

Included in this set are CGI effects for adding rain, snow and fog to your movie's scenes!

Particles can also be personalized and customized.

Particle clips in the **Particle Room** are tagged to categories, although you can also select **All Content** to see them all at once. When you click on a particle, you'll see its animation in your **Preview** window.

Among these **Particles** are a number of elements that will appear as stereoscopic 3D when added to a 3D project. But even those that do not include 3D objects can be modified so that they have depth and dimension when used in a 3D movie.

In addition to the default set of **Particles** included with PowerDirector, if you are logged into the **DirectorZone**, thousands of additional **Particles** can be downloaded free by clicking the **DZ** button in the **Downloaded** category of the panel. For more information on the **DirectorZone**, see page 200.

Most Particles have transparent backgrounds, so that they become a part of your video.

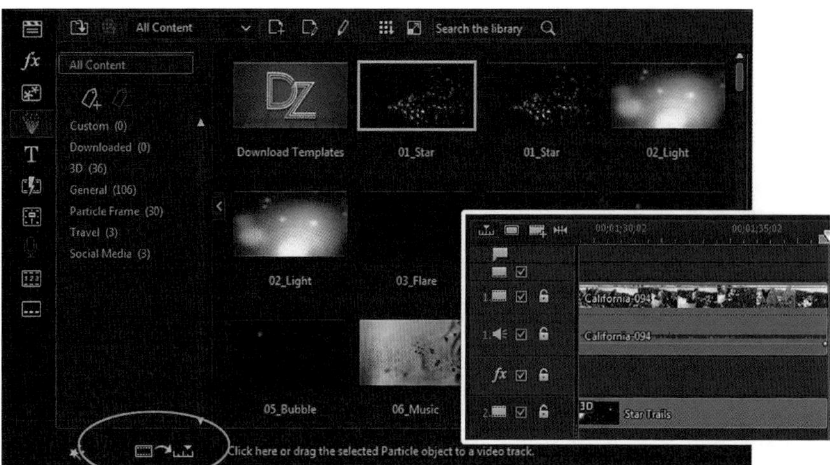

Drag the Particle effect to an available video track or click Insert on Selected Track.

Apply a Particle effect

Particles can used as is on the **Video 1** track – or they can be added alone to an "upper" video track (**Video 2, Video 3**, etc.), in which case they will overlay all of the video clips on **Video 1** or other lower video tracks.

A number of the **Particles** include **alpha**, which is a fancy name for transparency. The transparent areas of your **Particles** show as black in the **Particle Room** – and will appear as black if used on the **Video 1** track.

Particle clips that are not transparent (like **Planet, Star, Light, Flare, Bubble**, etc.) can be easily modified to make them transparent so that they can be used as foreground effects over your existing video, as discussed on page 105.

To add a **Particle** effect to your movie, either:

Drag the Particle from the Particle Room to an empty spot on your timeline. To use the **Particle** as an overlay or a foreground element, position the **Particle** clip on an upper video track. Or,

Select the track on your timeline you'd like to add the Particle clip to and position the **Timeline** playhead where you'd like the **Particle** clip to appear. Click the **Insert on Selected Track** button, as illustrated above.

If you add a **Particle** clip to an area of your timeline in which a clip already is placed, you will be prompted to select an overwrite or insert option, as discussed on page 58.

Particle clips are by default 10 seconds long. You can extend or trim your **Particle** clip to whatever length you'd like. If your **Particle** is animated, the animation will speed up or slow down to match the duration of the clip. In other words, if you extend your 10-second **Particle** clip to 20 seconds, the animation will appear at half its default speed. This, like every characteristic of a **Particle** clip can, of course, be modified in the **Particle Designer**.

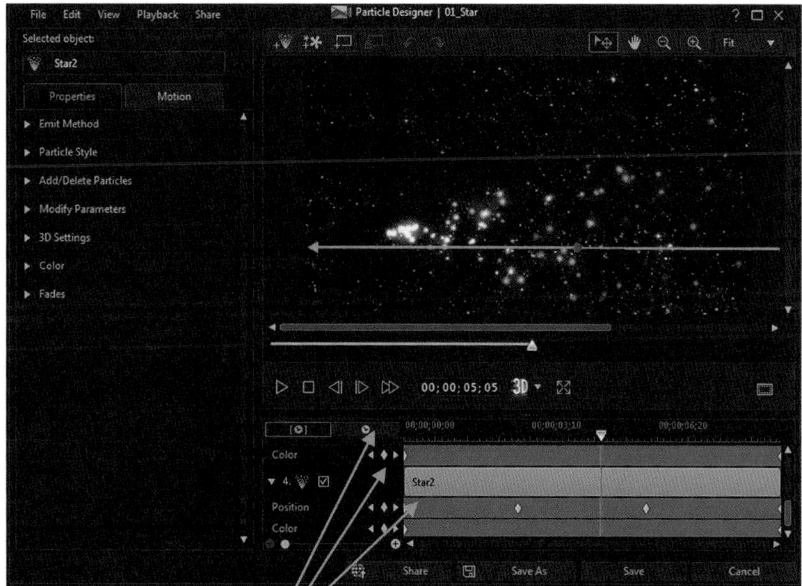

Particle clips are made up of objects, some animated and some that emit animated particles.

Modify a Particle

Every **Particle** effect can be customized, either in the **Particle Room** or on your timeline. If you customize a **Particle** clip while it's still in the **Particle Room**, you'll be prompted to save it as a new custom **Particle**, and it will be available for your use in any future project.

If a modification is made to a **Particle** clip on your timeline, on the other hand, it will only affect that particular usage of the **Particle**.

To open the **Particle Designer** so that you can modify a **Particle, double-click** the **Particle** in either the **Particle Room** or on your timeline.

Make a non-transparent Particle transparent

In the **Particle Designer**, the individual objects or elements that make up a **Particle** clip can be disabled or removed completely.

To make a **Particle** clip that includes a **Background** transparent, uncheck the box on the track header of the **Particle Designer Timeline** track that includes the **Background** object – or select the **Background** clip itself on this timeline and delete it.

Once you've removed your **Background** track, you'll also have the option of adding your own custom background image.

To do so, click the **Set Background** button above the **Preview** window.

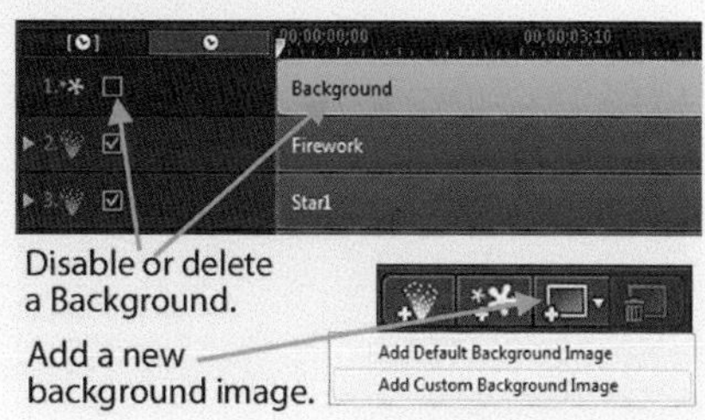

The **Particle Designer** is a workspace for customizing your **Particle** clip by adjusting the properties or characteristics of the particle objects, adding new particle objects, adding or changing a particle's animation and controlling the animation's timing.

To customize a particle object:

1 **Select the particle object**

Particle clips are made up of one or a number of particle **objects.** Each object is represented as a clip on the **Timeline** below the panel's **Preview** window.

Click to select an object clip on the **Particle Designer's Timeline.** When you do, the object will be indicated on the panel's **Preview** window as either an orange circle (if it is a stationary object) or a green line (if it is animated), as illustrated below.

2 **Set the object's properties**

Particle Properties include an **Emit Method** (the shape of the particles emitted), a **Particle Style** (the pattern of the particles' movements) and controls for setting the object's color and other parameters. Some of these parameters can be pretty high-level, and they include settings for how many particles are emitted from your object, how long they last, how much they vary in size, etc.

Again, remember that an object is only one element in your **Particle** clip, and some **Particle** clips include a number of animated and stationary objects on their **Timelines.**

At the bottom of the **Properties** panel are checkboxes for setting whether the object fades in and/or out or merely appears in the **Particle** clip.

Objects can also be temporarily turned off or disabled so that you can focus on one object at a time. To disable an object, uncheck the box on the track header of the track where the object appears on the panel's **Timeline.**

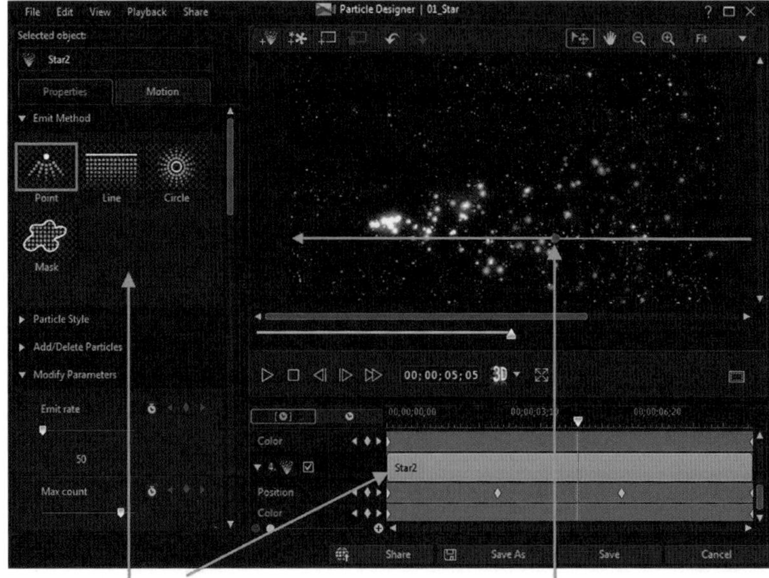

Selected object's properties.

Object's motion across the video frame.

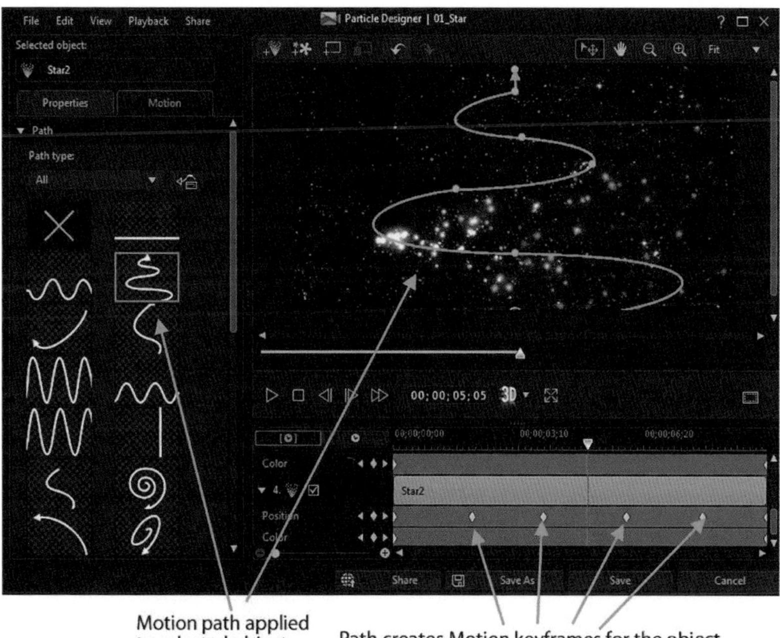

Motion path applied to selected object.

Path creates Motion keyframes for the object.

3 **Select a motion path**

With the object selected, click to select the **Motion** tab. This will give you access to a library of pre-created motion paths.

To apply a path to a selected object on the panel's timeline, click on your selected **Motion** path, as illustrated above.

This path will be added to your object and will appear as a keyframed property below the object on the **Particle Designers Timeline**.

Keyframes are tools for creating custom animations, and they appear throughout the program. Keyframes, including those on this panel, be easily created and modified.

You can speed up or slow down any object's motion by dragging the keyframes closer together or further apart. The closer these little diamond-shaped keyframes are on the timeline, the faster your animation will happen.

We discuss keyframing in more detail on page 109.

4 **Add another animated object**

To add a new animated object to your **Particle** clip, click the **Add New Particle Object** button above the **Preview** window.

A new track will be added to the panel's **Timeline** and a generic particle object will appear on this track as a stationary object (with animated "particles" emitting from it).

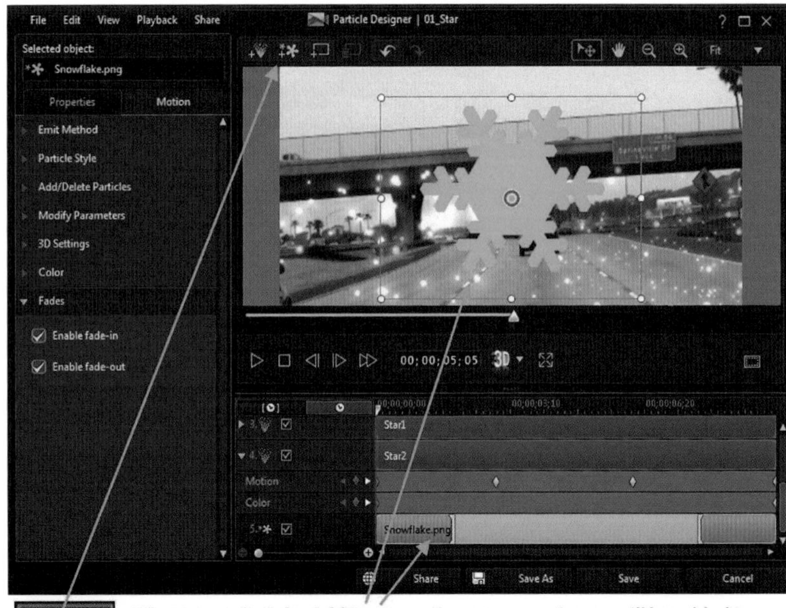

When you select the Add Image option, your new image will be added to a new track on the panel's timeline. By default, this new object will have Fade In and Fade Out applied to it.

If you select this object, you'll have the option to customize it **Properties** and **Motion** as discussed in **Step 2** and **Step 3**.

5 **Add custom images to your Particle clip**

To add a new custom object or image to your **Particle** clip, click the **Add Image** button above the Preview window.

A new track will be added to the panel's timeline and your still image will appear on this track as a stationary object.

If you select this object, you'll have the option to customize its **Motion** as discussed in **Step 3.**

Non-square objects

If you add a TIF or JPEG to your particle (or to your movie) as an object or you add an image to your movie or as a Particle object, it will most likely come in as a rectangular image – even if the graphic itself is, as illustrated above, non-square in shape.

In order to add your non-square graphic to your movie without the rectangular background, you'll need to create a graphic with no background layer in a program like Photoshop or PhotoDirector, and then save it in a graphic format that supports alpha, or transparency.

PNGs and GIFs are the two most popular formats for saving graphics with alpha channels.

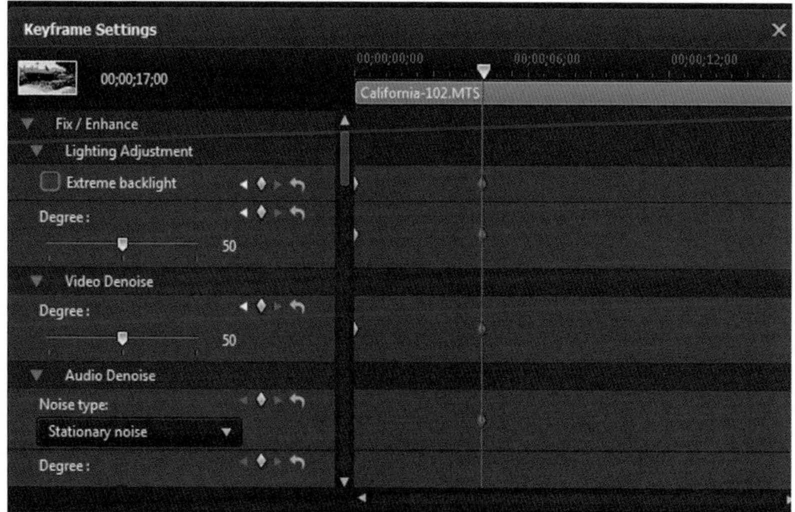

Keyframing

Keyframing is one of the most powerful tools in the PowerDirector toolkit. In fact, you'll find it represented throughout the program.

Keyframing can be used to create custom animations or motion paths, or to create effects that change characteristics or properties settings over the course of a clip. Keyframes are also used to vary audio levels on your clips so that you can, for instance, mix several audio sources, raising and lowering their volume levels as needed (as discussed on page 118).

The basic principles of keyframing are remarkably simple. And once you learn them, you'll see keyframing throughout the program and you'll suddenly find yourself able to create all kinds of cool animations and effects.

Keyframes are little diamond-shaped markers that are added to a clip's timeline. Each keyframe represents a different setting for an effect, level or position. And, as you add keyframe's to a clip's timeline, the program will create the animation or transition between these settings.

On page 68, we showed you how to use two keyframes added to the **Black and White** effect to create a video clip that transitions from black & white to color. On page 63, we showed you how keyframed **Opacity** levels create **Fade Ins** and **Fade Outs**.

To show you how keyframes work, we'll create a simple pan & zoom motion path over a still photo in the **PiP Designer.**

1 **Open the PiP Designer**

As seen in the illustration at the top of the following page, the **PiP Designer** is a workspace for adding a number of effects and adding the **3D to 2D** effect as well as for making adjustments to the basic image properties of **Opacity, Scale, Rotation, Motion, Freeform** and **3D Depth.**

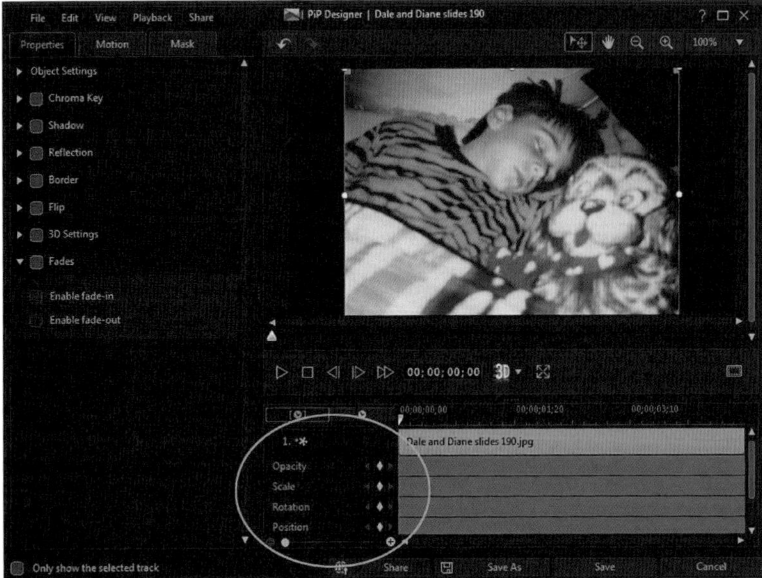

To open a still on your timeline in the **PiP Designer,** just **double-click** on it. (This method only works with photos. To create a pan & zoom over a *video clip,* keyframe the animation in **The Video Crop panel,** as discussed on page 113.)

2 **Create an initial motion path position**

Until you enable keyframing for a property, any changes you make to any settings or property will affect the entire clip evenly.

To resize the clip in the video frame, drag in or out on its corner handles.

To start with a close-up of the boy's face, first enlarge the photo's **Scale** so that only the boy's face is in the video frame. To do this, drag outward on the picture's corner handles. (If you need more room to drag these handles out, click on the zoom controls to make the video frame smaller in the panel.)

In order to see where the edges of the video frame are, toggle on the **Grid Lines** by clicking the button along the lower right of the **Preview** window, as in the illustration to the right.

Once you've **Scaled** the image enough to get a good, tight view of the boy's face, click and drag the image into position within the video frame.

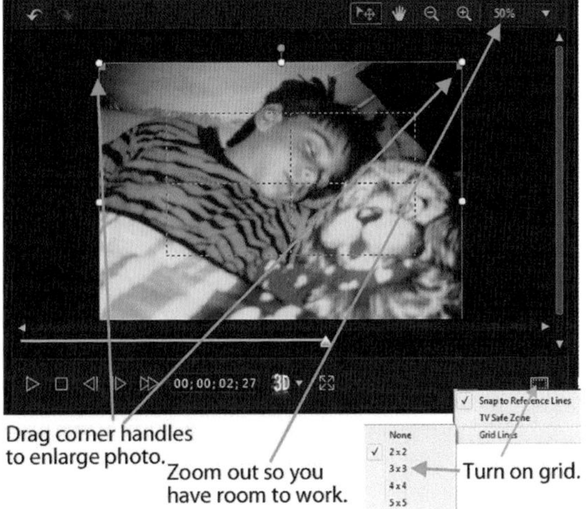

Ensure that the playhead is at the beginning of the clip's **Timeline** in the panel.

3 Enable keyframing

To enable keyframing for this timeline, click on the **Add/ Remove Keyframe** button on the right side of the track headers for **Scale, Rotation and Motion.**

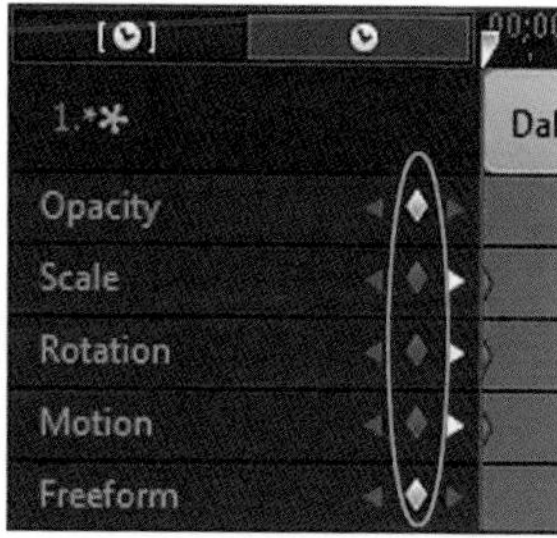

When you do this, little diamond-shaped keyframes appear under the playhead. These little diamonds are keyframes representing the current settings for the scale and position of this image in the video frame.

4 Create second keyframes

To create additional keyframes, drag the playhead down the panel's **Timeline**. Then drag the corner handles in to resize the photo so that it fits and fills the video frame, dragging across the photo as necessary to center it in the video frame.

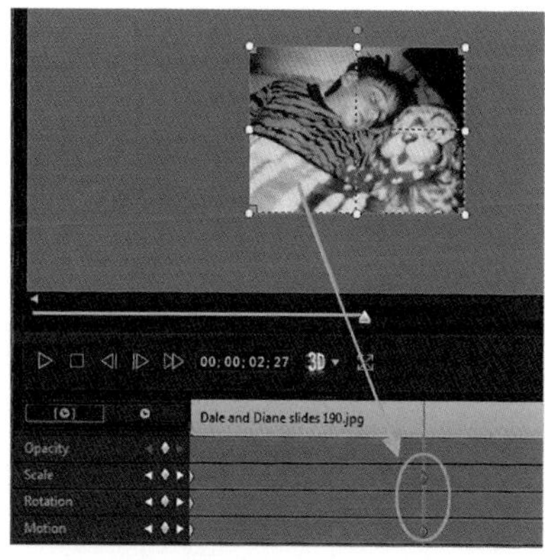

As you do this, new keyframes, representing these new settings for **Scale** and **Motion** will be created on the panel's **Timeline**.

When you play the clip, you should a nice, smooth animation, beginning with a close-up of the boy's face and zooming back to reveal the entire picture.

Some things to note about keyframes:

Keyframes can be dragged to other positions on the Timeline. The nearer the keyframes are to each other, the faster the animation between them will be.

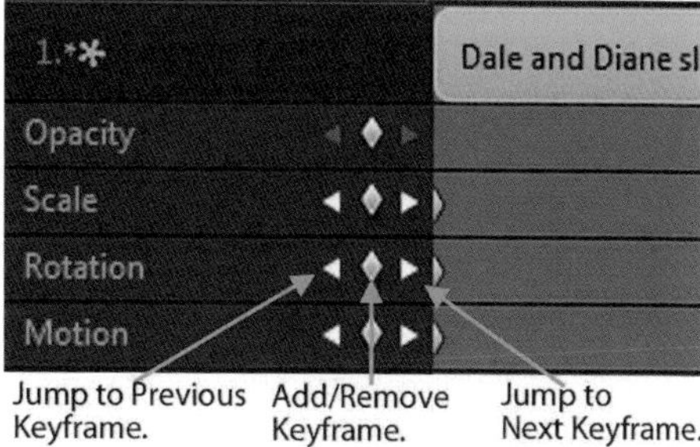

Keyframes can be overwritten with new settings. To overwrite a keyframe's current settings, drag the playhead over it. When you are directly over a keyframe, the yellow diamond will turn red. When you change a setting or reposition an image in the video frame, the settings that this keyframe represents will be automatically updated.

Clicking on a keyframe button on the track headers, illustrated to the right, either creates a **New Keyframe**, jumps to a **Previous Keyframe** or jumps to the **Next Keyframe.** If you are sitting on a keyframe, clicking the **Make Keyframe** button will delete that keyframe.

The paths under the **Motion** tab in the **PiP Designer** are actually presets of keyframed motion. If you apply a **Motion** path to a clip, you will see its **Motion** keyframes appear on the panel's **Timeline**.

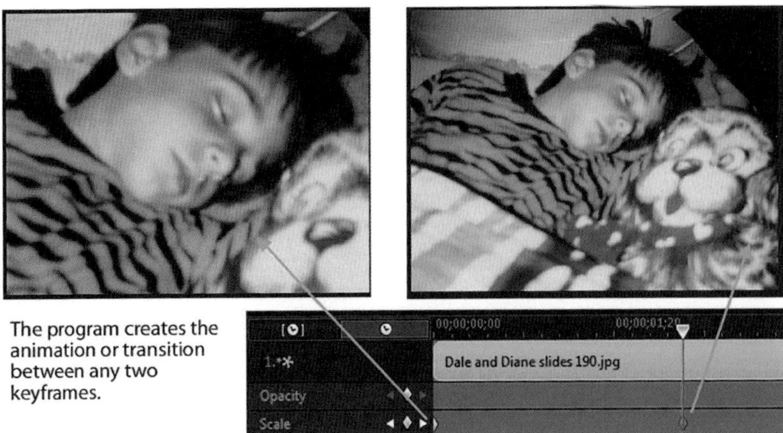

The program creates the animation or transition between any two keyframes.

Once you've applied a **Motion** path preset to your clip, you can reshape its path by dragging the little orange "waypoints" of the **Motion's** pattern on the panel's **Preview** window.

In addition to the **PiP Designer**, a number of other panels offer access to keyframing timelines.

Keyframe Settings for effects and enhancements

The **Keyframe Settings** panel can be opened three ways:

Click the Keyframe button on the Effects Settings panel. The **Effects Settings** panel is opened when you have selected a clip to which effects have been applied and you click the **Effect** function button along the top of the **Timeline** (as discussed on page 93).

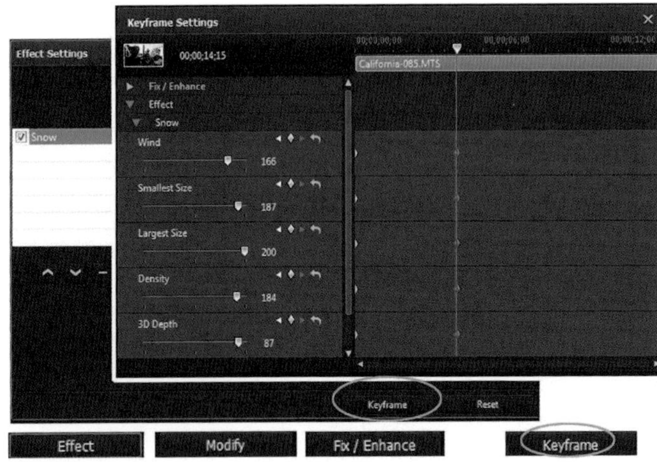

Click the Keyframe button on the Fix/Enhance panel. The **Fix/Enhance** panel is opened when you select a clip on the timeline and click the **Fix/Enhance** function button (as discussed on page 64).

Click the Keyframe function button along the top of the Timeline when you have a clip on the timeline selected.

No matter which of these three methods you use, you get to the same **Keyframe Settings** panel. On this panel, you can create keyframed transitions or animations to any **Fix/Enhance** adjustment (**Lighting, Video Denoise, Audio Denoise, Color Adjustment** or **White Balance**) or to the settings of any **Effect's** you've applied to your clip.

In addition you'll find a keyframing timeline for making animations based on **Clip Attributes** like **Opacity, Scale, Rotation** and **Motion**. These are the same attributes you can keyframe in the **PiP Designer**, as we did on page 109. In fact, any keyframing you've created in the **PiP Designer** will be displayed on this keyframing timeline, and vice versa.

Additionally, you can use this panel to keyframe audio **Volume** for a clip.

Although there is another – usually preferred – way to set audio volume keyframes and to mix your audio. We show it to you on page 118.

The Crop/Zoom panel

The **Crop/Zoom** panel is a simple area for cropping off the sides and/or top or bottom of your video. It's also a great place to create an animated motion path over your video, using a process very similar to the way we created a pan & zoom motion path over a photo on page 109. (Note that this tool is only available for video. You can't use it to create pan & zooms for photos, unfortunately.)

1 **Open the Crop/Zoom panel**

Select a clip and select the **Power Tools** option from the **Tools** button along the top of the **Timeline** (as discussed on page 65).

On the **Power Tools** panel, check and select the **Crop & Zoom** Power Tool.

Click the **Crop/Zoom** button.

The **Crop/Zoom** panel will open.

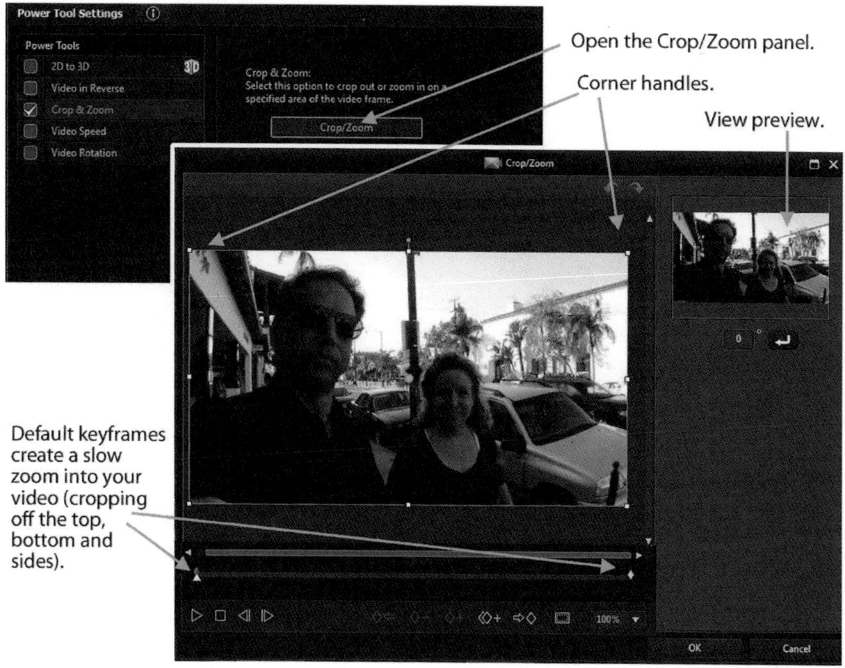

As illustrated at the right, under the **Preview** window on this panel is a timeline representing the duration of your video clip. It automatically has two keyframes already added to it, on either end of its **Timeline.** This creates an animation that begins with your video fully in the frame and ends with a cropped, slightly zoomed in view of your video.

The rectangular overlay represents the area of your video visible in the video frame. As you make adjustments to its size, the new view will be previewed in the little preview window in the upper right of the panel.

2 **Adjust a keyframe**

In order to adjust the size and position of this rectangular overlay, you will need to either be on top of an existing keyframe or a keyframe you've added by clicking on the button along the bottom of the panel's **Timeline.**

If you are not at the beginning of the timeline or the first keyframe isn't highlighted red, click the **Previous Keyframe** button below the timeline, illustrated below.

Once you are on a keyframe, corner handles will appear on the rectangular overlay.

Drag these corner handles in or out to resize the view on your video. (Remember, the smaller this rectangular overlay, the larger your video will appear.) Drag the center blue dot to change the rectangle's position. Drag over the green dot at the top to rotate the white rectangle.

The green arrow that appears from the rectangle's center indicates the motion path your crop animation will follow.

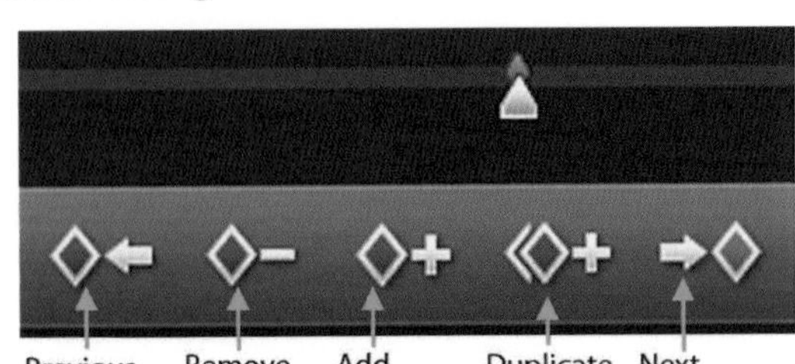

When you are directly over a keyframe, the keyframe will turn red, and any changes you make to your crop or position will be updated on this keyframe.

3 **Add a keyframe**

Move the playhead to the middle of the panel's timeline. Click the **Add Keyframe** button below the timeline.

A new keyframe will appear on the timeline and the corner handles will again appear on the white rectangle.

Any adjustments you make to its size and position will be updated on this new keyframe.

Some additional information on **Crop Video** keyframes:

You can add as many keyframes as you'd like to the **Crop Video** panel's timeline.

With the exception of the beginning and ending keyframes, you can drag keyframes to different positions on the panel's **Timeline**.

The closer your keyframes are together, the faster the animation will be between them.

Use the **Previous Keyframe** and **Next Keyframe** buttons (illustrated on page 111) to jump from keyframe to keyframe.

Click the **Remove Selected Keyframe** button to remove the keyframe positioned directly under the playhead. (The default keyframes at the beginning and end of the panel's **Timeline** can be modified – but not moved or removed.)

Mixing Audio with the Audio Mixer

Mixing Audio with Keyframes

Detecting Beats in Your Music

Adding Effects with WaveEditor

Chapter 10

Audio Editing

Mixing audio and adding audio effects

As an element of your movie, audio is at least as important as your video.

You want your projects to have good, clean audio – and you want this audio to have the same excitement and tone as your video.

Though not quite as feature-rich as its video tool set, CyberLink PowerDirector includes a number of terrific tools for creating, mixing and adding effects to your audio.

Additionally, all versions of PowerDirector come bundled with WaveEditor, a powerful audio editing program that works as a standalone audio editor as well as interfacing directly with your PowerDirector project.

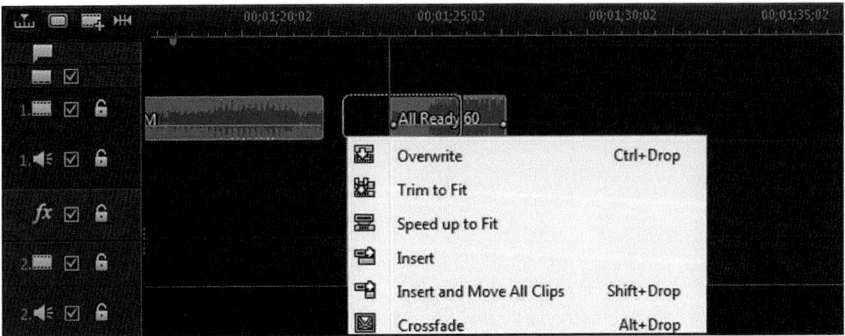

Add audio and music clips to your timeline

Adding audio clips to your timeline is essentially the same as adding video to your timeline. You just drag your audio clips from the **Media Room** to an audio track on the **Timeline**. If you attempt to place an audio clip on a track where it will overlap another audio clip, you will work with the insert/overwrite options, as illustrated above and detailed in page 58.

Like video clips, your audio clips can be trimmed and split (see pages 58-59). And, if you delete a clip from your timeline, you must choose from the same set of ripple options as you do when you delete video (see page 60).

PowerDirector's **Timeline** includes designated tracks for music and voice/narration. However, you can place any audio clip on any audio track.

Mix your audio levels with keyframes

You'll often be mixing audio from several sources in your PowerDirector project. And, when you do, you'll want to properly mix this audio – ensuring that one audio source dominates, for instance, while the other audio sources play in the background or mute completely.

Create custom music tracks for your movie

Bundled with PowerDirector is **Magic Music**, a great little tool for creating custom, royalty-free soundtracks and music clips for your movies.

For more information on this cool tool, see **Magic Music** on page 86.

A typical example of this is when you have three audio sources – the audio that's included with your video, a musical soundtrack and a narration track.

In this case, you'd like your musical track to dominate when there is no narration. And, when the narration comes in, you'd like your music to fade back so that the narration can dominate and be clearly heard.

Mixing audio is usually best done with keyframes. **Keyframing** is a feature that you'll find throughout the program as a way to control and customize a number of effects and animations (as discussed on page 109).

Keyframing audio means setting audio levels at specific points in your movie – varying your volume levels as needed to properly mix your audio levels.

In the illustration above, I've got a short video movie that consists of several video clips (with their accompanying audio), a music soundtrack and a couple of short narration clips.

Because the audio on my video clips isn't relevant, I'm going to mute it completely.

Then I'll mix the voice and music tracks so that music fades down whenever the narration is playing.

There are a couple of ways to do this in PowerDirector: Adding keyframes with the **Audio Mixer**, as we discuss below; creating **Gain** keyframes right on the **Timeline**, as we discuss on page 122; and setting the audio levels on the **Keyframe Settings** panel, as we discuss on page 123.

Adding keyframes with the Audio Mixer

This method uses the sliders in the **Audio Mixing Room** to keyframe your clip's **Gain** levels.

1 **Open the Audio Mixing Room**

   PowerDirector's audio mixer can be opened by clicking the **Audio Mixing Room** tab along the upper left of the program.

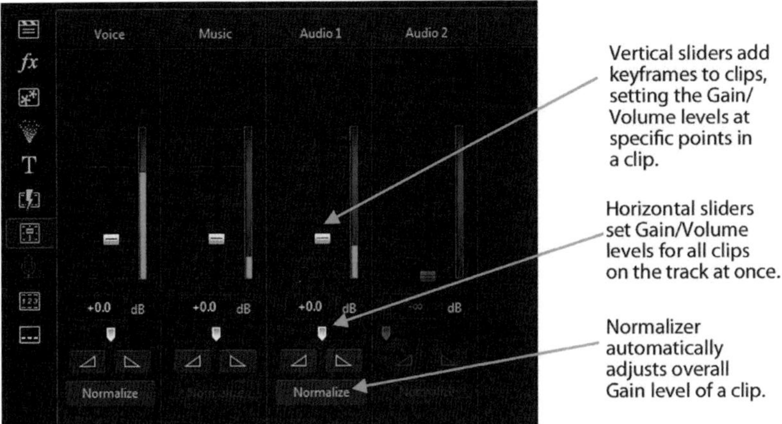

This panel will display sliders for the **Timeline's** audio tracks. Tracks that have audio on them will be highlighted and active. (If the timeline's playhead is not over a clip on an audio track – say, it is between narration clips – that slider will also not be active.)

2 **Mute the Audio 1 track**

The easiest way to mute an entire track is to use the **Master Audio** slider in the **Audio Mixing Room**. This is the little *horizontal* slider below the track's vertical slider.

As you move this slider left for the **Audio 1** track, you will see the horizontal line that runs through *all audio clips* on **Audio 1** lowering. This horizontal line through your audio clips is represents your clips' **Gain** level (essentially the audio clip's volume).

To mute an audio track, slide the **Master Audio** slider completely to the left as illustrated at the top of the facing page.

The reason this is a preferred way to mute the audio on a track is because, as opposed to, say, disabling the audio track (unchecking the **Disable/ Enable** box on the track header) or muting the clips (by selecting the option on each clip's **right-click** menu), setting the master level simply reduces the overall **Gain** for the clips on this track.

If you need to, you can still drag the **Gain** level line up for a certain clip if you'd like to feature its audio.

3 **Add a keyframe to begin the fade down**

Position the playhead on the **Timeline** to just before first **Narration** clip begins.

On the **Audio Mixer**, click on the handle on the **Music** track's slider (but don't actually move it). This will add a little dot to the **Gain** line on your music clip. This dot, or keyframe, will be the beginning of our fade down.

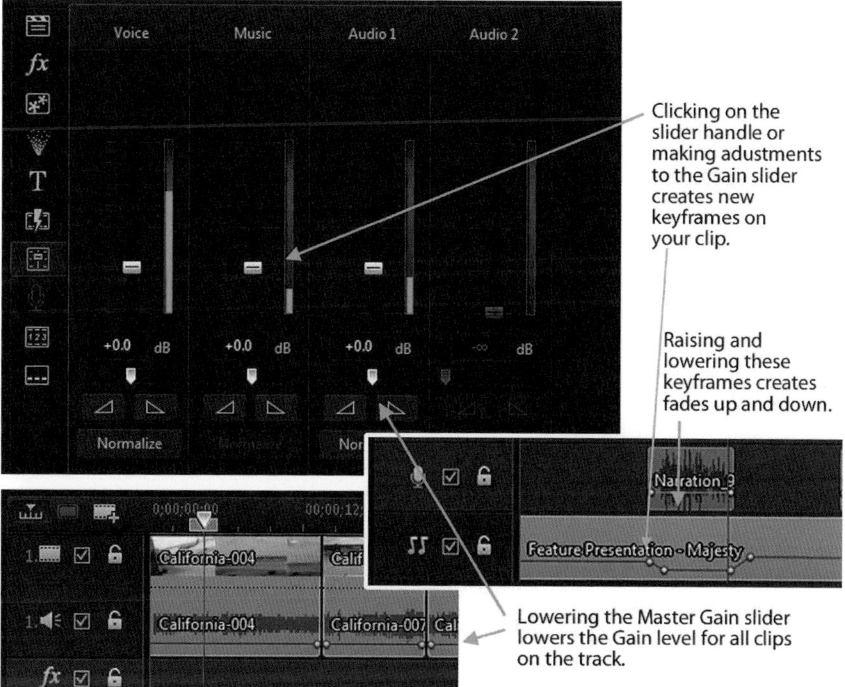

4 **Add a fade down Gain keyframe**

Move the playhead to the very beginning of the **Narration**. Drag the **Audio Mixing** slider down to reduce the gain level to about -8.0 (or type -8.0 in the **dB** box). This will create a new keyframe that is slightly lower on the music clip than the initial keyframe, as illustrated above.

5 **Add a keyframe to begin the fade up**

Move the playhead to just before the **Narration** ends.

In the **Audio Mixer**, click on the handle on the **Music** track's slider again (and, once again, don't actually move it). This will add another keyframe to the **Gain** line on the music clip. This keyframe should be at the same -8.0 dB level as the previous keyframe.

6 **Add the fade up Gain keyframe**

Move the playhead to just after the **Narration** ends. Move the slider in the **Audio Mixer** or type in numbers to set the **Music** clip's **Gain** back to 0.0.

A new keyframe will be added to the music clip, bringing the **Gain** level back to where it was before we faded it back.

The little "hammock" we've created between these keyframes will trigger the fade down, then fade back up, of the music clip as our narration clip is playing.

The -8.0 **Gain** level is, of course, just a general setting for your music's fade-back level. You can use whatever **Gain** level best mixes your audio.

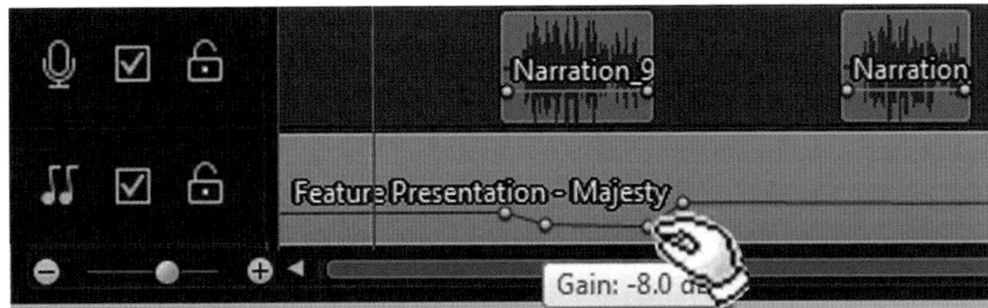

Keyframes can also be created simply by clicking and dragging on the Gain level line.

Creating Gain keyframes right on the Timeline

Audio level, or **Gain**, keyframes can also be created right on the **Timeline** – and many people find this method the least cumbersome way to mix audio.

1 **Add keyframes to your music clip**

Click on the horizontal **Gain** level line that runs through the music clip. This will create a little dot – a keyframe.

Create a total of four keyframes – one just before the **Narration** starts, one just as the **Narration** starts, one just before the **Narration** ends and one just after the **Narration** ends, as illustrated above.

2 **Position the fade down keyframe**

Drag down on the second keyframe you created. An indicator will appear, showing you the **Gain** level you are setting. Drag it to approximately -8.0 dB.

3 **Position the begin fade up keyframe**

Drag down on the third keyframe you created. Drag it to approximately the same **Gain** level as you did the previous keyframe (-8.0 dB).

You should end up with the same "hammock" keyframe configuration as we did when we used the sliders in the **Audio Mixing Room**. The **Gain** level for the music fades down when the **Narration** clip is playing, then fades back up to its previous level after the **Narration** ends.

Normalize your audio volume

Normalizing is an automatic way of correcting your clips' **Gain** levels.

When you click the **Normalize** button in the **Audio Mixing Room** (as illustrated at the top of page 120), the program will analyze the **Gain** levels of your clips and, if necessary, raise or lower them to a "normal" level.

The challenge, of course, is that you may have loud and quiet audio in the same clip. **Normalizing** is an overall adjustment – and it will base its settings on the clip's loudest sounds. It will not compensate for variations in the sound levels on a clip.

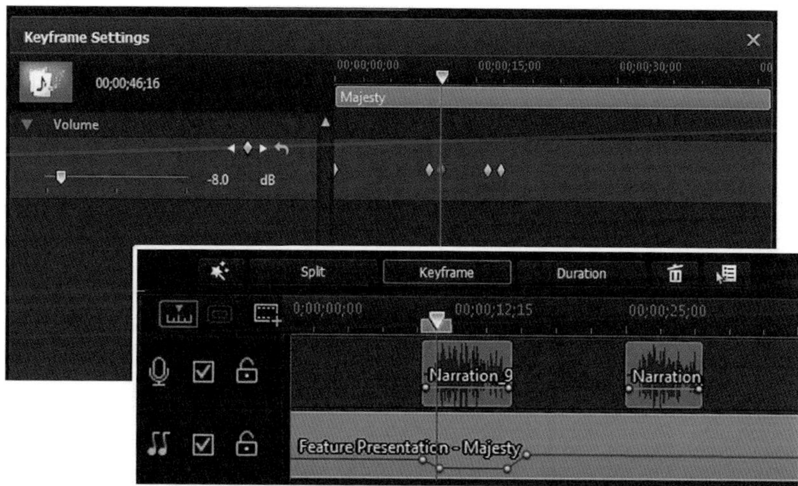

Keyframes in the Keyframe Settings panel correspond to keyframes on the clip itself.

Setting audio levels with Keyframe Settings

A clip's **Gain** level can also be keyframed in the **Keyframe Settings** panel. To open this panel, select an audio clip and click the **Keyframe** function button along the top of the **Timeline**, as illustrated above.

Click the little triangular toggle to the left of the **Volume** listing to open the volume settings slider and timeline.

Add Keyframe.

Previous Keyframe.

Next Keyframe.

To create **Gain** keyframes in this panel:

1 **Create a keyframe to begin the fade down**

Position the playhead on the panel's **Timeline** to just before where you'd like your fade down to begin. (The playhead on the program's main **Timeline** moves in sync with the panel timeline's playhead – so drag the playhead in the **Keyframe Settings** panel until the playhead on the main **Timeline** is just before the **Narration** begins.)

Click the **Add Keyframe** button on the **Keyframed Settings Timeline**. This will add a keyframe to the panel's **Timeline** as well as to the music clip on your main **Timeline**.

This keyframe will be the beginning of your fade down.

2 **Add a fade down Gain keyframe**

Align the playhead with the beginning of the **Narration**. Drag the **Volume** slider to reduce the gain level to about -8.0 (or type -8.0 in the ***dB*** box). This will create a new keyframe that is slightly lower on the music clip than the previous keyframe.

3 **Add a keyframe to begin the fade up**

Move the playhead to just before the **Narration** ends.

Click on **Add Keyframe** button to create another keyframe. This keyframe should be at the same -8.0 dB level as the previous.

4 **Add the fade up Gain keyframe**

Move the playhead to just after the **Narration** ends. Move the slider or type in numbers to set the **Volume** back to 0.0 dB.

A new keyframe will be added to the music clip and on the panel's **Timeline**, bringing the **Gain** level back to where it was before we faded it back.

Keyframes can be dragged to new positions (left and right as well as up and down), as needed to tweak how and when they fade up and down the audio.

Remove a clip's audio keyframes

To remove all audio keyframes applied to an audio clip on your timeline, **right-click** on the clip and select **Restore to Original Audio Level**.

Record a Voice-Over or narration

PowerDirector includes tools for recording narration or a voice-over directly to your project's timeline.

To record narration or a voice-over:

1 **Open the Voice-Over Recording Room**

PowerDirector's recording workspace can be opened by clicking the **Voice-Over Recording Room** tab along the upper left of the program.

2 **Configure your microphone**

If a microphone is operating on your computer, the little microphone icon on this tab should be highlighted.

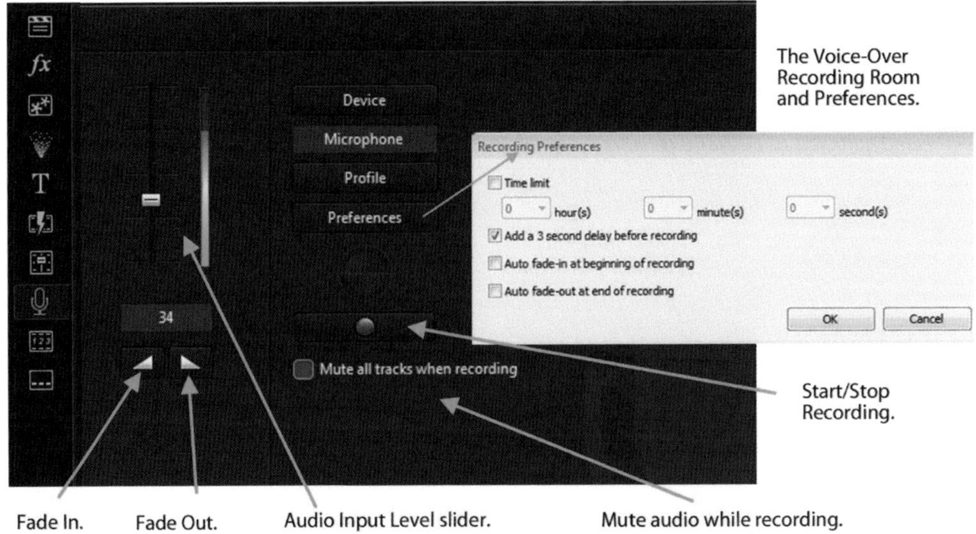

The Voice-Over Recording Room and Preferences.

Start/Stop Recording.

Fade In.

Fade Out.

Audio Input Level slider.

Mute audio while recording.

If it is not, you will need to ensure your microphone is properly configured in Windows.

If your have more than one microphone attached to your computer (Say, for instance, you have a microphone on your webcam in addition to your recording microphone), make sure that the correct device is configured for your **Voice-Over**. Click the panel's **Device** button and select your recording microphone from the **Audio Device** drop-down menu, as illustrated.

The **VU meter** on the left side of the panel will show the level of your microphone's input.

Speak or read into your microphone and ensure that VU shows a full green line but does not peak out at red. A red VU is an indication that your microphone is too "hot", and this could result in distorted audio.

Use the **Audio Input Level** slider to set a good level for your voice.

Click the **Preferences** button to set up your recording preferences. Among the choices on this panel is the option to precede your recording with a 3-second countdown.

If you don't select this option, recording will begin immediately when you click the **Record** button.

You also have options to limit the length of your **Voice-Over** and to add a fade in or out at the beginning and/or end of your recording.

You can also add a fade in or fade out to your recording manually by clicking the buttons below the **Audio Input Level** slider on the panel, as in the illustration on the facing page.

3 **Record your Voice-Over**

Position the playhead on the **Timeline** at the point you'd like your **Voice-Over** to begin.

Use the **Mute All Tracks When Recording** checkbox on the panel to set whether you do or do not want to hear your movie as you're recording your **Voice-Over**.

Click the red dot **Record** button and, unless you've set the 3-second countdown preference, immediately begin your **Voice-Over.**

4 **Stop recording**

When you're finished, click the red dot **Record** button again to stop recording. The program will process and save your recording and then add it to your timeline.

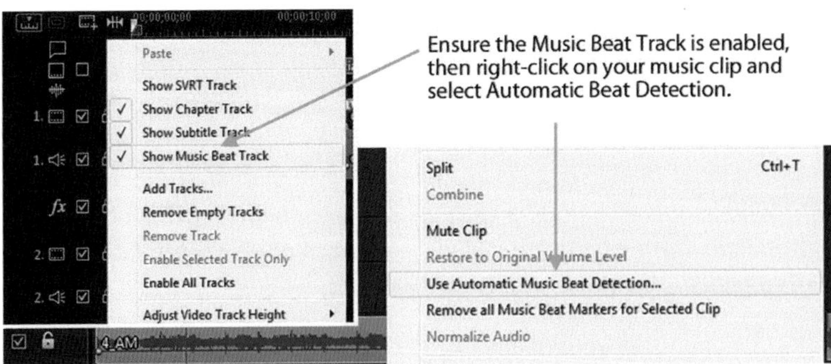

Detect beats in your music

Among the cool features in PowerDirector is a tool for automatically detecting the beats in a musical clip. Detected beats can be used as a great reference for, say, creating a slideshow or adding video clips that cut to the rhythm of a song.

To use the **Automatic Beat Detection**:

1. **Ensure the Detect Beats track is visible**

   The **Music Beat Track** is an optional track that runs along the top of the **Timeline**.

   To enable it, **right-click** on the **Timeline's** track headers and, in the context menu, check the **Show Music Beat Track** option.

2. **Launch Auto Beat Detection**

   Right-click on a music clip on your timeline and select the option to **Use Automatic Beat Detection**.

   The **Automatic Beat Detection** panel will open, as illustrated at the top of the facing page. Your musical clip will be represented as a waveform on the panel's **Timeline**.

3. **Detect beats**

   Click the panel's **Detect** button. The program will analyze your music and create a series of beat markers above the panel's timeline.

4. **Test drive the beat markers**

   Click the **Play** button on the panel's timeline and evaluate how well the tool has tracked the beats. You may want to **zoom** in on the timeline so that you can better see the individual beat markers.

   If you're happy with the results, click **Apply**.

As an alternative to **Automatic Beat Detection**, you can manually add beat markers to your clip.

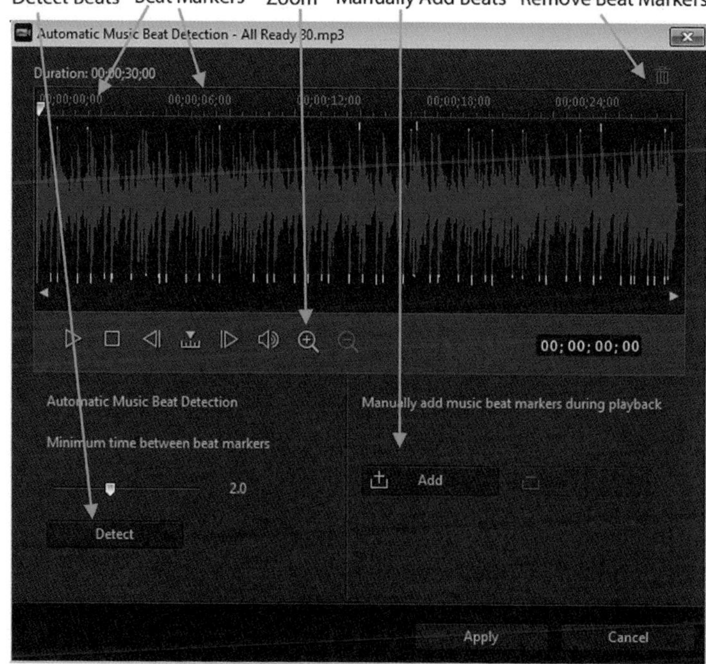

To do this, click the **trashcan** icon in the upper right of the **Automatic Music Beat Detection** panel to remove the current keyframes. Then play the music and click on the **Add** button in rhythm with the music. (As an alternative, you can click the **Add** button to create the first beat marker, then tap the "**A**" key on your keyboard to create the rest.)

When you're happy with the results, click **Apply.**

The beat markers will appear on the **Music Beat Track** at the top of the **Timeline.** These markers are assigned to the music clip they detected beats for. If you drag the music clip to another position on your timeline, the markers will follow it.

These markers also create invisible "snap-to" guides on the **Timeline.**

When you add or trim a clip on your timeline, the beginning or end point of the clip will "snap" to the marker's position.

When you add or trim a clip on your timeline, the cut will "snap" to the beat marker.

When launched from PowerDirector, WaveEditor opens to a copy of the selected audio clip on your PowerDirector timeline.

Edit your audio with WaveEditor

Though technically its own separate program, WaveEditor is a sound editing program that comes bundled with all versions of CyberLink PowerDirector – and is dynamically linked to it.

WaveEditor can be used to remove noise, add dynamics, equalize or add special effects to your audio.

Open a PowerDirector audio clip in WaveEditor

To open a PowerDirector clip's audio in WaveEditor, select an audio clip or a video clip that includes audio on your timeline.

Click the **Edit Audio** function button along the top of the **Timeline** and select **Wave Editor...**

The WaveEditor program will open and the audio from your selected clip will open in it. (PowerDirector will be temporarily disabled while you're editing this audio.)

Two very important things to note about this audio, however:

This is audio from the clip *as it appears on your Timeline.* In other words, if you have a longer clip that's been trimmed on your timeline, only the trimmed segment – the segment of the clip that actually appears on your timeline – will open in WaveEditor.

The audio that opens in WaveEditor is a *copy* of the clip's audio. So don't worry about overwriting your original clip's audio.

In WaveEditor, you can add your **Effects** to all or a portion of this clip.

If you do not have a Range selected in this clip, your **Effect** will be applied to the entire clip.

If you have a Range selected (highlighted in yellow, as in the illustration), the **Effect** will only be applied to that segment.

Selected **Ranges**, by the way, can also be cut, copied and pasted to another area of this clip by using **Ctrl+x, Ctrl+c** and **Ctrl+v** or by clicking on the buttons along the top of the panel.

To apply an effect, select the **Effect** from the listing along the left side of the program or from the **Effect** menu at the top of the program. (They give you the same options.)

When you apply an effect, an option screen will open in which you can set various levels for the effect. If you check the **Preview** box at the bottom of a panel, you'll be able to test drive the effect and your settings.

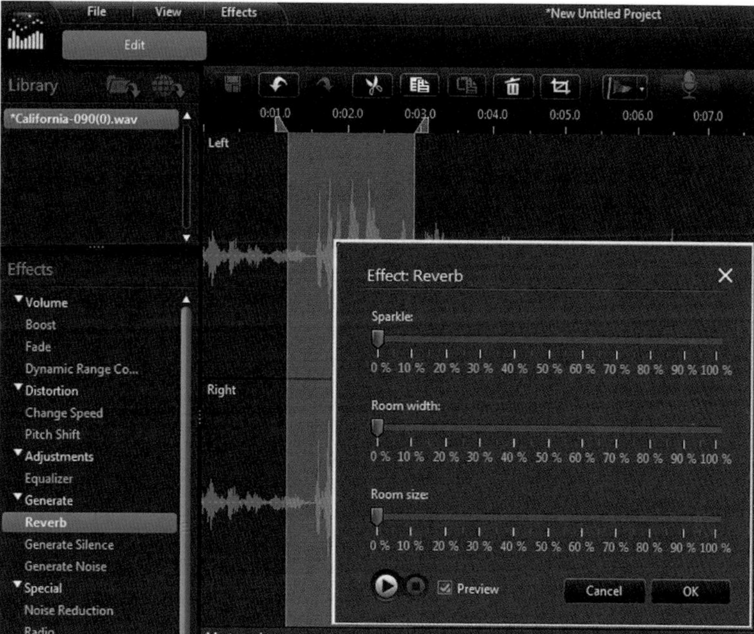

Effects can be applied to the entire clip or to a selected region only (highlighted in yellow-green). To test drive an effect's settings before applying them, check the Preview box at the bottom of the effect's option panel.

Among the audio effects available are:

Volume, which includes **Boost** (to raise the volume level of your clip), **Fade** (to create a transition from louder to quieter or vice versa) and **Dynamic Range Compression** (which reduces the difference between the loudest and quietest sounds in your audio).

Distortion, which can be used to change the playback speed of your clip or to shift its pitch higher or lower.

Adjustments, which includes an **Equalizer** for fine tuning the levels of your audio at various frequencies of bass, midrange and treble.

Generate, which includes the **Reverb** effect for creating echoes as well tools for replacing portions of your audio with silence or a buzzing noise.

- **Special Effects,** which include tools for reducing noise in your audio (similar to the **Audio Denoiser** in the **Magic Fix** on page 82-83) as well as tools for making your audio sound as if it's coming from a cheap radio, a telephone or speaker phone. You'll also find a tool here for playing your clip in **Reverse** and a **Vocal Eraser** tool for removing vocals from songs in order to create your own karaoke music.

The program also has facilities for adding third-party **VST** (Virtual Studio Technology) effects to its toolkit.

To add **VST** plug-ins to the program, install the effects on your computer and then go to the **Effects** menu at the top of the program and select **VST**, then **Import VST Effects.** Browse to create a link to the effects.

Naturally, you can add more than one effect to a clip at a time.

When you're done editing your audio, close the program by clicking the **X** in the panel's upper right corner. A pop-up will ask you if you want to save your audio track. Click **Yes.**

The audio for your selected clip is replaced with a WAV file to which effects have been applied.

The program will save your effected audio clip as a *new audio file* and then automatically use this audio file to replace the selected audio clip in your PowerDirector project. (Once again, note that this is a *copy* of your original audio. Although PowerDirector will use it to replace your audio clip on your timeline, your original media file hasn't been changed in any way.)

If the audio file you've edited was the audio portion of a video clip, the audio portion of the clip on your timeline will be replaced with this new WAV file, as illustrated above right.

If you want to go back to your original audio file, just delete the clip from your timeline and re-add the original clip from your **Media Room** library.

Use WaveEditor as a standalone audio editor

To use WaveEditor as a standalone auditor editor, launch the program from your operating system and then select **Import Track** from its **File** menu to open the audio file you want to edit.

When you're finished editing, select **File/Save Track As** to save your edited file as a WAV, WMA, MP3 or M4A audio file.

Creating Picture-in-Picture Effects

The PiP Designer

Working with Multiple Tracks of Video

Using and Creating PiP Objects

Animating Lines in the Paint Designer

Chapter 11

PiPs and Multi-Track Video Effects

Working with layers of video

Many cool visual effects can be created by layering video on top of video.

With 100 video and audio tracks available, PowerDirector offers lots of opportunities to create interesting picture-in-picture and other multi-track effects.

Compositing is the process of combining several tracks of video to create a visual effect.

When video clips are placed on separate tracks above one another, they behave as if in a stack. The clip on the top track is the most visible, with the clips on tracks below it visible around and through transparent areas in it.

Multi-layer video effects include **Picture-in-Picture** effects, **Chroma Key**, J-cuts and L-cuts and video grids (like what we call the "Brady Bunch effect").

Create a Picture-in-Picture effect

A **Picture-in-Picture** composition is a video in which one or more smaller videos are overlayed onto a main video as an inset or as a smaller video visible in the corner of the screen.

There are two ways to create **Picture-in-Picture** effects: You can create the effect directly on the **Timeline**, or you can use the very powerful **PiP Designer**.

Create a Picture-in-Picture effect on the timeline

The simplest way to create a **Picture-in-Picture** composition is to layer a video over another video on your timeline, and then resize and re-position the upper track video using tools right in the program's **Preview** window.

1 **Place your video clips**

Place your main or background video on the **Video 1** track. Place the video you will use as your **Picture-in-Picture** (PiP) on the **Video 2** track, overlaying it, as illustrated at the top of the facing page.

Remember that, in PowerDirector, the track layers are represented on the **Timeline** "upside-down." In other words, video on **Video 2** will appear *over* video on **Video 1** in your movie, even though on the **Timeline** itself they are placed *under* it.

Because PiP video clip on **Video 2** currently fills the video frame, you will only see this video in the **Preview** window at this time.

Chroma Key

Chroma Key is a powerful multiple track effect in which you take a video of an actor and replace its background with any real or fantasy background.

For more information on this cool tool, see **Apply Chroma Key** on page 95.

Place the video you will use as your PiP on Video 2, directly over your background video, on Video 1.

2 **Resize the PiP video**

Click to select the PiP video clip on your timeline. Corner handles will appear around the outside of this video in the **Preview** window, and a blue crosshair will appear over the video's center as illustrated below right.

Drag these corner handles in to resize the PiP video. This will reveal the video on **Video 1** behind it.

When a clip is selected on your timeline, you can scale and position it by dragging on the corner handles and center point in the Preview window.

3 **Position your PiP**

Click on the blue crosshair in the center of the PiP video and drag the clip into position in your video frame.

Several layers of video tracks can be used to create as many PiPs as you'd like (or a grid, as we show you on pages 141-142). Just select the clip you want to resize and reposition on the **Timeline** to activate its corner handles.

The scale and position of your **Picture-in-Picture** can also be animated using keyframes – an effect that can be created using the **Clip Attributes** in the **Keyframe Settings** window (see page 109) or by using the **PiP Designer** (as we show you on page 135).

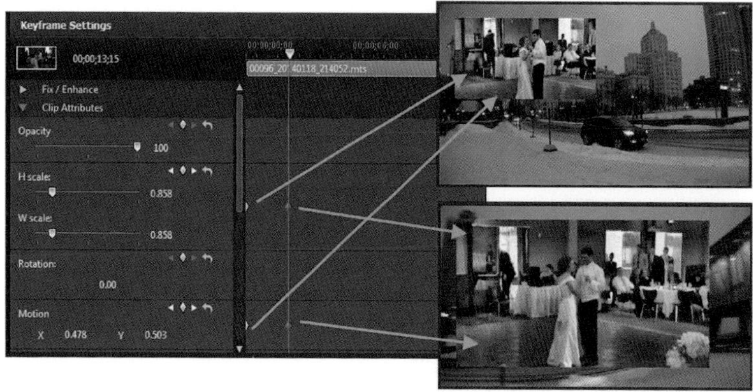

Create a Picture-in-Picture effect in the PiP Designer

The **PiP Designer** is a powerful workspace for creating effects on multiple tracks or layers of video.

To open the **PiP Designer**, select a clip and click the **Modify** function button along the top of the **Timeline** – or simply **double-click** a clip on your timeline.

The **PiP Designer** includes a set of **Properties** tools for affecting how your PiP affects the clips below it, **Motion** tools for creating movement for your PiP over the clips below it and **Mask** tools for "cookie cuttering" your clip into various shapes or making areas of your clip transparent.

Additionally, the **PiP Designer** includes tools for scaling and positioning your **Picture-in-Picture** video as well as a **Timeline** for animating these PiP settings.

Safe Zones

Whenever you're compositing images or text in a video frame, it's a good idea to work with the **TV Safe Zone** turned on in your **Preview** window.

The TV Safe Zone is a rectangular guide that appears over your **Preview** window, indicating the area you should keep all of your text and relevant video in. This helps protect important parts of your video or text from being cut off when shown on a TV.

For more information on the **TV Safe Zone**, see the sidebar on page 153.

To create a **Picture-in-Picture** in the **PiP Designer**, begin with your background video on the **Video 1** track and the video you want to use for your **Picture-in-Picture** on **Video 2**, as illustrated at the top of page 133.

1 **Open the PiP Designer**

Select the PiP clip on **Video 2** and click the **Modify** function button along the top of the **Timeline** – or simply **double-click** on the PiP clip.

The **PiP Designer** will open, and the PiP clip will appear in the panel's **Preview** window with handles on each corner.

2 **Scale and position the PiP**

Drag on the corner handles to change the PiP's size in the video frame – then click and drag it into position.

Animate your Picture-In-Picture in the PiP Designer

By default, the changes you make to the clip's **Scale, Motion, Opacity** and **Rotation** are made for the duration of the clip. In other words, if you position your PiP in the upper left corner of your video frame, it will remain in that position for the entire clip.

You can, of course, also **keyframe** animation for any of these properties so that your PiP changes size and position over the course of the clip.

For instance, let's take our PiP of the couple dancing in the upper left of the video frame and animate so that this PiP begins in this upper corner, then shrinks down and disappears in the center of the video frame.

1 **Create your PiP's initial position**

Ensure that the playhead on the **PiP Designer** is at the beginning of the panel's **Timeline**.

Drag your PiP's corner handles to scale and position the clip in the upper left of the video frame (as we discussed on the facing page).

2 **Create your initial keyframe**

Click the white, diamond-shaped **Add Keyframe** button on the track headers for **Scale** and **Motion** (or whatever properties you plan to animate), as illustrated to the right.

Diamond-shaped keyframes will be created at the position of the playhead on the panel's timeline.

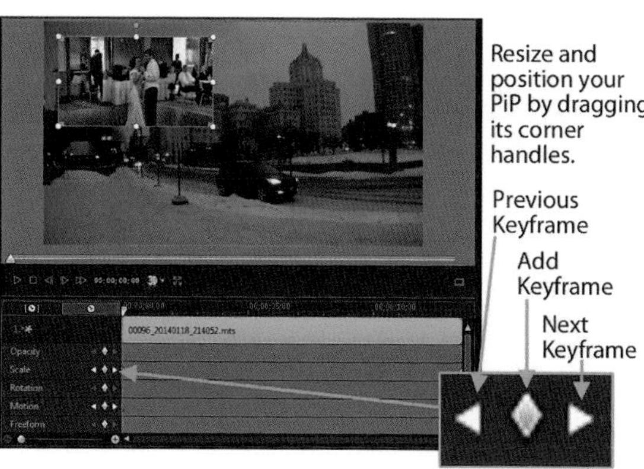

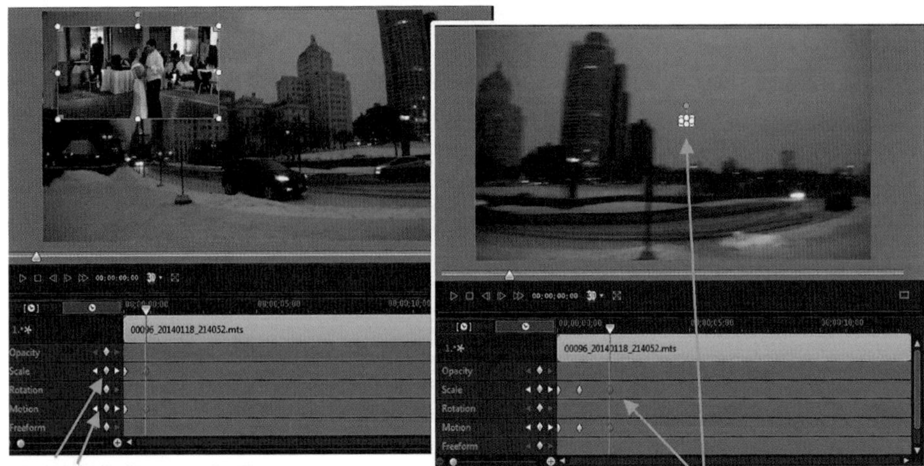

Click Add Keyframe to duplicate previous keyframe settings.

Scale and reposition the PiP and the program will automatically create new keyframes.

3 **Create a second keyframe that duplicates the first's settings**

Move the playhead a second or two down the panel's **Timeline**.

If we were to create a keyframe with different **Scale** and **Motion** settings at this position, the program would create an immediate transition from the first keyframe's settings to this keyframe's settings.

So, rather than beginning our animation immediately, let's create a second keyframe with the same settings as the first – so that our PiP will remain in its position for the first second or two of the clip.

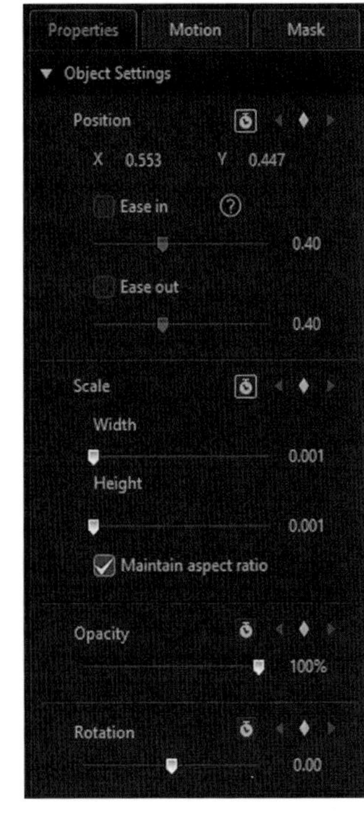

Click the **Add Keyframe** buttons again for **Scale** and **Motion**. New keyframes will be created at the playhead's current position, as in the illustration.

4 **Create a zoom out keyframe**

Drag the playhead another second down the panel's **Timeline**.

Drag the PiP video into the center of the video frame. (A new **Motion** keyframe will be created automatically.)

Drag the PiP's corner handles in until the clip disappears completely, as on the facing page. Better yet, as illustrated at the bottom of page 136, toggle open the **Object Settings** on the **Properties** panel, drag the **Scale** settings for **Width** and **Height** down to zero (technically 0.0001, the lowest setting possible).

We've now created an animation in which our PiP begins in the upper left corner of our video frame, stays there for a moment, then zooms out and vanishes into the center of our video frame.

For more information on creating animations, see **Keyframing** on page 109.

PiP Designer Properties

In addition to **Object Settings** for creating **Scale**, **Motion** and **Rotation** animations, the **PiP Designer** includes tools for creating a number of **Picture-in-Picture** effects.

Under the panel's **Properties** tab, you'll find settings for controlling and keyframing how your PiP is sized or positioned and how it reacts with the video clips that are under it on your PowerDirector **Timeline**.

Object Settings include settings for the **Position** of your video in your video frame, its **Scale**, **Opacity** and **Rotation**.

Chroma Key is an effect which creates transparency through your video clip, based on a color range you designate. We show you how to use this tool in **Apply Chroma Key** on page 95.

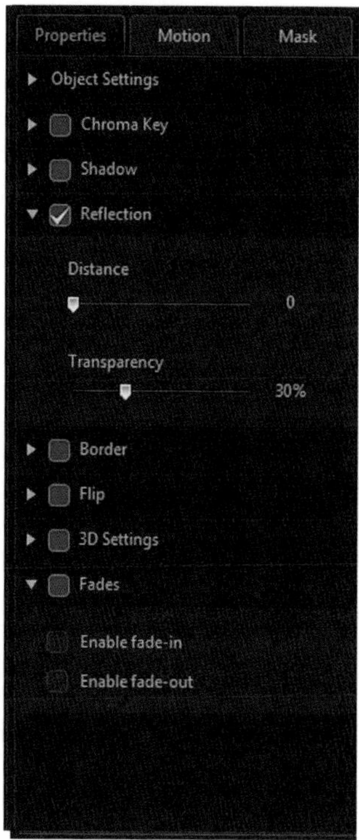

Shadow adds a drop shadow under your PiP. Settings control how far this shadow falls from your PiP, how blurry or transparent your shadow is and which direction the shadow falls.

Reflection creates a reflection of your PiP below it in your video frame. Settings control the distance the reflection is from your PiP and how transparent it is.

Border adds a border, or outline, around your PiP.

Flip flips your PiP horizontally or vertically.

Aspect Ratio constrains the shape of your PiP.

3D Settings include a control for adding 3D depth – making your PiP look closer than the videos under it – when used in a 3D project.

Fades add a one-second **Fade In** or **Fade Out** to your PiP. Fading, it should be noted, affects the clip's opacity or transparency level. So a **Fade** will, in effect, make your PiP appear to *dissolve* in or *dissolve* out of your video frame rather than fade in from or out to black.

PiP Designer Motion presets

Under the **PiP Designer's Motion** tab, you'll find **Path** presets for creating animation movement of your PiP over your other videos.

Applying a **Path** to your PiP is as simple as clicking on a **Path** preset on this panel. (To remove a **Path**, click the **X** in the upper left corner.)

These **Motion Paths** don't change the **Scale** of your PiP – so by default your PiP remains at 100% its size as it follows the **Path**. To **Scale** or even keyframe an animated **Scale** change to your PiP, follow the steps in **Create a Picture-in-Picture in the PiP Designer** on page 134 or **Animate Your Picture-in-Picture in the PiP Designer** on page 135.

When you add a **Path** to your PiP, diamond-shaped keyframes are added to the **Motion Timeline** below the panel's **Preview** window. The **Path** itself will also be visible in the **Preview** window, indicated as a curved line with two or more orange "way points."

Keyframes on the **Timeline** can be moved around to affect the speed of your **Path**. The closer your keyframes are together, the faster your animation will occur.

(For more information on creating and customizing keyframed animations, see **Keyframing** on page 109.)

The "waypoints" on your path are also customizable. Drag them in the panel's **Preview** window to reshape your **Path**.

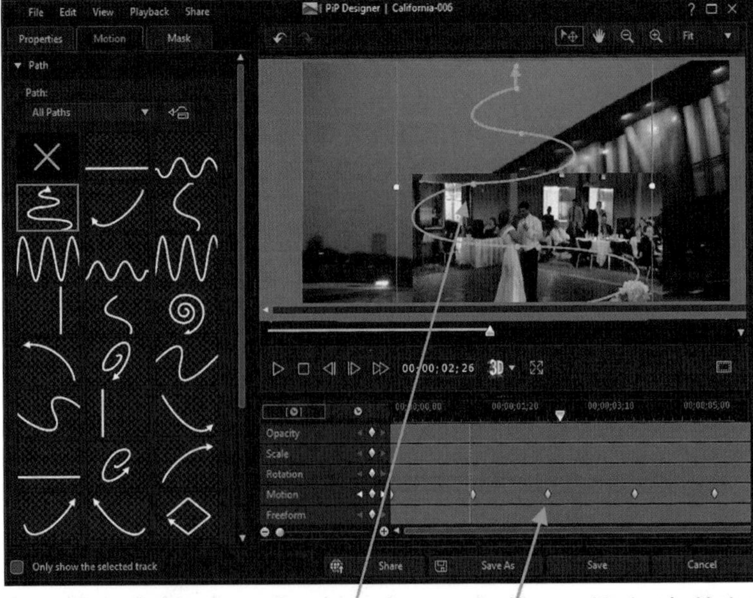

Once a Motion Path has been selected, it can be customized by repositioning the Motion keyframes or dragging the Path's "waypoints" to new positions.

PiP Designer Masks

Masks are presets for making certain areas of your video transparent.

They can be used as "cookie cutters" to cut your video into custom shapes. And they can be applied to video clips on the **Video 1** track as well as applied to PiPs.

Applying a **Mask** to your PiP is as simple as clicking on a **Mask** preset on this panel. (To remove your **Mask**, click the **X** in the upper left corner.)

The panel also includes tools for customizing your **Mask's Transparency** (how much the video outside the **Mask's** shape can be seen) and **Feather Radius** (how soft the edge of the Mask's shape is).

In addition to the **Masks** on this panel, you can import your own custom shape for use as a mask.

The shape need only be a white shape on top of transparent background, usually in a PNG format. For information on creating files with transparent backgrounds, see **Non-Square objects** on page 118.

You can combine a **Mask** and a **Motion Path** on the same clip.

When working on a **Chroma Key** shot, **Masks** can be used as "garbage mattes" to remove unwanted areas of your key shot. For more information on this technique, see the sidebar on page 97.

Masks cut your video into a shape, making the areas outside the shape transparent.

Tell stories with multiple video tracks

Although you can create some terrific movies with a single track of video, there are some very powerful and professional storytelling techniques at your disposal when you composite several tracks of audio and video.

Think of multiple tracks of video as a stack, like a stack of photos. In most cases, only the uppermost track in the stack will be visible.

However, if you change the size and position of the images on the uppermost track – or on several tracks – or you make portions of the images on upper tracks transparent, you can display video on several tracks at once and create some very interesting compositions.

You can also add a video clip to an upper track so that your movie cuts away to a separate visual sequence while still playing audio from the track under it.

L-cuts and J-cuts

In addition to the **Picture-in-Picture** techniques discussed earlier in this chapter, multiple tracks of video can be used to create **L-cuts** and **J-cuts**, powerful ways to add visual interest to your movies.

L-cuts and **J-cuts** begin or end with an on-screen storyteller. As he or she speaks, the movie cuts away to related video, supplementing the story he or she is telling with visuals.

Think of a TV news report that features video of a reporter standing in front of a burned-out building, describing the fire that destroyed it.

As he continues speaking, the video cuts away to footage shot earlier of the fire itself. That's an **L-cut**.

A **J-cut**, on the other hand, begins with video of the fire and the reporter's voice describing it – then cuts to video of the reporter finishing his report.

The techniques are similar and the principle is the same: As audio continues from one scene, the video cuts away to another scene.

L-cuts and **J-cuts** are so named because, back in the "primitive" days of film editing, when a segment of film had to be removed and the audio left in place to allow for the placement of alternate video, the cut resembled an "L" – or a "J," depending on whether the beginning or end of the visual portion was replaced with new footage.

Creating an **L-cut** or a **J-cut** is easy with multi-track editing.

1 **Place the main video on the Video 1 track**

   This would be the clip of the reporter speaking to the camera or, as in my illustration, the person being interviewed.

2 **Place the cutaway video on an upper video track**

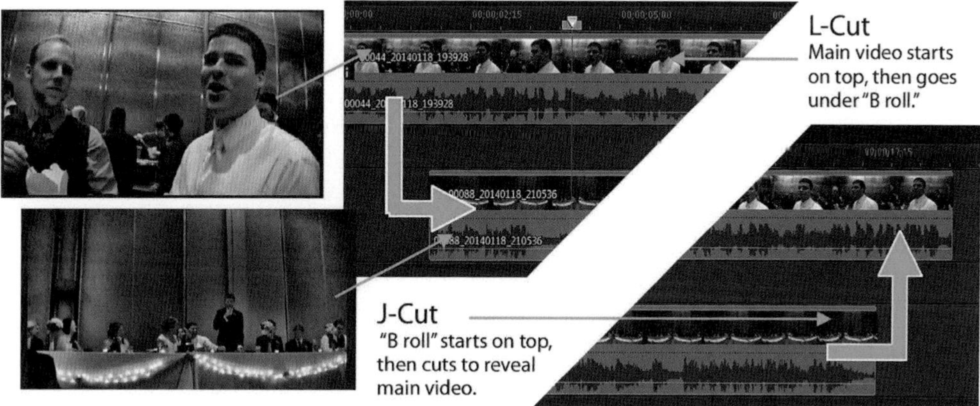

As audio from the main clip continues, video cuts away to or from "B roll" footage.

Place the cutaway video – the video illustrating what the reporter or the interviewee is talking about– on the **Video 2** track, overlaying the main video (below it, on the PowerDirector **Timeline**).

The cutaway video should be offset from the main video slightly, so that we begin or end – or both – with the main video of the reporter or the interviewee speaking.

Voila! Tweak **Clip B**'s position for maximum effect and you're done! We begin with the reporter or interviewee speaking to the camera and, as he continues to speak, we cut away to footage of what he's describing.

L-cuts and **J-cuts** are very effective for news-style reports as well as for interviews, in which you cut away from the person speaking to separately shot footage of the story he or she is telling.

It's a great way to reinforce, with images, what's being presented verbally.

By the way, here's some professional vocabulary to impress your friends with. That secondary footage that plays as the main video's audio continues? It's commonly called "**B-roll footage**", a relic from the days when this kind of editing actually did involve pasting in footage from a separate roll of film or video.

Create the "Brady Bunch effect"

Your **Picture-in-Picture** effects need not be limited to a single image. You can resize and position several tracks of video in your video frame to create a split screen or to show several images at once.

Using a number of video tracks and some precise scaling and positioning, you can even create a grid of video images – something we at Muvipix.com call the "Brady Bunch effect."

1 **Place each video source on a separate track**

Stack up the videos you want to use in your grid by placing each on a separate video track on the **Timeline**, one above the other.

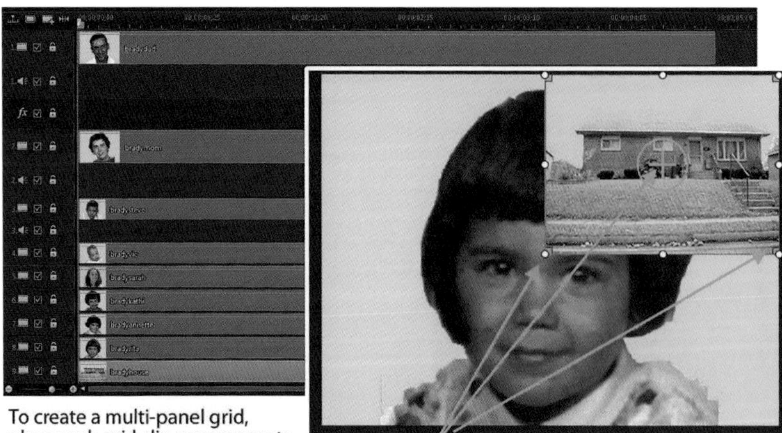

To create a multi-panel grid, place each grid clip on a separate video track, one above the other.

When a clip is selected on the Timeline or in the Preview window, you'll be able to resize and position it using the corner handles center point that appear.

2 **Scale and position each clip**

Select a video clip on your timeline or in the **Preview** window. Use the corner handles and center point that appear when your clip is selected to size and position the clip in the video frame.

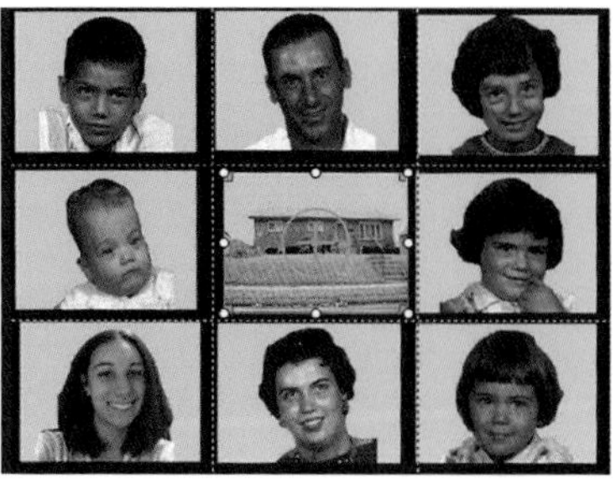

Use Grids as guides

Built into PowerDirector's **Preview** window are a number of grid patterns which you can use to help you in your layouts.

To access these **Grid** overlays, **right-click** on the video in the **Preview** window and select one of the **Grid** options.

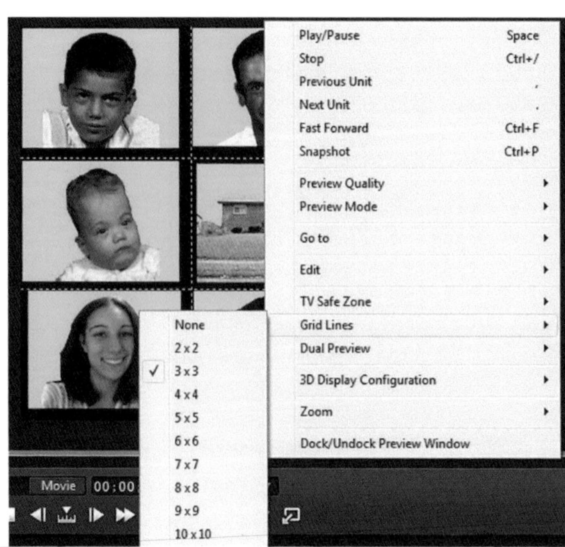

This **Preview** window also includes a **TV Safe Zone** guide for ensuring that text and other relevant information isn't cut off when viewed on a TV. We show you how to use it on page 153.

The PiP Object Room

PowerDirector comes loaded with dozens of pieces of video "clip art" that can be used in and over your videos. A great many of these clips are animated, and a couple will even display as 3D when used in a stereoscopic 3D project.

To access this library of clips, click the **PiP Object Room** tab along the upper left of the program. A **Search the Library** box in the upper right of the **Room** allows you to real-time search for a specific **PiP Object** (see page 19).

PiP Object clips are tagged to categories, although you can also select **All Content** to see them all at once. When you click on a **PiP Object**, you'll see its animation in your **Preview** window.

In additional to the default set of **PiP Objects** included with PowerDirector, if you are logged into the **DirectorZone**, thousands of additional **Objects** can be downloaded free by clicking the **DZ** button in the **Downloaded** category of the panel. For more information on the **DirectorZone**, see the sidebar on page 200.

When **PiP Objects** are added to an "upper" video track (**Video 2, Video 3**, etc., which are actually *below* the **Video 1** track on the PowerDirector **Timeline**), they will overlay any video on **Video 1** or other lower video tracks.

You can create and save your own custom-created, animated **PiP Objects** to this room using the **Paint Designer**, as we show you on page 144.

You also have the option of opening any existing **PiP Object** in the **Paint Designer** and modifying it by adding your own animation.

To open a **PiP Object** in the **Paint Designer**, select the object in the **PiP Object Room** and click **Modify Selected Paint Object** at the top of the panel.

As with **Particles**, you can also add your own graphics (as we show you on page 108) to this room by clicking **Create a PiP Object from an Image**. Browse to your graphics file or image and it will open your graphic in the **PiP Designer,** where you can customize its look and add animation.

Select a tool, width and size.

Click to start and stop recording your drawing.

Create and animate graphics with the Paint Designer

The **Paint Designer** is a cool little tool that makes adding animated paint and pencil lines to your videos simple and fun.

Open the **Paint Designer** by going to the **PiP Objects Room**, then clicking the pencil icon at the top of the room's panel (as illustrated on page 143).

In the **Paint Designer**, select a drawing **Tool** (pencil, chalk, marker, crayon, pen or eraser), set its width and select a color.

Begin recording the animation by clicking the red dot **Record** button below the panel's **Preview** window.

Draw across your video frame. Click the red dot again to stop recording. Then click the **Save** button and name your animation.

Your animated clip will appear as a custom overlay in the **Pip Object Room** library.

When added to the timeline above another video, the line you've drawn will appear animated, as if being drawn in real time!

You can also customize existing **PiP Objects** by selecting the object in the **PiP Object Room** and clicking **Modify Selected Paint Object** at the top of the Room's panel.

Your customized object will be saved as a new, Custom **PiP Object**.

Title Room Templates

The Title Designer

Text Masking Effects

The TV Safe Zone for Titles

Chapter 12

Add Text and Titles

Working with layers of video

With Titles, you can create opening or closing credits for your movie.

You can also use on-screen text to tell or help clarify your movie's story.

Titles and other text can be used to tell your video's story – or to give credit where credit is due.

CyberLink PowerDirector comes loaded with title templates in a variety of categories. Many of these templates include animation, and a number of them come complete with colorful backgrounds.

Existing title templates can be customized. And new titles, complete with 3D-like animation, can be created in the **Title Designer**.

The Title Room

The **Title Room** includes over 100 title templates, many of which include animation, styled text, graphics and backgrounds. The **Ending Credits** template, for instance, is a pre-animated credit roll, which you can customize with your cast and crew's names.

To access this library of title templates, click the **Title Room** tab along the upper left of the program. A **Search the Library** box in the upper right of the **Room** allows you to real-time search for a specific title (see page 19).

Title templates are tagged to categories – although you can also select **All Content** to see them all at once. When you click on a template, you'll see its animation in your **Preview** window.

In addition to the default set of title templates included with PowerDirector, if you are logged into the **DirectorZone**, thousands of additional title templates can be downloaded free by clicking the **DZ** button in the upper left of this room. For more information on the **DirectorZone**, see page 200.

Create or modify a Title Template.

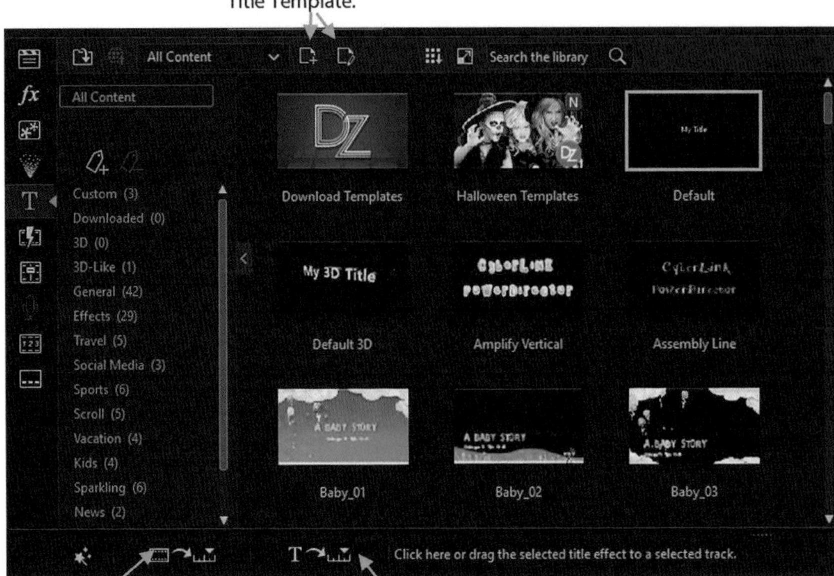

Insert template to the selected track.

Add template to the Title track.

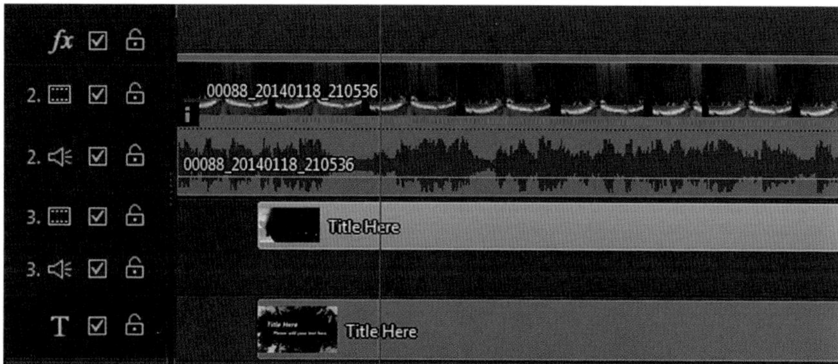

Titles can be added to Video 1, to the Title track or to any video track overlaying your video.

Add a title from the Title Room

Title templates can be added to the **Video 1** track, or they can be used on an upper video track, overlaying your video.

There are three ways to add a template from the **Title Room** to your timeline.

Drag a template from the Title Room to wherever you'd like it to appear on your timeline.

Select a template in the Title Room and click the Insert on Selected Track button. The title will be added to the video track you have selected at the position of the **Timeline** playhead. If you attempt to add a title to a position already occupied by a clip, you will be prompted to select a ripple option, as described in **Add Media Clips to the Timeline** on page 58.

Select a template in the Title Room and click the Add to Title Track button. The title will be added to the **Title track** (see page 10) at the position of the **Timeline** playhead.

Once you've added a title to your timeline, you can customize its duration and content.

To change a title's duration on your timeline, drag on the title clip's endpoint to extend or shorten it.

If your title includes text animation, extending its length will slow your text animation (a credit roll, for instance). Shortening the title will make the text animation run faster.

Extending or shortening your title clip will not, however, affect the speed of any other animated elements or objects in the template.

To customize the text or the template for a title on your timeline, **double-click** on it – or **right-click** on the title and select **Edit Title.** This will open the **Title Designer.**

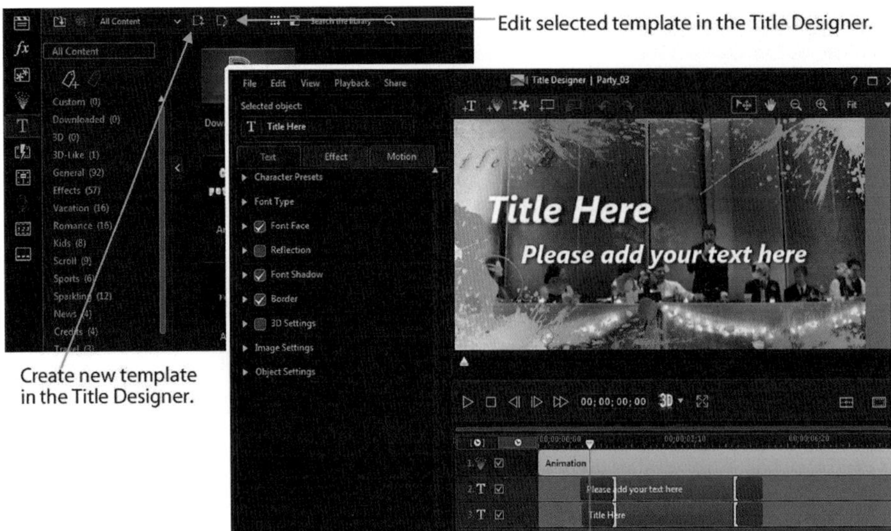

The Title Designer

The **Title Designer** is a workspace for creating and customizing your title templates. In this workspace, you can customize a template's text and text style; add, remove and edit graphic elements in the template; and add, remove or edit animation in the template.

The **Title Designer** can be used to customize a title on your timeline or it can be used to edit an existing template in the **Title Room**, in which case your customized title will be permanently added to the **Title Room** for use in a future project.

To open a title on your timeline in the Title Designer, double-click on the title – or **right-click** on the title and select **Edit Title.**

To create a custom title based on an existing template, double-click on a template in the **Title Room** or select a template and click the **Modify Selected Template** button at the top of the panel.

To create a template from scratch, click on the **Create a New Title Template** at the top of the **Title Room** panel, as illustrated above.

The **Title Designer** workspace includes a **Timeline** for creating custom animations, a **Text** panel for customizing your text attributes and a panel with a library of animated **Motion** presets.

If you've edited a template from the **Title Room**, once you click **Save** or **Save As** in the **Title Designer**, your customized template will be added to the **Custom** category in the **Title Room**.

If you've edited a title clip on your timeline, clicking **Save** will update only the instance of your title template as it appears on your project **Timeline**.

Select the text to customize it and to add or change its properties.

Customize your template's text

To customize the text in a title, select the existing text in the panel's **Preview** window and type over it.

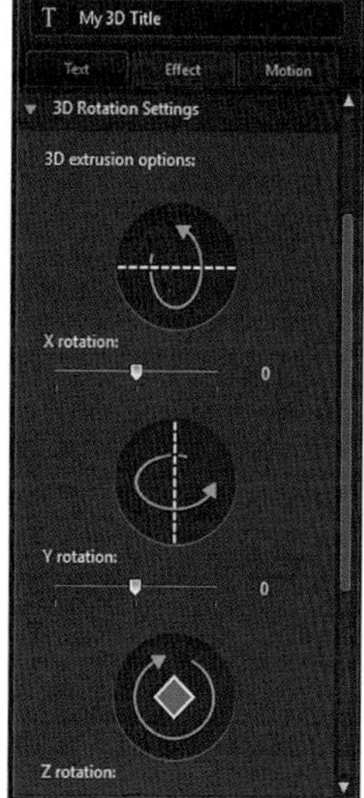

With all or part of the text selected, you can also change its characteristics by using the options on the **Text** panel on the panel's left side. This panel includes a number of styled **Character Presets** as well as options for setting the text's font and size, if it has a font face or border or if it casts a reflection or drop-shadow. If you are using the title in a stereoscopic 3D project, you also have the option of setting its **3D Depth** – how much it seems to float over the background video.

If you are editing the **3D-Like/Default 3D** template, you'll also find options in this panel for rotating your title in 3D space (as illustrated to the right) and for adding 3D textures.

Many titles include animation that is built right into its default text. You really can't edit this animation, other than controlling its speed.

If your animated text on the panel's **Timeline** has a shaded area over its beginning or end (as in the illustration above), this is an indication of an animation that is programmed into part of the title. You can control how fast this animation occurs by widening or shortening this shaded area.

You may also remove this existing text entirely (if you want, for instance, to replace it with your own custom-created animation) by selecting it on the **Title Designer's Timeline** and pressing the **Delete** key on your keyboard.

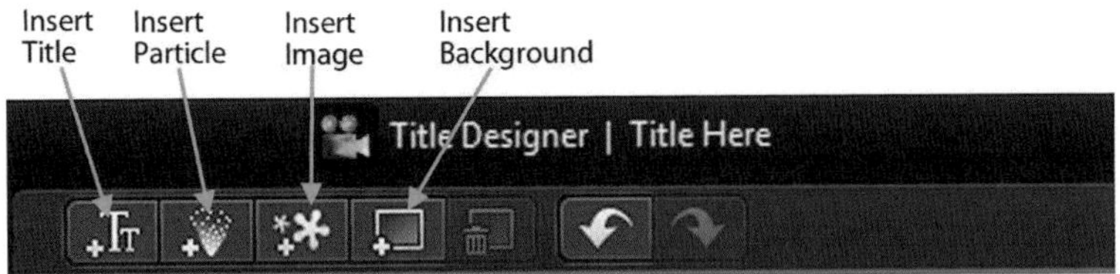

New Elements are added to the panel's Timeline, where they can be trimmed, respositioned re-ordered or deleted.

Add more blocks of text to your title

To add or create text in your title template, click the **Insert Title** button at the top of the **Title Designer** panel (as illustrated at the top of the next page) – then click in the **Preview** window and start typing. You can also simply **double-click** in the **Preview** window and start typing.

Once you've added text, it can be styled and colored using the properties listed under the **Text** tab, as we discuss on page 149.

Add Motion to your text

Paths are animation presets that move your text block(s) around your video frame. To add an animated **Path** to a text block in a title template, select the text on the panel's **Timeline** and then select an animation preset from under the **Motion** tab.

When you select a **Path** preset for your selected text, a preview of the effect will appear in the **Preview** window.

To remove any of these animation effects, click the big blue **No Effect X** at the top left of the **Motion** panel.

Add an animated Particle to your title

If you click the **Insert Particle** button at the top of the panel (as illustrated above), the program will open into your **Particle Room** (see page 103). The **Particle** you select will be added as an animated element in your title.

This **Particle** effect will appear as a clip on the panel's **Timeline**. By trimming and positioning this **Particle** clip, you can set when, in your title, this effect begins and ends.

Add a custom image or background to your title

The **Insert Image** and **Insert Background** buttons at the top of the panel give you the option of importing custom still photos or graphics into your title.

For information on adding a non-square graphic with no background to your project, see the sidebar on page 108.

Edit elements from your title template

Once added to the panel's **Timeline**, elements can be trimmed and positioned to start or end at a given point.

By dragging on the **Timeline's** track headers, you can rearrange the stacking order of these elements.

To remove text, a background, a graphic or a **Particle** animation from your title template, select that element on the **Title Designer's Timeline** and press the **Delete** key on your keyboard.

Add a Starting or Ending Effect to your title's text

The **Title Designer** includes a number of cool, animated effects for your text blocks. These animations can be added as **Starting Effects**, flying or animating your text into the video frame, or **Ending Effects**, flying or animating your text out of the video frame – or both!

To access this library of animations, as well as a tool for adding **Motion Blur** to these animations, select a text block in the **Title Designer** and select the **Effect** tab to the left of the panel.

Under this tab you will find over 75 **Starting Effects** and over 75 **Ending Effects.** To preview the animation of any effect, hover your mouse over the effect's thumbnail. To test drive it with the text in your title, click on the effect's thumbnail.

If your title template already includes animation, its **Effect** will already be selected on this panel. You may replace this animation **Effect** with any other **Starting** or **Ending Effect** – or remove the animation completely.

Once you click on a **Starting** or **Ending Effect**, it is applied to the selected text block in your title. Selecting another effect automatically replaces the previously-selected effect. However, any combination of **Starting Effect** and **Ending Effect** can be added to a block of text – and, of course, different effects can be used on each block of text in your title.

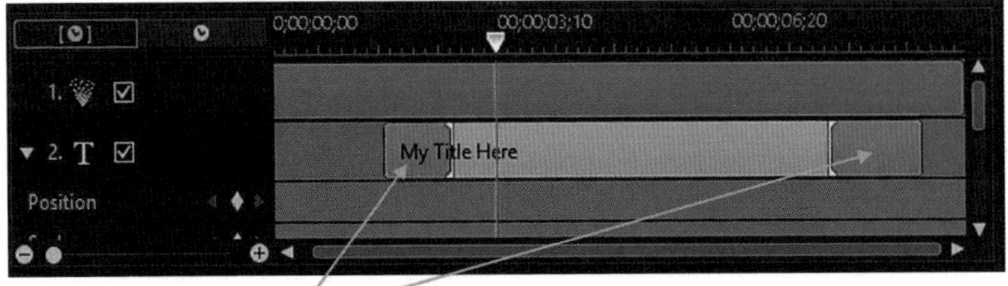

Fade In/Out indicators appear on any element added to the Title Designer timeline.

To remove an effect, click on the large **X No Effect** thumbnail.

To apply a **Motion Blur** to your animation, check the option at the bottom of the **Effects** panel. (You may need to scroll a long way down to see it.) The **Motion Blur** effect includes controls for setting the intensity of the blur.

Fade text or other elements in or out on your title

By default, a one-second **Fade In** and a one-second **Fade Out** are added to any text or other element on your title. These **Fades** are represented as adjustable overlays at either end of the text block or graphic element clip on the **Title Designer's** timeline.

These **Fade** segments are adjustable. Just drag them longer or shorter right on the timeline. They can also be removed completely by dragging them to the end of the text box or graphic on the timeline.

In fact, the entire clips representing the text or other elements can also be extended, shortened or removed by trimming, dragging or deleting them to meet your custom need.

Text Masking

In addition to the title templates in the **Title Room**, PowerDirector includes a number of **Text Masking** effects.

The TV Safe Zone

All TVs, including today's modern LCDs and plasma sets, cut a little off the sides off your video. This is an effect called overscan – and some TVs do it more than others.

To ensure that you don't lose any important video information through this effect – especially text – PowerDirector includes an overlay which indicates the **TV Safe Zone** within which you should keep all of your vital video information.

To turn it on in the main **Preview** window, select a video clip on your **Video 1** track, then **right-click** on the **Preview** window and select the option to turn on the **TV Safe Zone**. (Strangely, this overlay is only visible when a clip on **Video 1** is selected.)

You'll also find a switch for turning on the **TV Safe Zone** in the **Title Designer**, right under that panel's **Preview** window.

We highly recommend you keep your titles and subtitles within this **TV Safe Zone**. Otherwise you risk your title "Gone With the Wind" appearing on some TVs as "one With the Win".

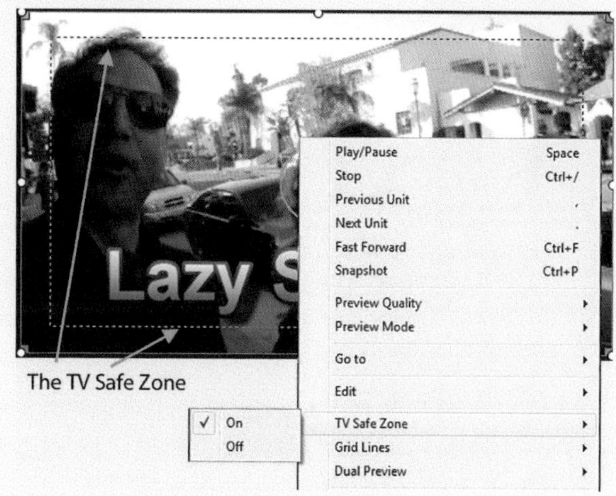

The TV Safe Zone

Text Blur Masking

Text Sepia Masking

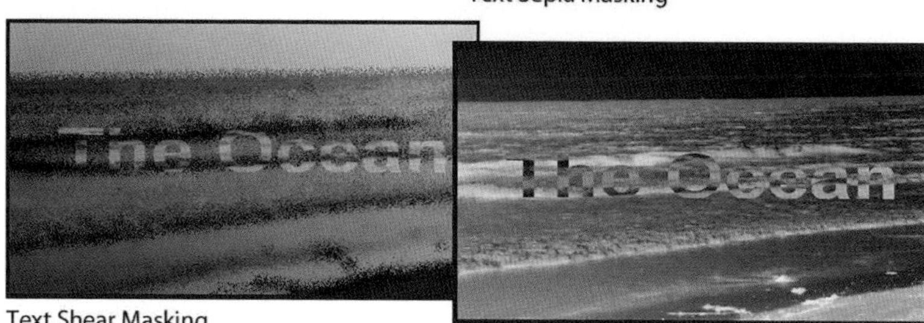
Text Shear Masking

Text X-Ray Masking

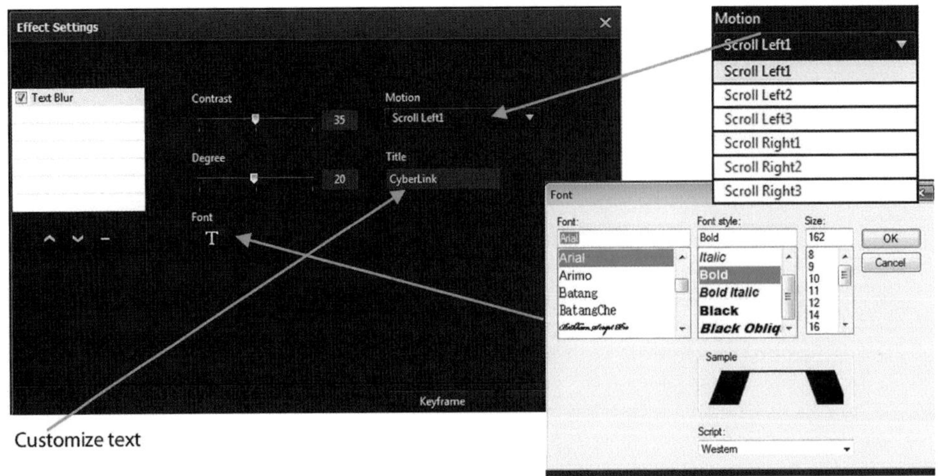

Customize text

Text Masking templates are found in the **Text Masking** category of the program's video effects, accessed by clicking the **FX Room** tab in the upper left of the program (see page 91).

Text Masking cuts your video into the shape of your title and applies a video effect to the video outside this shape – then applies an animation to it, as illustrated at the bottom of the facing page.

As with any effect applied to a clip, **Text Masking** can be customized in the **Effects Settings** panel (see page 85).

To open the **Effects Settings** panel for a clip, select the clip to which **Text Masking** has been applied and then click the **Effect** function button along the top of the **Timeline**.

On the left of the **Effects Settings** panel, you will see the applied **Text Masking** effect as well as any other effects that have been applied to this clip.

Select the **Text Masking** effect from this list.

To customize the text that will be used in this effect, type over the word **CyberLink** under the **Title** property.

Other properties for the effect can be customized by using the sliders – or, for **Motion** animation, you can select an option from the drop-down menu.

When you first attempt to modify any of these properties, a box will pop up warning you that **This operation resets all of the keyframes in this effect. Do you want to continue?** Click **OK**. Otherwise you won't be able to customize your effect at all.

To change your text's font, style or size, click the "**T**" under the **Font** property listing.

Fade Ins and Fade Outs

Crossfades

The Transitions Room

Customizing Transitions

Add Transitions to Your Whole Movie at Once

The Transition Designer

Chapter 13

Add Transitions

Effects for getting from one clip to another

Transitions are fun ways to get from one clip, or one scene, to another.

They can be subtle or showy – fun or barely noticeable.

Transitions add to the tone and feel of your movies.

There are lots of ways to get from one clip to the next in a movie.

The most basic way is the cut, in which we simply and abruptly move from one clip to another on our timeline. This, most simple "transition" serves its purpose: It is, for the most part, invisible.

More elaborate transitions draw attention to themselves to varying degrees. Some transitions are subtle and are hardly even noticed. Others are showy and can't help but be noticed.

In any event, a transition is just another storytelling element. It can be used to tell your audience that time has passed between scenes, or that we're moving from one location or point-of-view to another. Good transitions – like a movie's color tone and music – add to your movie's mood and style.

Fade ins and fade outs

Fading into and out of a scene is like raising and lowering a curtain in a stage show. It tells your audience that a major sequence – or maybe the entire show – is beginning or ending.

Fade Ins and **Fade Outs** are added to individual clips on your timeline in PowerDirector.

The simplest way to add a **Fade** to a clip on your timeline is in the **PiP Designer**, which is launched when you **double-click** on a clip on your timeline.

At the bottom of the **Properties** panel on the **PiP Designer** are the options for **Enabling a Fade-In** or **Enabling a Fade-Out** on your clip.

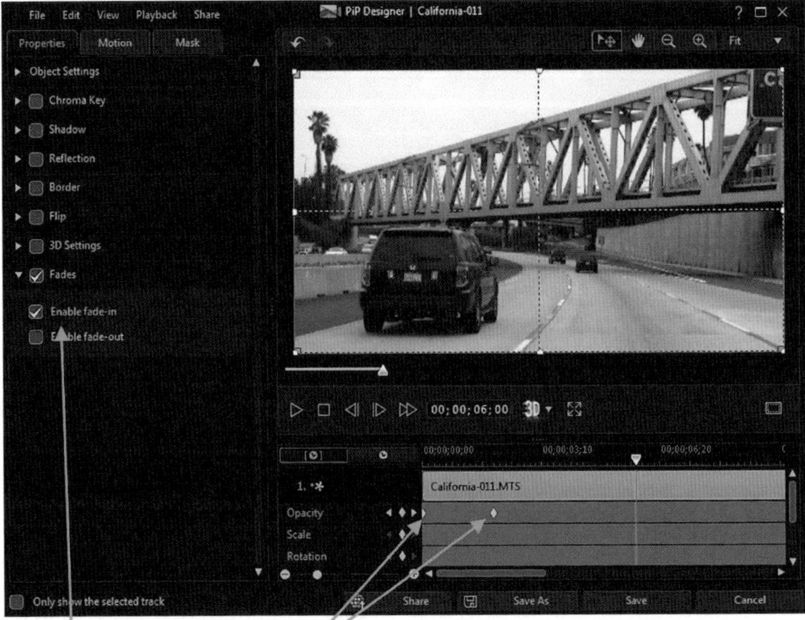

Selecting the option to Enable Fade-In or Enable Fade-Out in the PiP Designer, adds a keyframed transition to the Opacity property.

When you select one of these **Fade** options, diamond-shaped keyframes are added to the **Opacity** property on the **PIP Designer's Timeline**, below its **Preview** window.

By default, these keyframes will create a two-second **Fade-In** animation from 0% to 100% **Opacity** at the beginning of the clip or a **Fade-Out** animation from 100% to 0% **Opacity** at the end of the clip.

By moving the middle keyframe nearer to or farther from the beginning or the end of the clip, you can extend or shorten the length of the **Fade**. (For more information on keyframing in the **PiP Designer**, see **Animate Your Picture-in-Picture** on page 135.)

An important note about **Fade-Ins** and **Fade-Outs** is that they are the results of animations of the **Opacity** property. In other words, when a **Fade In** goes from 0% to 100% **Opacity**, even if it looks like a fade in from black, it is actually an animation from 100% *transparency*.

If your video clip is on the **Video 1** track, then, this animation In will appear to be a fade in from blackness (since there is nothing on a track below your clip). However, if the video you are applying this animation to is on an upper video track and there is another video on a video track below it, your **Fade-In** will appear more like a *dissolve* from the video on the lower track to this video clip rather than a fade in from black.

We see this happening when a **Fade** is applied to a **Picture-in-Picture,** as we discuss in **PiP Designer Properties** on page 137.

Add a Crossfade

Whenever you add a video clip to your timeline or you shift the position of a clip on your timeline so that it overlaps another clip, a pop-up screen will offer you a number of options (as we discuss on page 58).

If you select the **Crossfade** option, the program will create a dissolve the length of the overlap from one clip to the other.

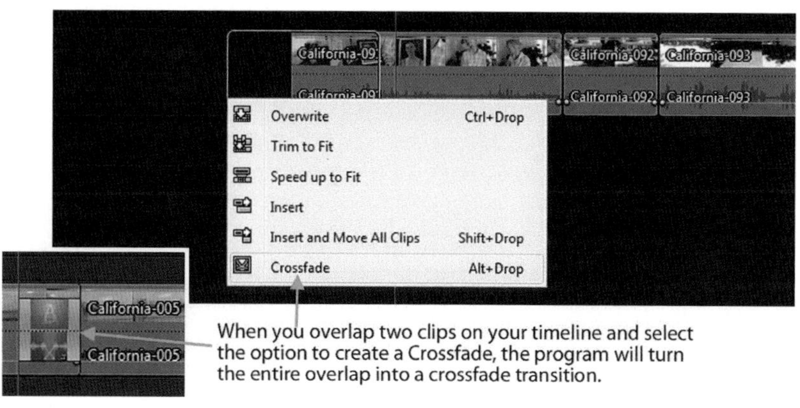

When you overlap two clips on your timeline and select the option to create a Crossfade, the program will turn the entire overlap into a crossfade transition.

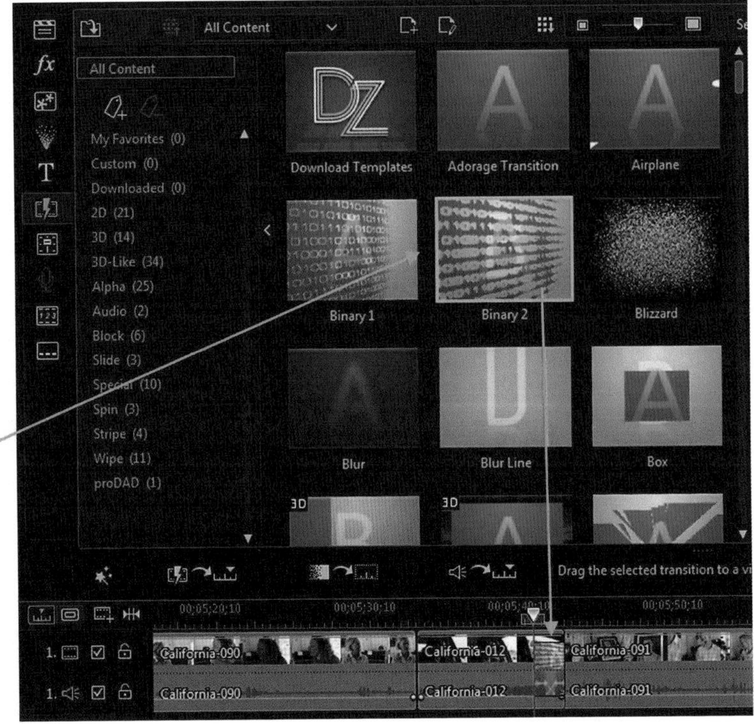

To apply a transition, drag it from the Transition Room to the intersection of two clips.

To replace a transition, simply drag a new one over the existing transition.

If you click on this overlapped area, you'll see an indicator showing the **Crossfade** transition between the two clips. **Right-click** on this **Crossfade** and select **Modify Transition** to customize its behavior in the **Transition Settings** panel, as we discuss on page 160.

You can also replace a **Crossfade** with another transition by dragging your new selection from the **Transition Room** onto the **Crossfade** on your timeline. This new transition will be the same length as the **Crossfade** was.

The Transition Room

CyberLink PowerDirector, illustrated above, includes a library of over 120 animated transitions.

To access this library of transitions, click the **Transition Room** tab along the upper left of the program. A **Search the Library** box in the upper right of the **Room** allows you to real-time search for a specific transition (see page 19).

The transitions in this room are tagged to categories – although you can also select **All Content** to see them all at once.

When you hover your mouse over a transition, you'll see its animation in your **Preview** window.

A number of these transitions are 3D, which means that, when used in a project set up for stereoscopic 3D, the transition's animated elements will appear to fly right off the screen!

Among the library of transitions are two audio transitions, **Constant Gain** and **Constant Power.** Both of these transitions do essentially the same thing – create a smooth audio dissolve from one audio clip to another.

Which you use is up to you. They're very similar. Although most experts agree **Constant Gain** makes for a slightly smoother transition.

Apply a transition

To apply a video transition between two clips on your timeline, simply drag it from the **Transition Room** onto the intersection of the clips.

A two-second transition will be added between the clips.

If the clip has both audio and video, a **Constrain Gain** audio transition will also be added automatically to the audio.

Customize a transition

To change the length of an applied transition, **double-click** on it and, in the pop-up option panel, change its **Duration Settings**.

When you add your transition directly between two clips, you may notice that the second clip shifts left two seconds so that the clips overlap during the transition. This is called an **Overlap** transition, and it is the type of transition behavior the program applies by default.

Although this behavior sometimes drives users crazy, since it changes the duration of their clips every time they add a transition, this shift also provides the program the footage it needs to create the transition.

When you add a transition between two clips, the second clip will jump left to form a 2-second overlap which the program can use to create the transitional segment.

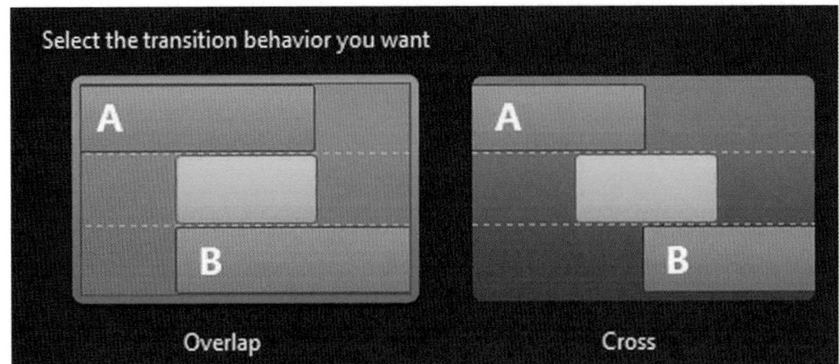

An Overlap transition creates the transitional segment by overlapping the two clips. A Cross transition transitions to black from one clip then transitions out of black for the other.

This is because, throughout any transition between two clips, both clips are on-screen at the same time. When one clip jumps left to overlap the other, this provides the program with the necessary footage from both clips to create this transitional segment.

As an alternative, PowerDirector also includes options for adding transitions without overlapping or shifting your clips' positions.

Drag your transition to one or the other clip rather than exactly between two. This will give one of the clips a transition in from black or a transition out to black – but the transition won't apply to both of your clips.

Add a Cross transition rather than Overlap transition. In a **Cross** transition, the clips remain in position and do not overlap. However, this behavior also creates a very different looking transition.

In a **Cross** transition, the transition you apply will take your first clip to black – and then this same transition will take your second clip back out of black.

Options for setting your transition to **Cross** or **Overlap** – as well as for customizing the other elements of your transition – are found in the **Transition Settings** panel, discussed in the next section of this chapter.

To replace one transition with another, simply drag your new selection from the **Transition Room** onto the existing transition on your timeline.

The Transition Settings panel

To launch the **Transition Settings** panel, either select the transition on your timeline and click the **Modify** Function button, or **right-click** on a transition that you've added to your timeline and select **Modify Transition**.

The settings and options available in this panel vary from transition to transition. In fact, some transitions offer only options for setting the transition's **Duration** and selecting whether the transition uses the **Cross** or **Overlap** behavior.

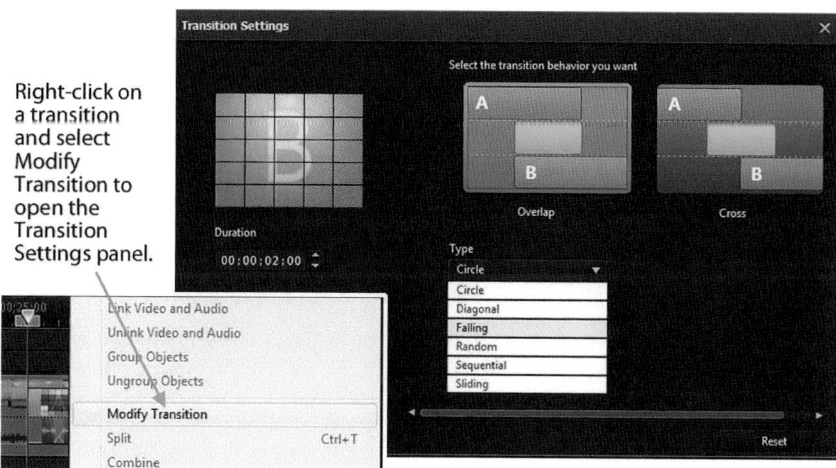

In the program's preferences, you can set the default properties for all of your transitions. To access these preferences, click the **Cog** at the top of the program's interface. Transition defaults are set on the **Editing** preferences page.

Add transitions to all of your movie at once

When you select a transition in the **Transition Room**, three **Apply to All** buttons appear along the top of the **Timeline** – none of which have anything to do with the particular transition you've selected.

If you click on any of these buttons, you'll be given four options for how it applies its transitions.

Prefix Transition, which adds a random transition or fade in to the beginning of your movie.

Postfix Transition, which adds a random transition or fade out to the end of your movie.

Cross Transition, which adds random transitions or fades so that each clip in your movie transitions from black and then transitions to black.

Overlap Transition, which shifts the positions of all of the clips on your timeline so that they all overlap, applying a random transition or fade from clip to clip.

Remove a transition

To delete a transition you've added between two clips on your timeline, click to select it and press the **Delete** key on your keyboard – or **right-click** on the transition and select **Remove.**

Design or customize a transition

The **Transition Designer** is a workspace for customizing and creating **Alpha Transitions.**

Alpha Transitions use the black and white values of an image to create a transitional pattern. The transitional pattern that the **Transition Designer** creates will be based on a dissolve from the blackest black in the image to the whitest white.

In other words, if you provide the **Transition Designer** a gradient image that is black in the center and white around the sides (as illustrated at the top of the facing page), the **Transition Designer** will create from it a transition that begins in the center of the video frame and then widens out.

To customize an existing transition, select the transition in the **Transition Room** and click the **Modify Selected Alpha Transition** button at the top center of the panel, as illustrated below. (Note that not all of the transitions can be modified.)

To create a new transition from scratch, click the **Create a New Alpha Transition** at the top center of the **Transition Room.**

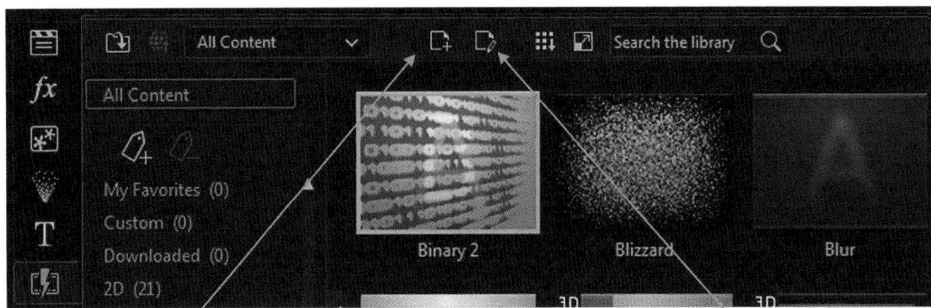

Create a New Alpha Transition

Modify Selected Alpha Transition.

Either button launches the **Transition Designer.** However, when you click the **Create a New Alpha Transition** button, you will be prompted to select an image to base your transition on. You can use any color or black & white image to build a transition from – however using an image that is made up of only black, white and shades of gray makes it easier to determine the animation pattern your transition will use.

At Muvipix.com, we have designed a batch of free, black & white patterns you can download and use to create your transitions. Just type "Gradient Wipe Pack" in the product search box.

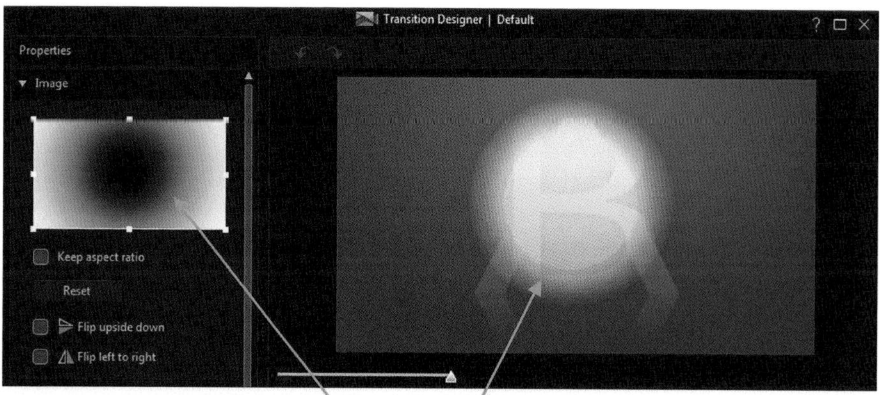

Your newly created Alpha Transition will create a transitional animation from clip to clip based on the pattern you provide, from the blackest black to the whitest white in your image.

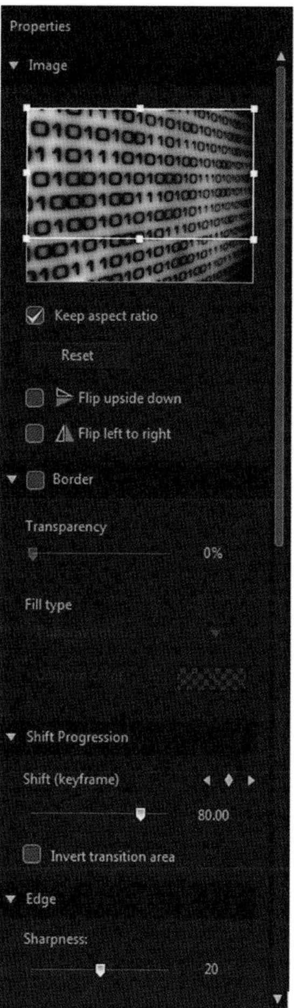

Whether you're modifying an existing transition or creating a custom transition based on your own pattern, the **Transition Designer's Properties** panel (at left) offers you a number of options, including the option to flip the transition's pattern, to add a border between the transitioning clips and to adjust the sharpness of the edge between the transitioning clips.

Shift Progression controls the timing of the transition from one clip to another. By adding a keyframe mid-way through the progression (or dragging at the point of the playhead on the **Progression** timeline, as illustrated below), you can interpolate the transition to vary the speed of the transition's progress.

Once you've created or modified a transition you can load it to the **DirectorZone** or to your personal **CyberLink Cloud** account (see page 204).

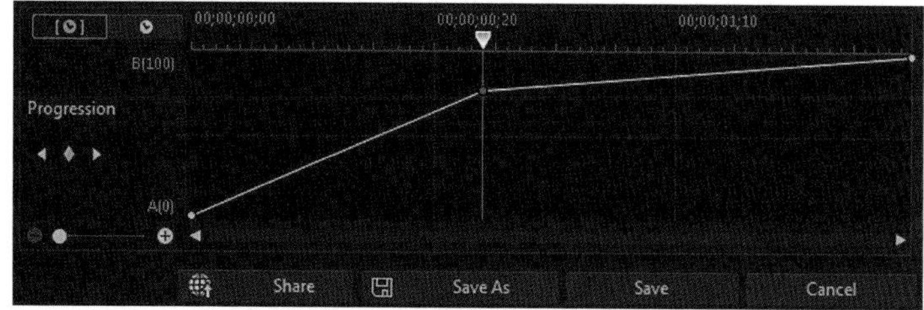

With keyframes on the Progression timeline, you can interpolate the transition to animate more quickly or more slowly at the beginning or end.

Creating Subtitles in PowerDirector

Importing Subtitles Into Your Movie

Settings Subtitle Behavior

Chapter 14

Add Subtitles

Optional text for your movie

Subtitles are captions in your movie that are used to clarify a scene's dialog or translate it into another language.

PowerDirector's subtitles can be imprinted on your finished video, or offered as a selectable option for your viewer.

Optional subtitles are another one of those high-level features that come standard with CyberLink PowerDirector Ultimate.

Subtitles you add to your PowerDirector project can be imprinted onto the video itself or they can be added as a selectable option for your viewer.

Your subtitles can be typed right into PowerDirector, or they can be imported into the project from a text file.

Create subtitles in PowerDirector

To access the PowerDirector subtitle creation panel, click the **Subtitle Room** tab in the upper left of the program.

When you add text to your movie in the **Subtitle Room**, you'll need to designate when the subtitle begins in your movie and when it ends. Fortunately, the program makes this process fairly intuitive.

If your **Subtitle Track** isn't visible at the top of the **Timeline**, enable it by **right-clicking** on the **Timeline's** track headers and checking the **Show Subtitle Track** option.

1 **Locate your subtitle's start point**

Drag the playhead on your timeline to the point in your movie you'd like your subtitle to begin.

2 **Click the Add Subtitle button**

The **Add Subtitle** button is the **+** button in the lower left of the **Subtitle Room**.

A new subtitle listing will be added to this **Room**.

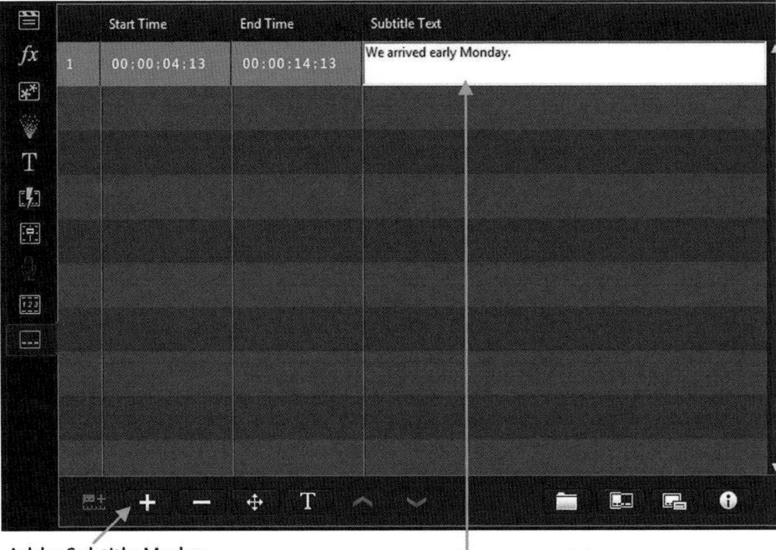

Add a Subtitle Marker. Double-click to add text.

The text clip is added to the Subtitle Track at the position of the Timeline playhead. Trim and position it in sync with your dialog or video.

3 **Create your subtitle**

Double-click where indicated in the **Subtitle Text** column.

Type your subtitle's text.

Click anywhere else in the **Subtitle Room** to save this subtitle.

For best results, keep it brief. You can add as many subtitles as you'd like to your project.

4 **Set the subtitle's duration**

By default, your subtitle will be 10 seconds long. However, you can trim it to any length by dragging the end of the subtitle inward on your timeline. You can also drag on the subtitle itself to reposition it on your timeline.

If your subtitle is a translation of your movie's dialog, you'll want to synchronize its start and end points to match the dialog.

5 **Select a font**

If you've created several subtitles already, click and drag across the **Subtitle Room** to select all of your existing subtitles.

By default, your subtitles will appear in the Courier font. To change the font and font size, click the "**T**" button at the bottom of the **Subtitle Room.**

Select your font, style and font size. These font settings will be applied to all of your selected subtitles. This font will also be applied automatically to any new subtitles you create in your project.

To ensure that none of your subtitles are cut off by TV overscan, it's best to work with **TV Safe Zone** turned on, as we discuss in the sidebar on page 153.

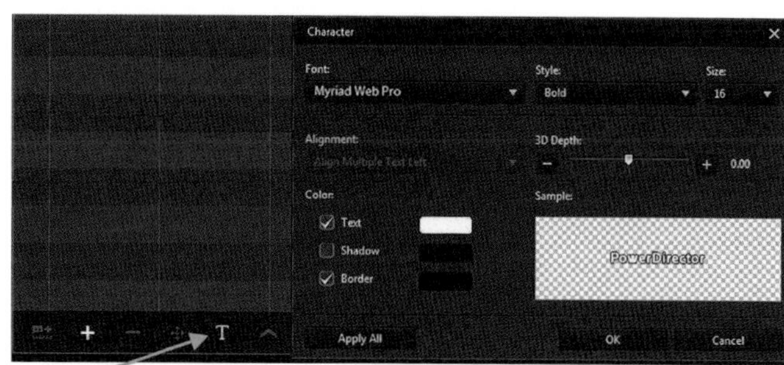

The font you select will be applied to all subtitles you have selected in the Subtitle Room as well as any new subtitles you create.

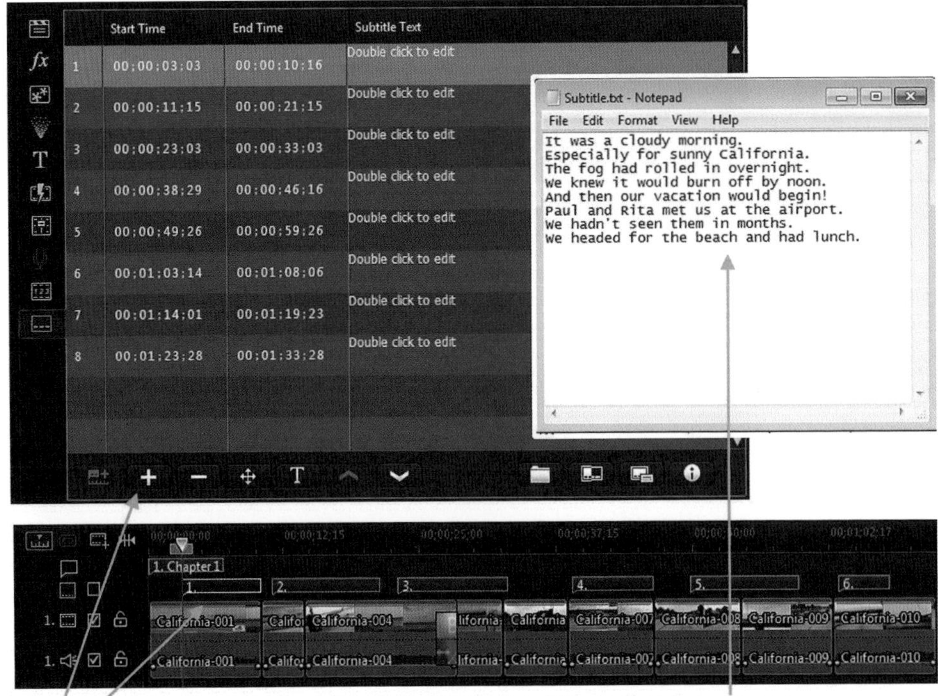

Create, size and position subtitle markers on the Timeline's Subtitle track, and prepare your subtitle text in a .txt or .srt file.

Import subtitles from a text file

Sometimes, rather than typing your subtitles one at a time into CyberLink PowerDirector, it's easier to work from a script, building all of your movie's subtitles into a text file and then importing that text file into your movie as subtitles.

An important thing to note about importing text is that your imported subtitles will overwrite any existing subtitle text you've added – so it's best to import any subtitles before you add any subtitle text manually.

1 **Create your text document**

In your document, add a line break between each subtitle.

Once you've got your subtitle document completed, save it in a format that PowerDirector can import into the **Subtitle Room**.

Your subtitle document must be saved as either a text (.txt) or SubRip (.srt) file. Virtually any word processor (even Windows Notepad) can save a text document as a .txt file.

2 **Create your subtitle markers**

Set the **Timeline** playhead where you'd like the first subtitle to begin. Click the **Add Subtitle** (**+**) button at the bottom of the **Subtitle Room**, as illustrated at the top of this page.

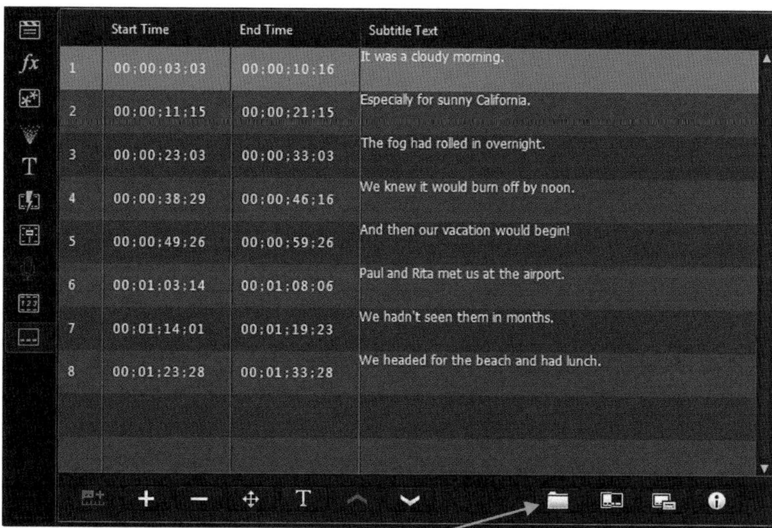

Import the .txt or .srt file into your Subtitle Room.

Move the playhead down the timeline and continue to create subtitle markers. You may need to also trim the markers' lengths in order to sync your subtitles with the movie's dialog or action.

3 **Import your text document**

Click the **Import Subtitles** (file folder) button at the lower-right of the **Subtitle Room.**

Browse to and open your text document. The text in your document will be automatically loaded into all of the subtitle markers you've created.

If you haven't got enough subtitle markers for your document's text, the program will warn you that not all of your subtitles were used.

If you'd like to manually create additional subtitles, use the steps described in **Create subtitles in PowerDirector** on page 166.

Set your subtitles' behavior

The subtitles you've added to your movie can be imprinted onto the video your output – in which case they will always be visible – or they can be set up as an option for your viewer.

To set your subtitle's behavior, click the **Select Type of Subtitles** button in the lower right of the **Subtitle Room**, as illustrated on page 170.

Create Subtitles for Discs/Files creates optional subtitles. Optional subtitles can be toggled on or off on DVDs, BluRays, AVCHD video and MKV video, when played on a compatible player.

Create Subtitles Imprinted on a Video File permanently prints your subtitles right onto your video.

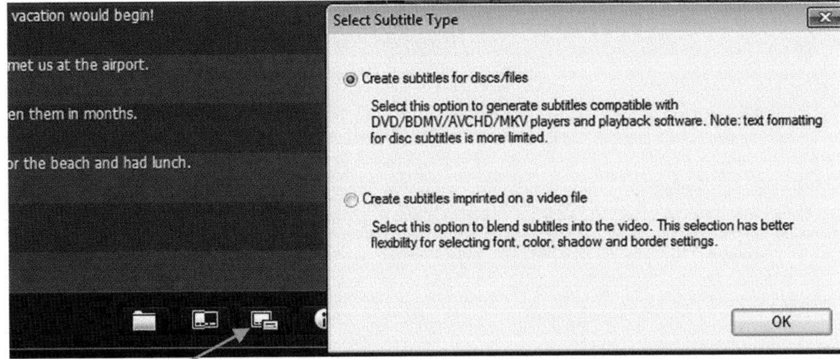

Select the type of subtitles you'd like to create.

When you select the **Create Subtitles for Discs/Files,** a sub-menu for turning on and off your subtitles will be automatically added to your disc menu structure.

For more information on disc menu options, see **Chapter 16, Disc Authoring**.

Section 4

Output Your Finished Movie

Produce a Video

Output a Video for a Device

Upload a Video to a Social Media Site

Chapter 15

Output a Video File

Sharing your movie

There are lots of ways to share your finished movie with the world.

You can create a disc; you can post it online – you can even output a file for viewing on a smartphone or other portable device.

PowerDirector includes easy tools for outputting an optimized movie for each of these destinations.

So your movie's finished. Now it's time to share your masterpiece with the world!

PowerDirector gives you a wealth of options for sharing your finished piece – including options for porting your video directly from the program to a number of popular video sharing sites.

In fact, there's such a wealth of output options available, it's often hard to decide which is the best for your particular situation.

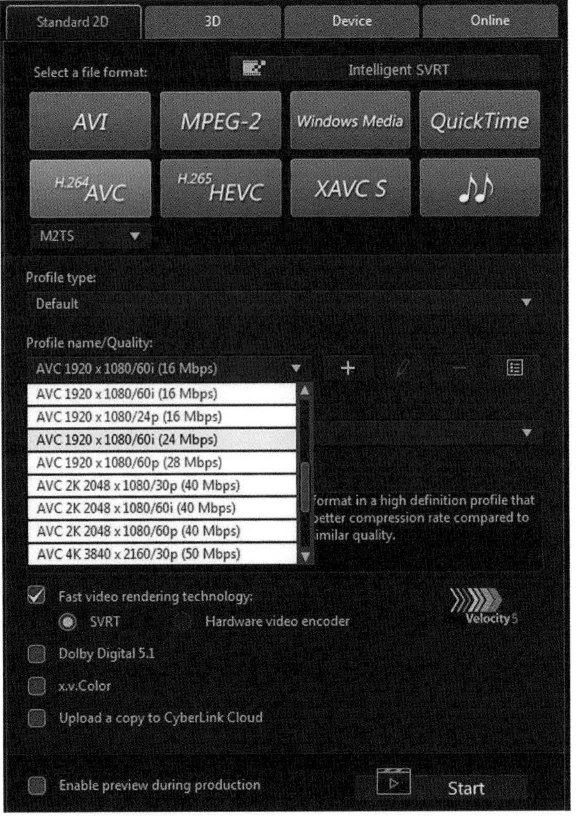

Produce a video file

PowerDirector offers you the option of outputting your video as any of seven popular video file formats.

To access your video output options, click the **Produce** button at the top of the interface.

To access the options for outputting non-3D video or audio, click on the **Standard 2D** tab.

Some profiles for these video formats are only available if your video is 4:3, some are only available if your video is 16:9.

AVI, the most common format for outputting editable standard definition video. For both 4:3 and 16:9 video, the DV-AVI profile will output editable video as NTSC 720x480 and PAL 720x576. This format can also be output as uncompressed Windows-AVI in 640x480 or lower resolution.

MPEG-2. A format that includes profiles for outputting DVD-ready 720x480, 720x576. 1280x720, 1440x1080 and BluRay-ready 1920x1080 at both 60i and 24p frame rates.

Windows Media produces a WMV file, typically used for video viewed online or on a computer. This format includes profiles for 320x180, 640x360, 1280x720, 1920x1080 and 4K video at 3840x2160 and 4096x2160.

Quicktime produces an MOV file, Apple's favorite workflow format. This format includes profiles for 160x90, 160x120, 320x180, 320x240, 640x360, 640x480, 960x540, 960x720, 1280x720, 1440x1080 and 1920x1080 at a variety of frame rates.

AVC. A high-quality H.264-compressed format that can output M2TS, MP4 and MKV video files with profiles for outputting 1440x1080 and 1920x1080, 2048x1080 as well as 4K video at 3840x2160 and 4096x2160 at a variety of frame rates. In a 4:3 project, you'll also find profiles for outputting standard definition 720x480 and 720x576 as well as higher definition 2048x1536 and 4096x3072 video.

HEVC uses the advanced H.265 codec to produce even higher-quality-per-size files than even AVC (H.264). This option will create M2TS, MP4 and MKV video files with profiles for outputting 1440x1080 and 1920x1080, 2048x1080 as well as 4K video at 3840x2160 and 4096x2160 at a variety of frame rates. In a 4:3 project, you'll also find profiles for outputting standard definition 720x480 and 720x576 as well as higher definition 2048x1536 and 4096x3072 video.

XAVC-S is a format for creating ultra-high definition and 4K video as an MP4. It includes profiles for outputting video at 1280x720, 1920x1080 and 3840x2160 at a number of frame rates.

Audio output formats (under the musical notes button) include **WMA** (Windows Media Audio), **WAV** and **MPEG-4** audio.

You also have the option of creating custom profiles for any video format.

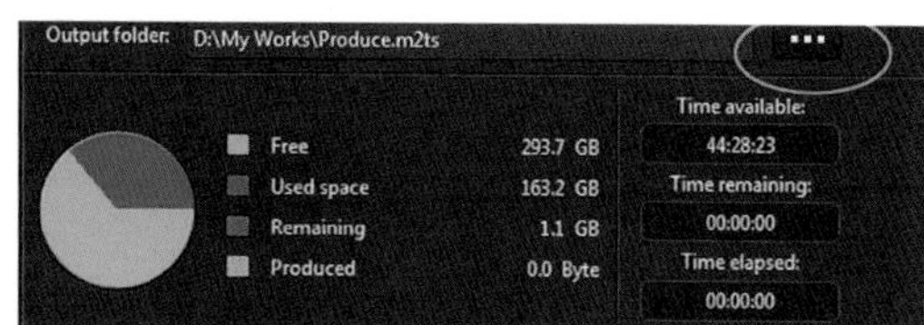

To set where your video will be saved to, click the **Output Folder...** button in the lower right of the **Produce** workspace and browse to a location.

To output your video, click the **Start** button at the bottom of the panel.

3D video outputs

If you're working on a project set up for stereoscopic 3D (see page 70), PowerDirector offers a number of options for sharing your video.

You can output your movie as:

A 3D movie. PowerDirector offers half a dozen formats for outputting your 3D video, in both anaglyphic (red/blue) and stereoscopic MVC (Multi-View Coding). For information on these options, see **Output your 3D video** on page 72.

YouTube 3D. PowerDirector also comes with facilities for loading your 3D video to YouTube. You'll find this option in the **Produce** workspace, under the **Online** tab. To upload your video in 3D, check the option box next to the **Profile** listing.

3D Disc. Finally, you can output your video as a 3D DVD or BluRay disc. To access these options, go to the **Create Disc** workspace and click on the **3D Disc** tab. Otherwise the process for creating your disc and its menus is the same as in **Chapter 16, Disc Authoring.** 3D discs can be output in a number of formats.

The **Anaglyphic** option will output your stereoscopic video channels and shades of red and cyan. Anaglyphic video can be viewed on any device, using inexpensive blue/red glasses.

The **Side-by-Side Half Width L/R** option will output your video with Multi-View Coding (MVC). Although MVC video can also be viewed as 2D on 2D equipment, viewing 3D MVC video requires a 3D monitor or television as well as 3D glasses.

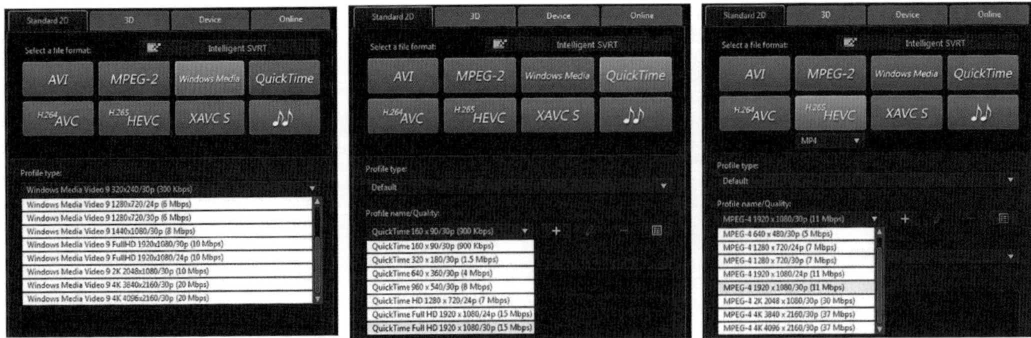

Each video format and profile has an optimum use.

Web video

WMVs and **MOVs** were originally designed to be delivery formats for video to be displayed on the internet. (Although MOVs can also be used as editable video, particularly on Mac software.) Highly compressed and small in size, virtually every streaming video on the Internet was either a Windows Media or a Quicktime file in the Web's early days.

AVC, HEVC and even **MKV** video (all of which can be output as .mp4 files) have more recently become the video formats of choice for video loaded to the Web, due to their smaller file size and higher quality video.

MP4 video (whether AVC, HEVC or MKV) is the ideal output format for video that you plan to upload to sites like **YouTube, Vimeo** and **Facebook**.

Editable video for use in another project

Editable video is video that you are outputting for use as source media in another project.

The **DV-AVI** profile of **AVI** is the ideal format for outputting video that will be used in a ***standard definition*** video project.

For high definition video, your best choice for outputting video to be used in another ***high-definition video*** project is the **AVC/M2TS** format with the **AVC 1920x1080 60i** or, if you'd prefer, 60p profile.

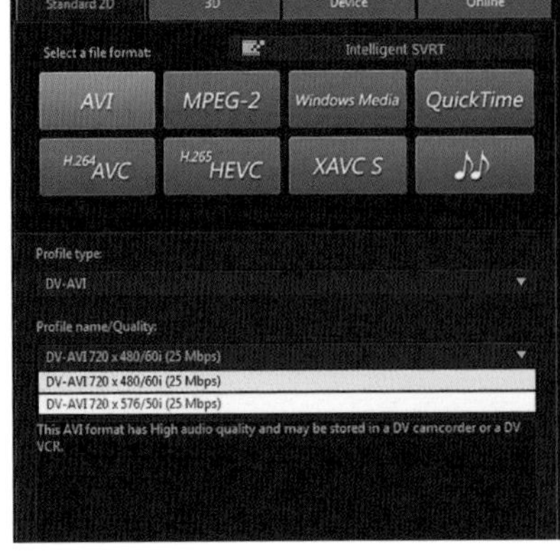

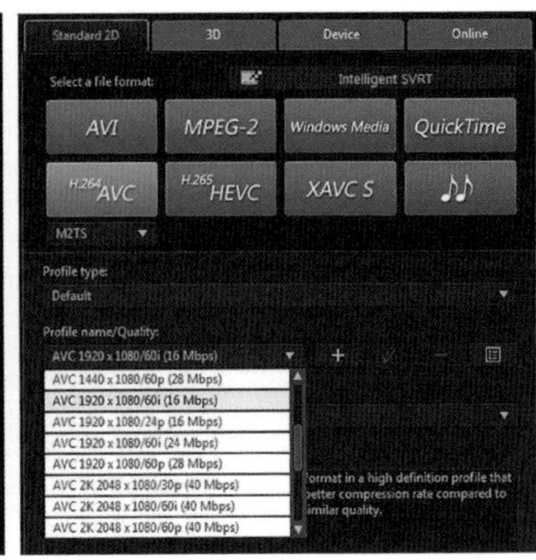

Disc-ready video

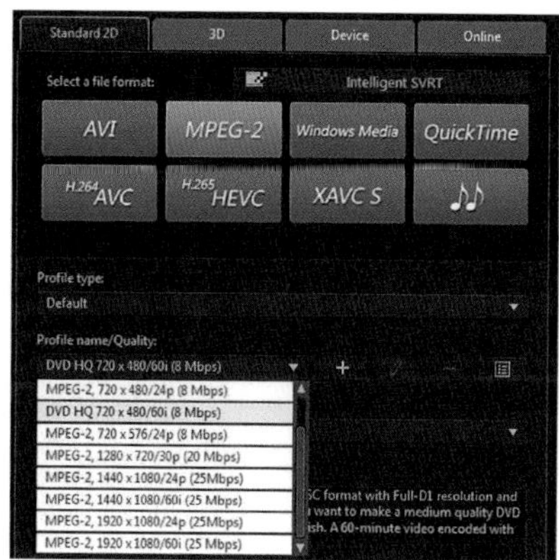

Video that you're going to use in a DVD or BluRay disc project should be output as MPEG-2s in order to function most efficiently in your disc authoring program. (In fact, they usually don't require re-encoding to a disc video format.)

For DVDs, the ideal MPEG-2 profile is DVD HQ 720x480.

For BluRay discs, the ideal MPEG-2 profile is MPEG-2 1920x1080/60i or 24p (depending on how your disc project is set up).

DVD-Ready and BluRay-ready **MPEG-2** videos may be burned directly to a disc (to create a menu-less DVD or BluRay) or may be ported to a disc-authoring program (like CyberLink's PowerDVD Ultra).

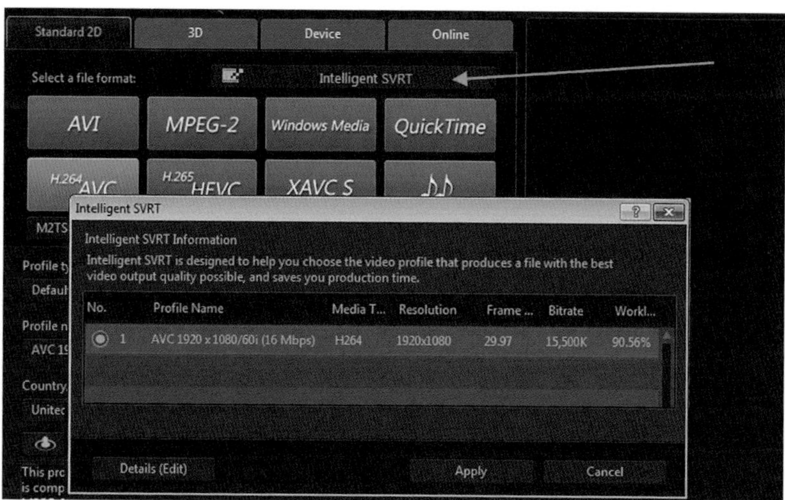

Intelligent SVRT

If you click the **Intelligent SVRT** button at the top of the **Standard 2D** panel, the program's **Smart Video Rendering Technology** software will analyze the video that makes up your movie and will recommend the best video format and profile for outputting your movie in the minimum amount of time in a format as close to your original as possible.

Note that this may not be the best format or profile for your video's particular use.

But is it a good way to determine the best output for any video that you may want to re-use in a future project.

Other video output options

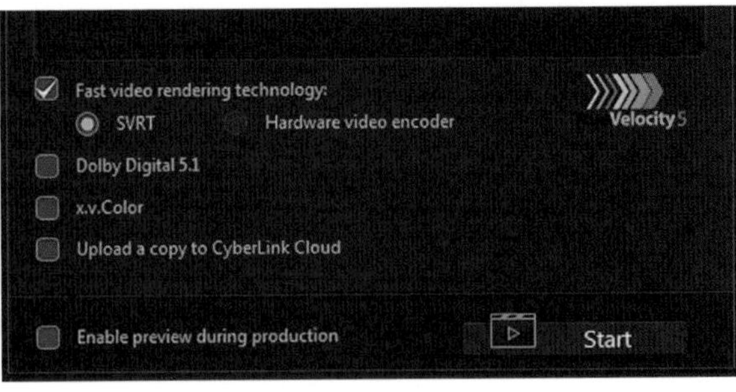

Along the bottom of many of the output panels in the **Produce** workspace panel are other options for your video output. Which options are available depends on the format you've chosen.

Fast Video Rendering Technology will optimize the process of rendering your finished video. Some formats allow you to apply **Smart Video Rendering Technology (SVRT)** and some offer you the option of utilizing the **Hardware Video Encoder.**

Dolby Digital 5.1. If your format allows for it, you have the option of creating a video with 5.1 surround sound. This type of audio, however, is most effective if your source video was actually recorded in 5.1 audio.

x.v.Color is a color system that can display a wider range of color than standard RGB. If this option is available for the video format you've selected, **x.v.Color** is nearly always a good choice.

Upload to the CyberLink Cloud. See the sidebar on page 204.

Output your video for a device

PowerDirector can create an optimized video for hard drive camcorders and portable playback devices, including smartphones, Apple products, Sony PSPs and Microsoft Zunes and XBoxes. It can also stream video back to your tape-based miniDV and HDV camcorder for archiving.

To access these output options, click the **Produce** button at the top of the interface, then select the **Device** tab.

The **DV** and **HDV** options record your video back to your miniDV or HDV tape-based camcorder. To use this output, you'll need to have a

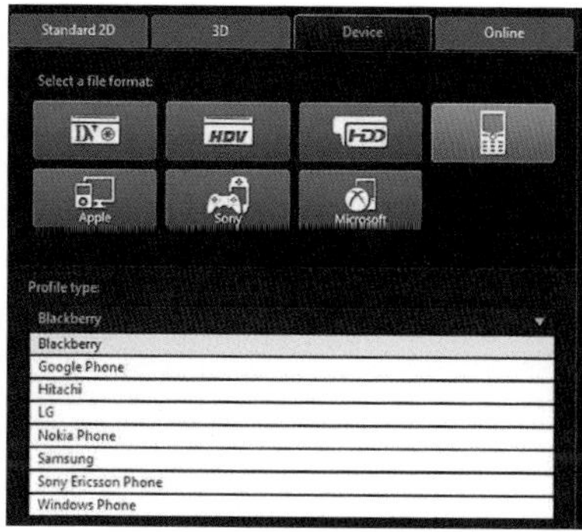

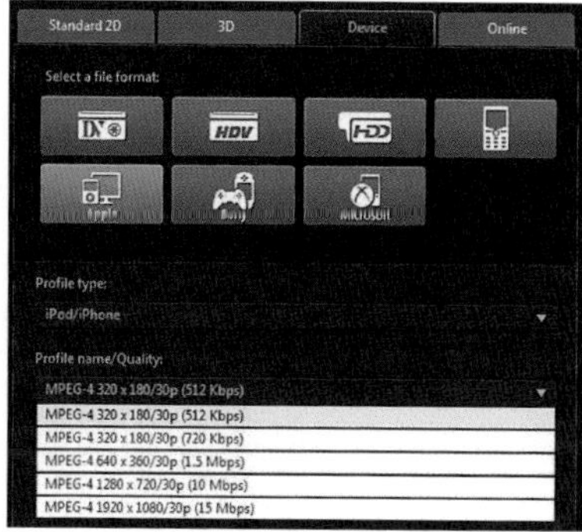

camcorder that's capable of recording video (most newer camcorders are not) and it must be connected to your computer through a FireWire/IEEE-1394 connection. Cue the tape in your camcorder to the point at which you'd like your recording to begin and then click the **Start** button at the bottom of the panel.

The **HDD** option creates a video file that you can later copy to your hard drive camcorder's storage drive or SD card. The video can be created as either 1440x1080 or 1920x1080 high-def, either NTSC or PAL.

The **MPEG-4 Portable** option creates an optimized video for playing on your smartphone. It includes specific profiles for outputting video for Blackberry, Google, LG, Nokia, Samsung, Sony Ericsson and Windows devices.

The **Apple** option creates optimized video for iPods, iPhones and iPads at 320x180, 640x360, 1280x720 and 1920x1080 resolutions.

The **Sony** option creates optimized video for Sony PSPs, PS Vitas, PS3s and video Walkmans.

The **Microsoft** option outputs optimized video for Zunes and XBox 360s.

Many output formats include additional options along the bottom of the panel. For more information on these options, see **Other video output options** at the top of page 178.

To set where your video will be saved to, click the **Output Folder...** button in the lower right of the **Produce** workspace and browse to a location.

To output your video, click the **Start** button at the bottom of the panel.

Post your video to a Social Media site

CyberLink PowerDirector includes tools for loading your videos directly to a number of popular video sharing sites under the **Online** tab.

Facebook, YouTube, Daily Motion, Vimeo and **Youku** include profiles for outputting 320x180, 320x240, 640x360, 640x480, 960x720, 1280x720, 2048x1080 and 2048x1536 video and even 4K at 3840x2160, 4096x2160 and 4096x3072.

Niconico includes profiles for outputting 523x384, 640x360, 800x600, 960x540, 1024x768, 1280x720 and 1920x1080.

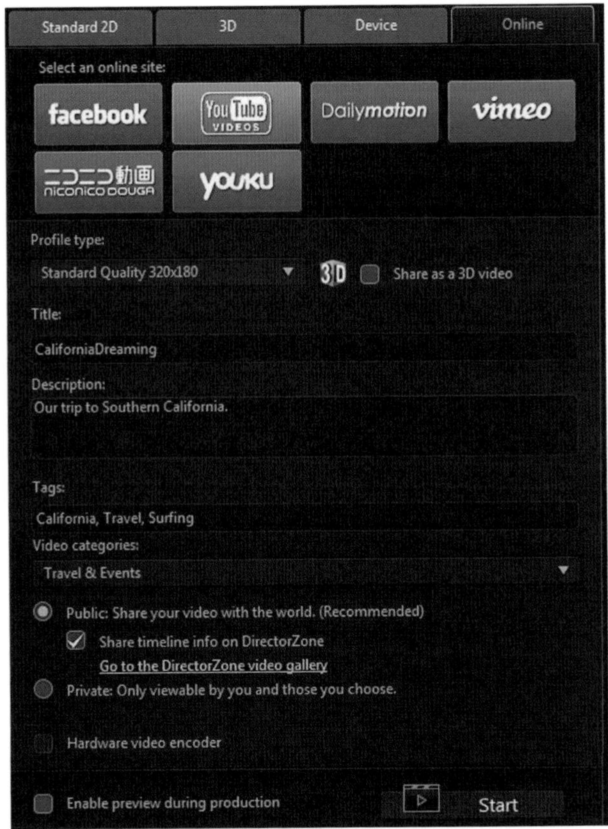

Which resolutions are available depend on whether your project is set up for 4:3 or 16:9.

Note that the **YouTube** uploader includes the option of uploading 3D video from a 3D project.

Once you've selected a site and a profile, give your video a title, description and, if applicable, add tags and select a video category. You can also select whether your video is viewable to the public or by invitation only.

The first time you use the program to interface with these sites, you will need to authorize it. To authorize the program, just follow the prompts, log in to the site and okay the authorization. After that, you'll be logged in every time.

Your output settings may include options for adding a title or tag words to your video, for posting it to a subject category or for setting whether your video is available to the public or to only invited viewers.

To upload your video to a site, click the **Start** button at the bottom of the panel.

Adding Chapters to Your Movie

Adding Content to Your Disc

Selecting a Disc Menu Template

Creating a Custom Menu Template

Saving your Disc Files to Your Hard Drive

2D an d 3D Disc Options

Chapter 16

Disc Authoring

Creating DVDs and BluRay discs

Among the most popular ways to share your movies is on DVDs or BluRay discs.

CyberLink PowerDirector includes a whole array of tools for developing menus and creating professional-looking discs.

The process of adding chapters, designing menus and menu systems and burning these completed videos to a DVD or BluRay disc is called **Disc Authoring**.

PowerDirector has a number of easy-to-use tools for creating great-looking discs with lots of cool elements.

Add Chapters to your video

Chapters are points in your movie you'd like your viewer to be able to jump directly to. When you create the menu for your DVD or BluRay disc, links to these **Chapters** will automatically be added to the menu pages as buttons.

In PowerDirector, as you add **Chapters** to your movie, they'll be indicated by markers on the **Chapter Track**, along the top of your Timeline.

If this track isn't visible, **right-click** on the **Timeline's** track headers and ensure that **Show Chapter Track** is checked.

To add **Chapters** to your movie:

1 **Open the Chapter Room**

This room can be opened by selecting the **Chapter Room** tab along the upper left of the program, as illustrated on the facing page.

The **Chapter Room** includes a number of tools for creating and naming your **Chapters**. Three of these options will add your **Chapters** automatically.

Chapters can be added automatically to every clip on your timeline.

Chapters can be added automatically at regular time intervals.

Chapters can be added automatically based on the number of **Chapters** you want in your movie. These **Chapters** will be evenly spread through your movie.

2 **Manually add Chapters**

Chapters can be manually added to and removed from your movie using the buttons along the lower left of the **Chapter Room**.

Timeline Markers

In addition to **Disc Chapter Markers**, you can also add **Timeline Markers** to your timeline. To create a **Timeline Marker, right-click** on the ticker along the top of the **Timeline** and select **Add Timeline Marker**. You'll be prompted to name the **Marker** and, when you click **OK**, a little blue **Marker** will be added to the ticker.

Unlike **Chapter Markers, Timeline Markers** will not link to your disc menus. However, they can be used as reference points for aligning your movie's clips and trims.

Markers can be deleted by **right-clicking** on them and selecting **Remove**.

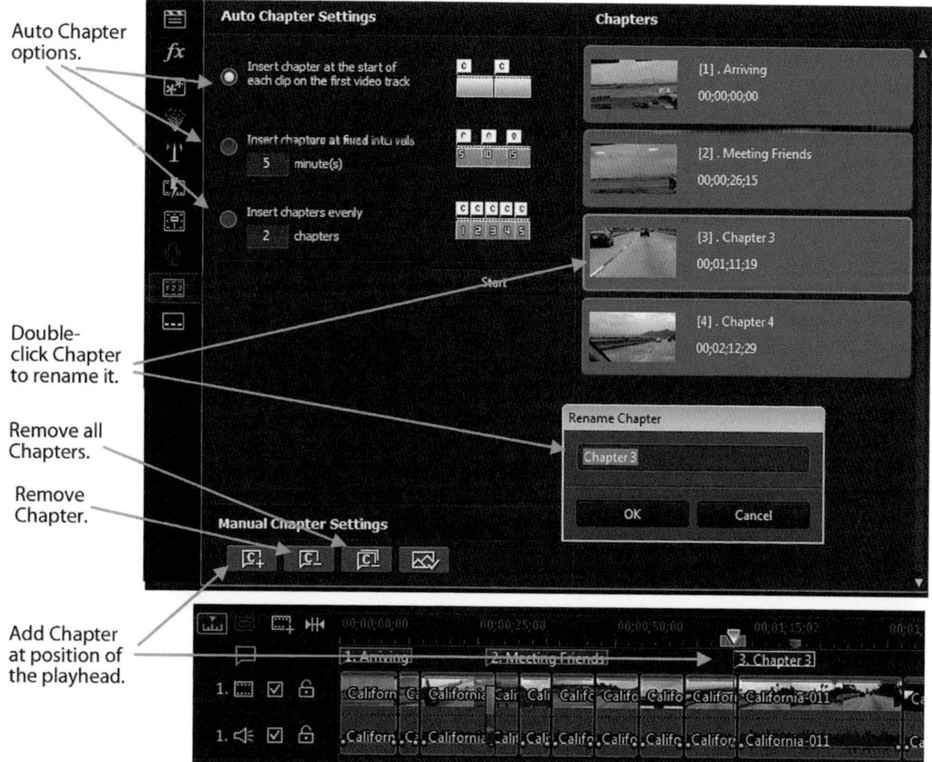

Position the **Timeline** playhead at the spot you'd like to place a **Chapter.** (Note that **Chapter 1** is added to your movie automatically.)

Click the **Add Chapter** button at the bottom of the **Chapter Room.** A **Chapter** will automatically be added to the **Chapter Track** and a thumbnail indicating this **Chapter** will appear in the right side of the **Chapter Room.**

The **Chapter** indicators that PowerDirector creates on your timeline are, of course, editable. You can slide them to a new position or, by clicking the button at the bottom of the **Chapter Room**, opt to remove one or all **Chapters** completely.

3D disc authoring

The process of creating menus and scenes for 3D DVDs and BluRay discs is essentially the same as that for authoring 2D discs.

The main difference is that, for full effect, you should select a 3D menu template – and/or you should adjust the 3D Depth (see page 202) for any text so that it appears to float over your menu page.

3 **Name your Chapters**

After you've created one or all of your movie's **Chapters**, you can customize how they'll appear on your DVD or BluRay menu.

Double-click on a **Chapter** listed on the right-side of the **Chapter Room** (as illustrated the previous page) to open the **Rename Chapter** panel. The name you type in this box will be the name that appears as the **Chapter** button on your disc menu.

4 **Customize your Chapter thumbnail**

Each **Chapter** will appear as text and thumbnail button on your disc's **Chapter** menu page(s).

By default, this thumbnail will be the frame of your video directly under the **Chapter** indicator. However, you can also customize it.

To change the thumbnail image for your **Chapter**, ensure that the **Chapter** is selected in the **Chapter Room** and then position the **Timeline** playhead so that the frame you want to use for your thumbnail is displayed in the **Preview** window.

Click the **Set Current Frame as Chapter Thumbnail** button at the bottom of the **Chapter Room**. Note that changing the thumbnail image does not change the location of the **Chapter** marker itself.

To select which image will appear on your menu button to represent a given Chapter, select the Chapter and position the playhead so that the image you want to appear as a thumbnail is visible in the Preview window – then click the Set Current Frame as Chapter Thumbnail button.

Create your disc menus

To select a menu template for your movie, click on the **Create Disc** button at the top of the program's interface to open the disc authoring workspace.

The left side of **Create Disc** workspace has four tabbed panels:

Content. This is where you'll load whatever videos you want to include on your

disc. The only limit to the number of videos you can add is how much space each takes up on your disc. An indicator at the bottom of the panel shows you approximately how much space your disc has left.

Menu Preferences. This where you'll select the menu template you'd like your disc to use. In addition to the templates on display in this panel, there are thousands more available for download from the **DirectorZone** – and you have the option of creating one from scratch!

2D Disc and **3D Disc**. This is where you'll set the properties for your disc.

On the right side of this workspace is a big **Preview** window in which you can customize the text and layout of your menus as well as tools for adding background music to a menu page, adding a video clip that shows before the first menu and arranging the order that the menu pages play.

Content

Under the **Content** tab, you can add "bonus" videos to your disc.

By default, your current video project will appear at the top of the list.

To include additional videos (say bonus features or a blooper reel), click the **Import Additional Videos** button at the top of the panel. (You can also add PowerDirector projects that haven't yet been output by clicking the **Import PowerDirector Projects** button.)

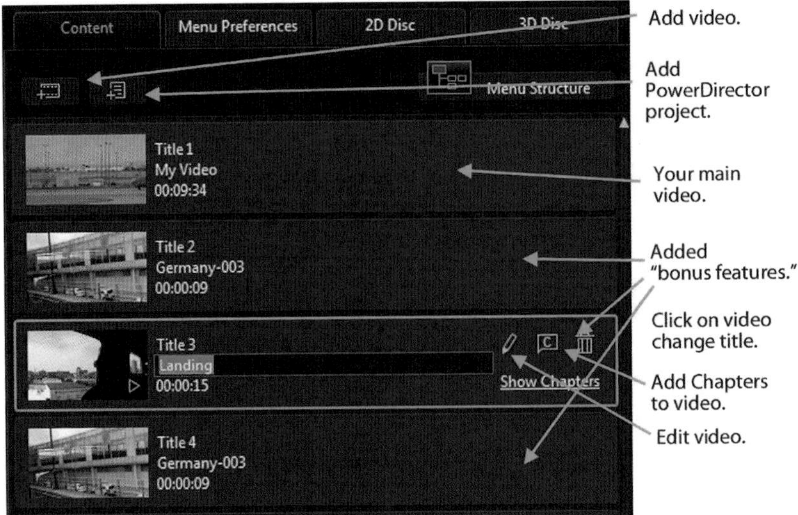

To preview any of these videos, select the video's listing in the **Content** panel and then click the Play button.

To rename a video (and simultaneously change how it will be listed on your disc menu), click on the center of the video's listing and overwrite its current name.

To edit a selected video, click the little pencil icon on the right side of the video's listing.

To add Chapters to a video, click the **Set Chapters** button on the right side of the video's listing.

To remove a video, click the trashcan icon on the right side of its listing or simply select it and press the **Delete** key on your keyboard.

Once you've gathered the videos you want to include on your disc, you can drag them into whatever order you'd like.

The first listed video will be the one that is launched when the **Play** button is clicked on your disc's main or **Root Menu**.

The other videos will be available via a sub-menu, opened by clicking a **Scenes** button on the **Root Menu**.

Select a menu Template

Under the **Menu Preferences** tab, you'll find a library of menu templates.

In addition to the default set of templates included with PowerDirector, if you are logged in to the **DirectorZone**, thousands of additional menu templates can be downloaded free by clicking the **DZ** button in the upper left of this panel. For more information on the **DirectorZone**, see the page 200.

You can also modify an existing template or create one from scratch in the **Menu Designer** (as we show you on page 190).

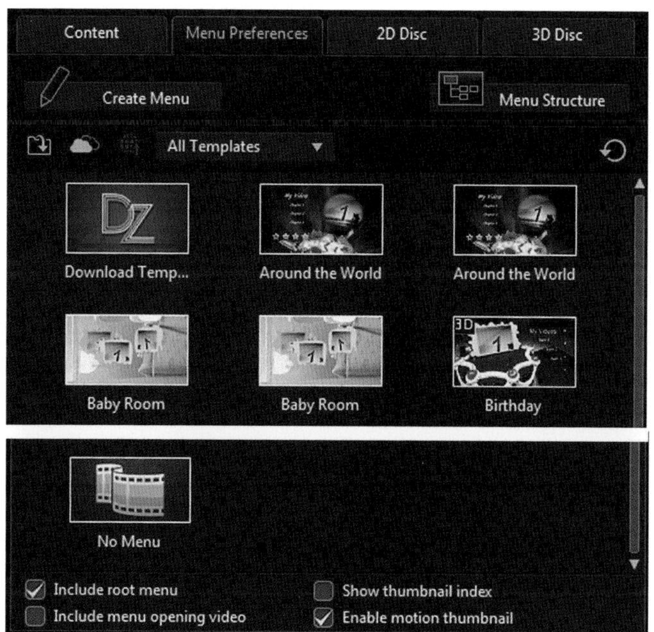

When you click to select a template on this panel, a pop-up panel will display a preview of its **Root Menu** and **Titles/Chapters Menu** designs (including its animation) and will offer you a couple of options:

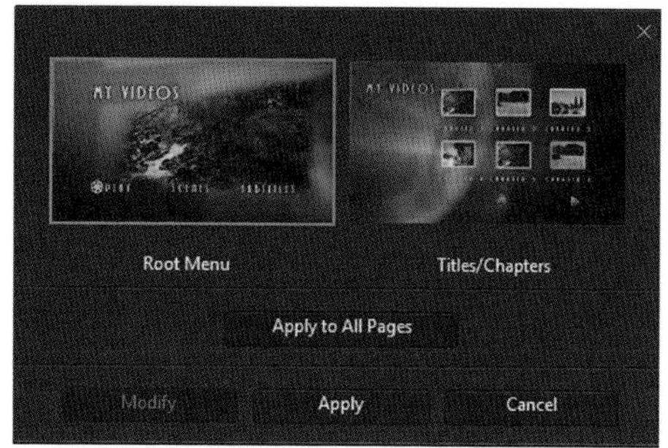

Apply to All Pages applies this menu template design to all menu pages on your disc.

Apply applies this template only to the menu page currently displayed in the **Preview** window.

Modify (available for some but not all templates) opens the template in the **Menu Designer** (see page 190) so that you can customize its look.

Many of these templates include rather elaborate opening animations, which you can watch by clicking the **Preview** button in the lower right of the interface. To opt not to include this opening animation and set your disc to go directly to your **Root Menu** page, check the **Remove Menu Opening Video** option at the bottom of the panel.

Many menu templates also include default music (which can also be replaced with your own music selection), as on page 189.

If you would prefer to create an "auto launch" disc that has no menus and plays as soon as it's loaded into your disc player, select the **No Menu** template option. A disc with no menus will auto-play as soon as it is loaded into a disc player and will play through all of its videos without menus or prompting.

If you have added optional **Subtitles** to your movie (see **Chapter 14**), the **Root Menu** will automatically include a link to a menu in which your viewer can turn these subtitles on or off.

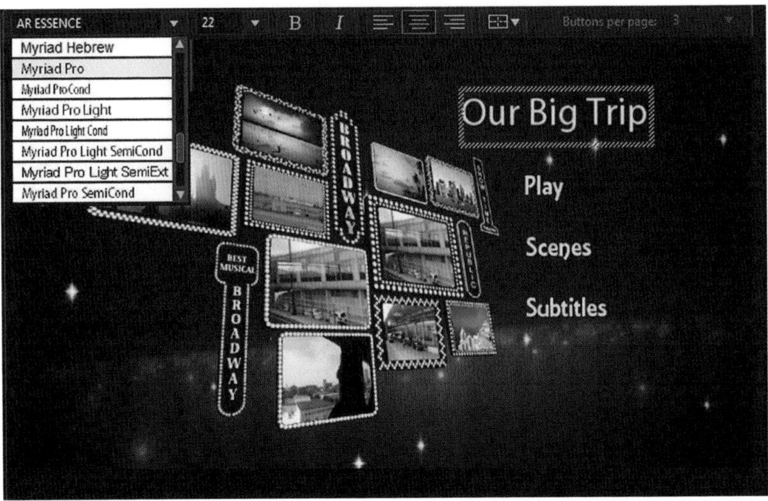

Edit your menu's text

To customize any text on your menu pages – including renaming buttons and links – click to select the text in the **Preview** window.

When a text box is selected in the **Preview** window, an option panel will appear along the top of this window in which you can set your font, size, style and paragraph alignment (as illustrated above).

When applying these text characteristics, you can select and apply them to one or several blocks of text at the same time.

Text blocks and links can also be dragged to any spot on your menu page.

Add menu background music and add a first play video

In the lower right of the **Create Disc** workspace are tools for adding **Background Music** or a **First Play Video** to your disc.

Most menu templates include music, and this music will be added as **Background Music** automatically. But if you'd like to add your own, custom music, you have two options.

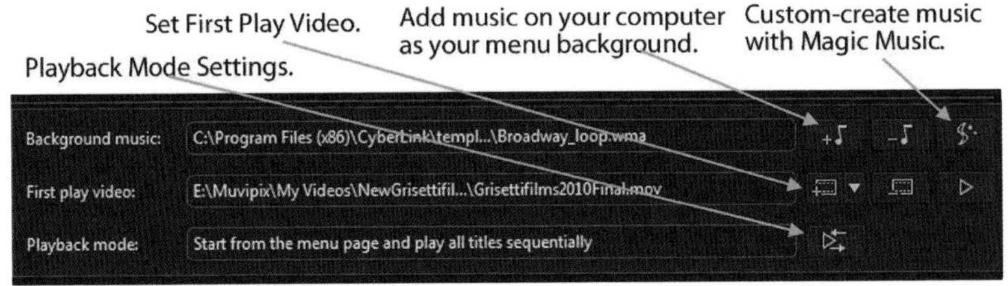

Click the **Set Background Music** button to browse to any music file on your computer's hard drive(s); or

Click the **Magic Music** button to create a custom-designed soundtrack for your disc menus. For more information on using the PowerDirector's **Magic Music**/SmartSound tool, see page 86.

First Play Videos are short videos (an animated logo, for instance) that play when your disc first loads, before the **Root Menu** appears.

To add a **First Play Video**, click the **Set First Play Video** button and browse to the video file on your computer.

Playback Mode is the order your videos and menus display on your disc.

On the **Playback Mode Settings** panel, for instance, you can set whether all of the videos linked to a menu page play one after another or if the viewer returns to the menu page after each video plays, as illustrated below.

Playback Mode, by the way, only affects the "bonus" videos you've added to your disc on the **Content** panel. When your viewer selects the option to jump to a **Chapter** in your movie, the video will *always* play through from that point to the end of your movie. It will not return to the menu at the end of that **Chapter**.

To open this option panel, click the **Playback Mode Settings** button in the lower right of the **Create Disc** workspace, as illustrated at the bottom of the facing page.

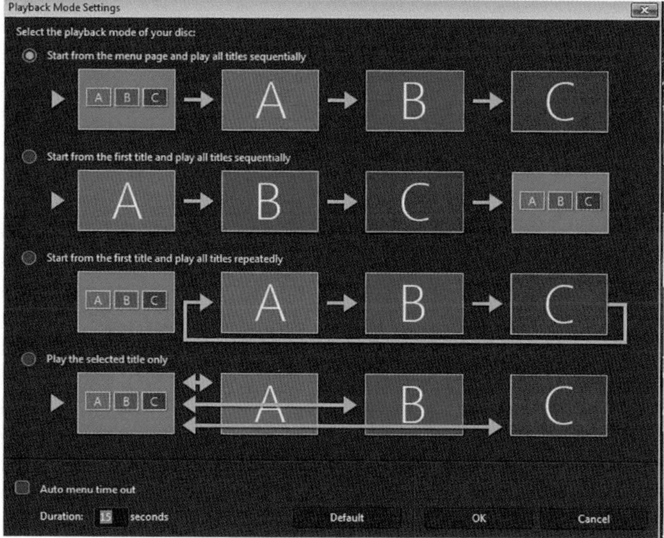

Navigate the disc's Menu Structure

At any point, as you're authoring your disc, you have the option of checking out the disc's **Menu Structure**. To open **Menu Structure** panel, click the button at the top of the **Content** or **Menu Preferences** panel.

The **Menu Structure** panel will display the pathways of your disc, spreading from the **Root Menu** to all of the individual menu pages and videos.

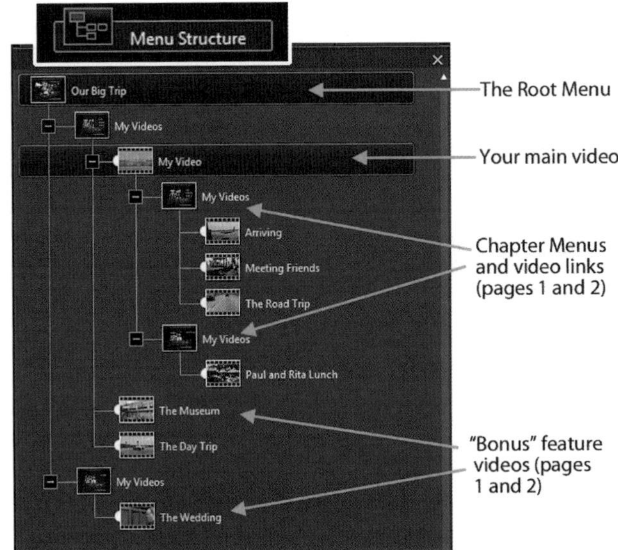

You can get a closer look at the layout of any of your menu pages by selecting it in the **Menu Structure** panel. This menu page will appear in the **Preview** window.

The **Menu Structure** panel is a great workspace for confirming and troubleshooting the arrangement of your disc's pages and links.

To close this panel and return to the **Content** or **Menu Preferences** panel, click the **X** in the upper right corner.

Preview your menus

Before you burn your disc, you'll want to take it for one final test drive.

To do so, click the **Preview** button in the lower right of the **Create Disc** workspace.

You'll be able to navigate using the various buttons and check out the disc's menu structure.

Create and modify templates in the Menu Designer

The **Menu Designer** is a workspace for customizing existing menu templates and creating new menu templates pretty much from scratch.

To modify an existing menu template, select the template on the **Menu Preferences** panel and, on the pop-option panel, click the **Modify** button. (Note that not all templates can be modified.)

To create a menu from scratch, click the **Create Menu** button at the top left of the **Menu Preferences** panel.

The **Menu Designer** will open to your selected template or to a generic **Root Menu** page with some basic objects and text over a black background.

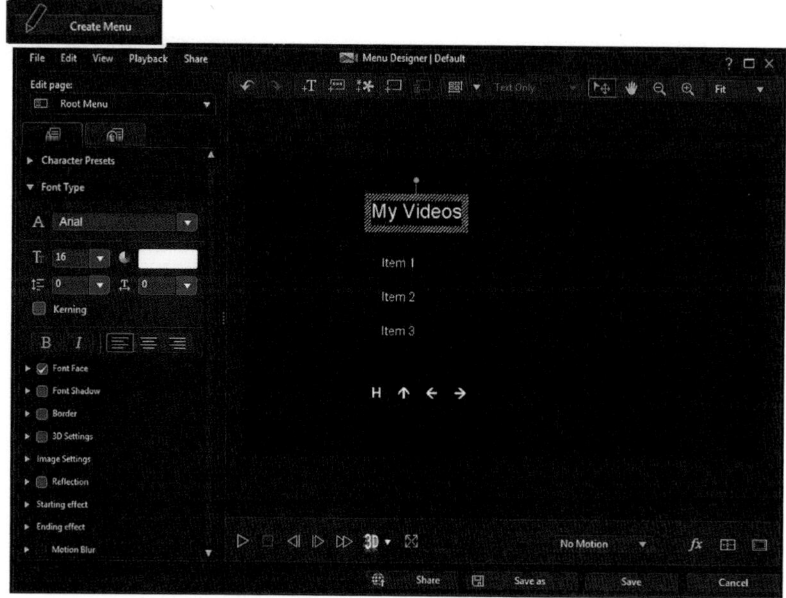

Design a Root Menu, Titles/Chapter Menu and Subtitle Menu

At the top left of the panel is an **Edit Page** drop-down menu. From this menu you can choose whether to edit the **Root Menu** template, the **Titles/Chapter Menu** template or the **Subtitles Menu** template. (All pages in your generated disc menus, other than the **Root Menu** and the **Subtitle Menu,** will be based on the **Titles/Chapter Menu** template.)

Text, objects and button highlights

On the panel to the left of the **Preview** window are three tabs in which you can add, remove and modify elements on your page.

Text Properties define the text characteristics of whatever text block you have selected in the **Preview** window. (You can also drag over or press **Ctrl+a** to select all at once.) On this properties panel you'll find **Character Presets** or text styles, fonts and font properties, **Font Face Settings** (which set the color, transparency and blurriness of the font), options for adding drop shadows under your text, borders around it or reflections under it. If you are working on a menu for a 3D disc, you can also make your text appear to float over the background by adjusting **3D Depth** under the **3D Settings** (see page 202).

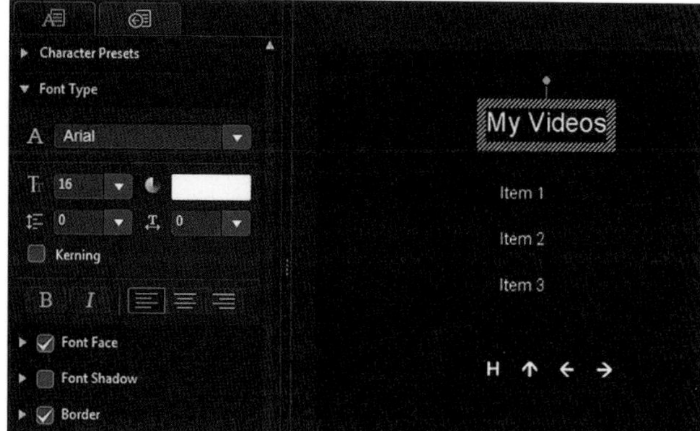

Among these properties are **Starting Effects** and **Ending Effects** from which you can select the animation effect, if any, your text uses to appear on or disappear from your menu page.

Button Properties

Button Properties is a library of custom **Navigation Button** looks, which you can use to replace a selected button on your menu template. The panel also includes a library of **Button Highlights** that you can select to appear as highlights when your viewer is navigating over your menu page.

Among the **Button Properties** are **Button Layout** templates for arranging the placement of the buttons on your menu page, as illustrated at the bottom of the facing page.

The four graphic buttons, by the way, that appear along the bottom of your menu page template are:

Home, which takes the viewer to the **Root Menu** page.

Up, which takes the viewer up one menu level.

Left and **Right**, which the viewer can use to go from page to page if, say, your disc includes several pages of **Chapter** buttons.

The menu background and additional objects

Along the top and bottom of the **Preview** window are more tools for adding and replacing elements on your menu page design.

Insert Text allows you to place additional text on the menu page. (After you click the button, click anywhere on the **Preview** window and start typing.)

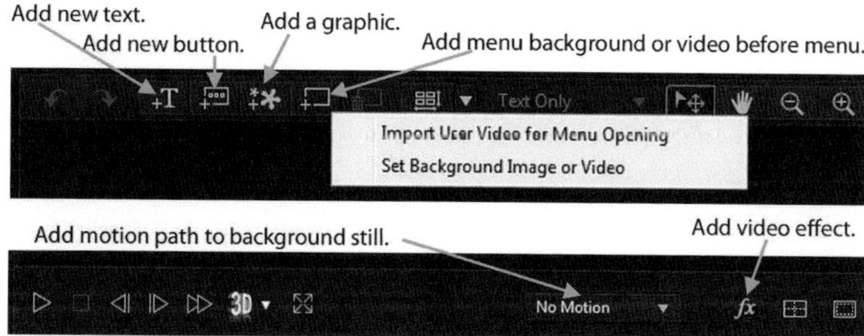

Add Button creates a new button on your menu page, increasing the number of **Chapters** or links to videos that can appear on any page.

Add Image allows you to import additional images or graphics for your menu page's design.

Set Background Image or Video gives you options for adding a video before the menu page or for adding a custom still photo or video as the menu page's background.

Additionally, in the lower right of the **Preview** window is a drop-down menu for adding motion to your menu background. (This feature is only available if you've added a still photo as your menu background.)

Motion options for **Background Image** include a **Pan, a Zoom, a Zoom and Pan** combination or a **Random** motion.

Background music for your menu is selected in the main **Create Disc** workspace rather than in the **Menu Designer** (see page 188).

When editing the Titles/Chapter Menu pages of your template, you can add, arrange customize the look of and resize your button thumbnails.

Final tweaks

At the lower right of the **Preview** window are additional tools for adding video effects, aligning any objects you have selected and a switch for toggling on the **TV Safe Zone** (see page 153).

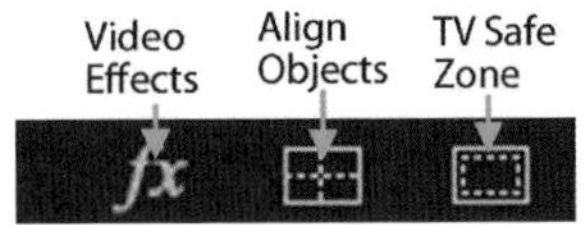

Click the **Play** button below the **Preview** window to test drive the menu page (including a video before the menu, if you've selected that option.)

Save your DVDs and BluRay disc files to your hard drive

PowerDirector offers you the option of burning your disc directly from the program, creating a **Folder** of your DVD or BluRay disc files or creating an **ISO** file.

An **ISO** is an image file, a format in which all of the video, audio and menu navigation is saved as a single file. Appropriately, this file will have .iso as its suffix.

ISO files and disc **folders** can be saved or archived to your computer's hard drive and then burned to a DVD or BluRay disc whenever you need to output a fresh copy.

To save your DVD or BluRay disc as an image file or as a set of folders, click on the **Burn in 2D** or **Burn in 3D button** in the lower right of the **Create Disc** workspace. On the option screen that opens, select the **Save as Disc Image** and/or **Create a Folder** option and set the save to location.

For information on burning an **ISO** or **folder** as a DVD or BluRay disc, see page 196.

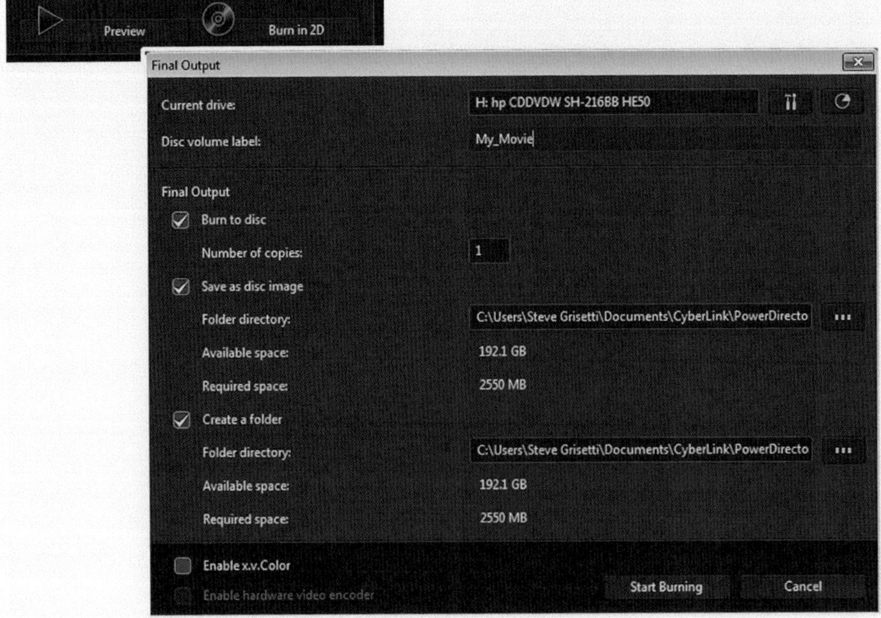

Save your template design

Remember that a complete menu template consists of a design for the **Root Menu**, a design for the **Titles/Chapter Menu** and a design for the **Subtitles Menu** (though they'll likely share a similar style or theme).

When you've finished these three page menu designs, click the **Save** button at the bottom of the panel and name your template. Your template will be saved to the **Custom Menu Preferences** library.

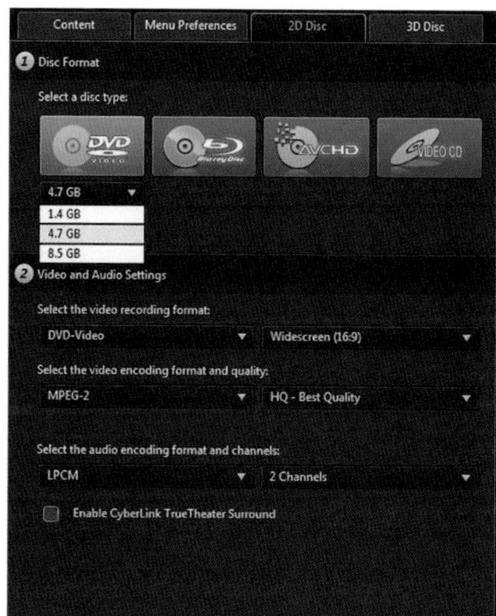

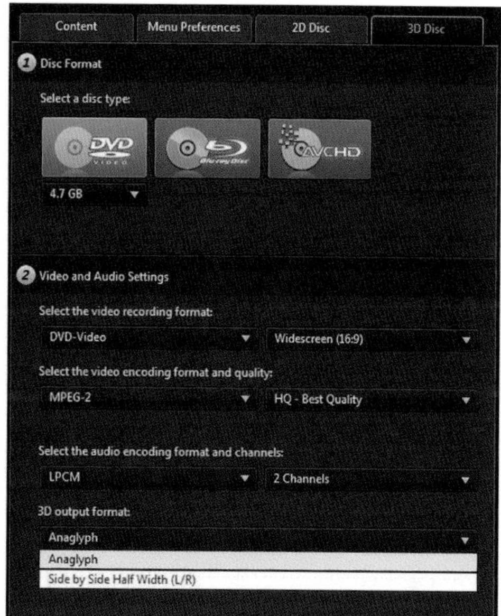

The 2D Disc and 3D Disc option panels

Under the **2D Disc** and **3D Disc** tabs are options for setting the type of disc you want to output and your audio and video preferences

A **DVD** is a standard definition video, the most common disc produced. DVDs can be burned to a 4.7 gigabyte disc, an 8.5 gigabyte dual-layer disc or, on rare occasions, a 1.4 gigabyte discs. Audio and video options for a DVD include the option for setting whether the disc is a 4:3 or 16:9 video and if the audio is 2-channel stereo or 5.1 surround sound.

A **BluRay Disc** is a high-definition video. BluRays can be burned to 25 gigabyte or 50 gigabyte discs and, on rare occasions, a 100 and a 128 gigabyte disc. A BluRay's video can be encoded as either H.264 (AVC) or MPEG-2. BluRay audio can be either 2-channel stereo or 5.1 surround sound.

An **AVCHD** disc is, essentially, a BluRay video burned to a DVD disc. This disc can only be played on a BluRay player (and not on all of them) and its audio can be either 2 channel stereo or 5.1 audio. AVCHD video can also be saved to a removable disc, memory card or memory stick and then played back on a computer.

A **Video CD** is a lower quality video that is burned to a CD. Video CDs can not be widescreen video and can not include 5.1 audio. In fact, Video CDs are really obsolete technology, and, in my not so humble opinion, you shouldn't even bother with them.

As a rule of thumb, a standard **DVD can hold about 70-80 minutes of video** at full quality. A dual-layer DVD can hold about twice that.

A 25 gigabyte **BluRay disc can hold about two hours of high-definition video**. A 50 gigabyte disc can hold about twice that.

A 4.7 gigabyte **DVD disc can old about 20 minutes of AVCHD video**, and an 8.5 gigabyte dual-layer DVD disc and hold about twice that.

Options for your 3D Disc properties are similar to those for 2D Discs, except that 3D Discs include an option for setting the disc's **3D Output Format**.

The **Anaglyphic** option will output your stereoscopic video channels as shades of red and cyan. Anaglyphic video can be viewed on any device, using inexpensive blue/red glasses.

The **Side-by-Side Half Width L/R** option will output your video with Multi-View Coding (MVC). MVC video requires a 3D monitor or TV to view in 3D (although this video will play as 2D on a standard TV also). This 3D format also does not support standard 2D disc menus or optional subtitles.

The **3D-BD** option is only available for BluRay discs and can only be played on a BD 3D player and viewed on a 3D television.

Burn a folder or ISO file to a disc

Most disc authoring tools (including Nero and CyberLink's PowerDVD) include features for creating DVDs or BluRay discs from a **VIDEO_TS folder** or an **ISO** file. Additionally, you can burn discs from these files using the indispensable free program **ImgBurn** (a free download from www.imgburn.com).

To burn a DVD or AVCHD disc from your **Burn to Folder** files using ImgBurn, select **Write Files/Folders to Disc** from the ImgBurn main menu. When the software opens, click the **Source/Folder** button and browse to and select the **VIDEO_TS** folder that was created when you burned your DVD or AVCHD files to a folder, then click the **Burn** button.

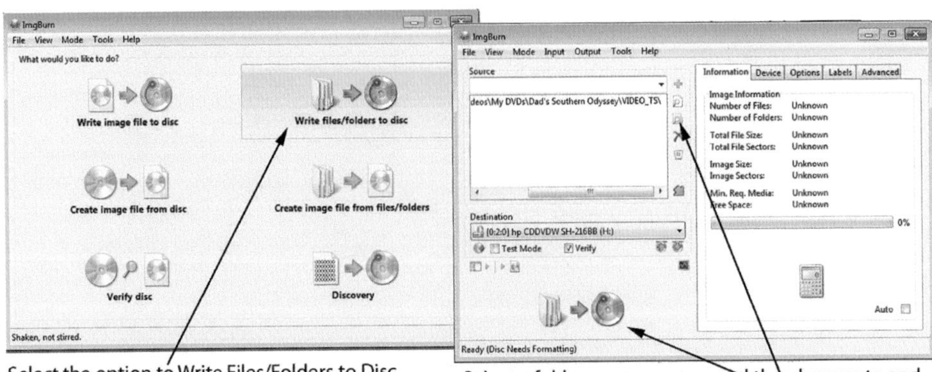

Select the option to Write Files/Folders to Disc from main ImgBurn page.

Select a folder as your source and then browse to and select your DVD's VIDEO_TS folder. Click Burn.

To burn a DVD, AVCHD disc or BluRay from your **Burn to ISO** files using ImgBurn, select **Write Image File to Disc** from the ImgBurn main menu. When the software opens, click the **Source** button and browse to and select the **ISO** file, then click the **Burn** button.

ImgBurn will automatically unpack the ISO file and create a playable DVD or BluRay, with menus, from its files.

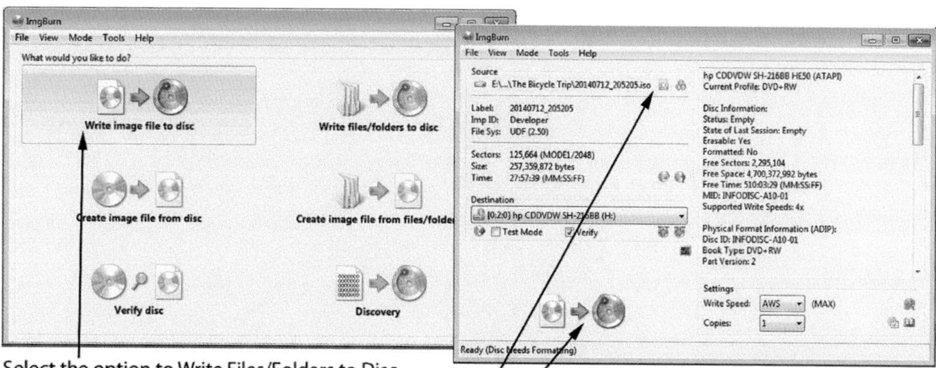

Select the option to Write Files/Folders to Disc from main ImgBurn page.

Browse to select your ISO file as your Source, then click Burn.

The DirectorZone and the CyberLink Cloud

Grabbing a Snapshot/Freeze Frame from Your Video

Using Shadow Files

Adding Favorites

Stereo and 5.1 Audio

Intelligent SRVT

Blurring a Face Like on TV's COPS

Chapter 17

An Appendix

More things worth knowing

In addition to the basic workings of the program, there are a number of additional things about the program worth knowing.

Here, in no particular order, is some extra knowledge for making your PowerDirector editing experience a little bit easier.

What's the difference between PowerDirector Deluxe, Ultra and Ultimate?

Some program features aren't included in the more basic Deluxe version (**MultiCam Editing, 3D Editing** and **Content Aware Editing**, for instance). But, for the most part, the main difference between the versions is the content (the effects package, for instance) included with it.

The Ultra and Ultimate versions of the program themselves function virtually identically.

The "suite" versions, like the Ultimate and top-of-the-line Director Suites, come bundled with additional programs (like ColorDirector and AudioDirector).

For a complete comparison of the versions of the program, go to: www.cyberlink.com/products/powerdirector and click the Comparison button.

What is the DirectorZone?

The **DirectorZone** is a free library of effects and templates, available to any PowerDirector user.

To access this library, simply click on the blue **DZ** button you'll find throughout the program.

To sign up or log in to the **DirectorZone**, click the **Sign In** button in the upper right of the PowerDirector interface or open the program's preferences (by clicking on the **cog** at the top center of the interface) and selecting the **DirectorZone** page.

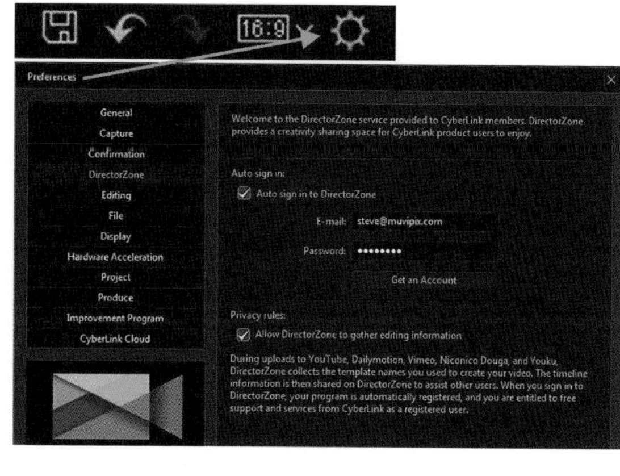

Among the cool stuff available at the **DZ** are **PiP Objects, Particle** effects, **Title** templates, **Disc Menu** templates, **Magic Movie** Styles, **Sound Clips** and sound effects and **Video Presets** for creating stylish video looks.

As of the writing of this book, there are over half a million templates and effects available.

Most of the effects and templates available at the **DirectorZone** were created by fellow users.

And, in fact, you can upload your own designs simply by clicking the **Share** button along the bottom of any **Designer** panel or by clicking the **Globe** icon at the top left of many of the **Rooms**, as discussed in **What is the CyberLink Cloud?** on page 204.

How can I grab a frame or take a snapshot of my video?

To save a still photo "snapshot" of the video currently visible in the **Preview** window, click the **Take Snapshot** (camera) button along the bottom of the Preview window.

A **Snapshot** can be saved from a 2D project as a .bmp, .jpg, .gif or .png. A **Snapshot** can be saved from a 3D project as an .mpo or .jps.

Once you save a **Snapshot** of your video, this still will be added to your **Media Room** library and you can then use it in your video project.

To select the type of image file your **Snapshot** will be saved as and where this file will be saved to, open the program's preferences (by click the **cog** at the top center of the interface) and go to the **File** page.

If you'd like to just freeze the playback of your video rather than grab a frame and save it as a still photo, you can simply **right-click** on a clip on your timeline and select **Edit Video/Image**, then **Freeze Frame**. A 5-second still of the current video frame will be inserted into your project's timeline.

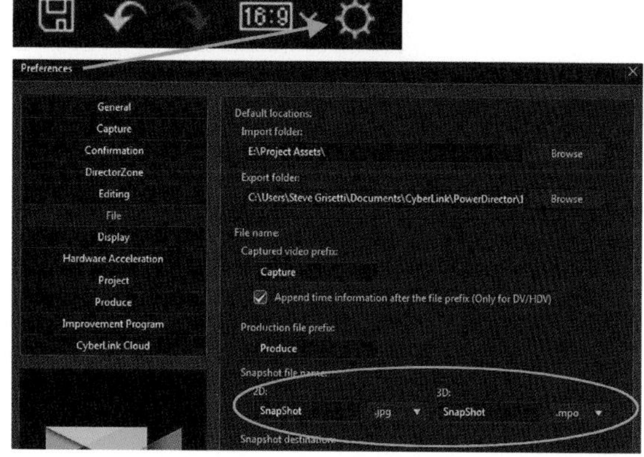

Also, in version 14, a much more sophisticated tool has been added for freezing your video as well as for adding cool time shift effects to your playback. For information on using this new **Freeze Frame** tool, see **The Video Speed Designer** on page 66.

What are "shadow files?"

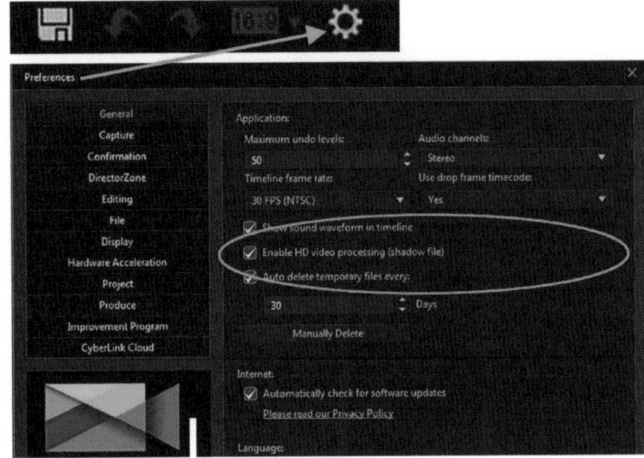

Shadow Files are proxy files that PowerDirector automatically creates in order to make the editing of high-resolution video more efficient.

While you are editing a high-definition video format that stresses your system resources, PowerDirector creates low resolution versions of your video file, which it uses in place of the larger, more challenging files throughout the editing process.

When you are ready to produce your finished video or disc, PowerDirector then applies your editing data to your original, full-definition video files in order to produce a full quality output.

To enable or disable **Shadow File** editing, open the program's preferences (click on the **Cog** at the top center of the interface) and go to the **General** page.

Where can I set my project to 5.1 surround sound rather than stereo?

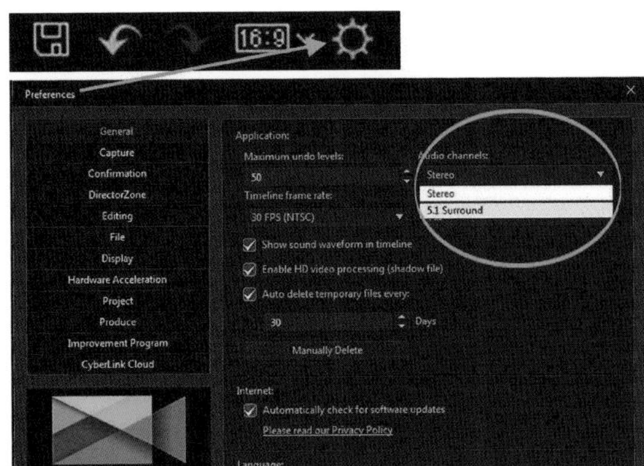

You can access this option by opening the program's preferences (by clicking on the **cog** at the top center of the interface) and going to the **Audio Channel** preference on the **General** page.

When you output your finished video, select the 5.1 option, as discussed on page 178 and page 195.

What is 3D Depth?

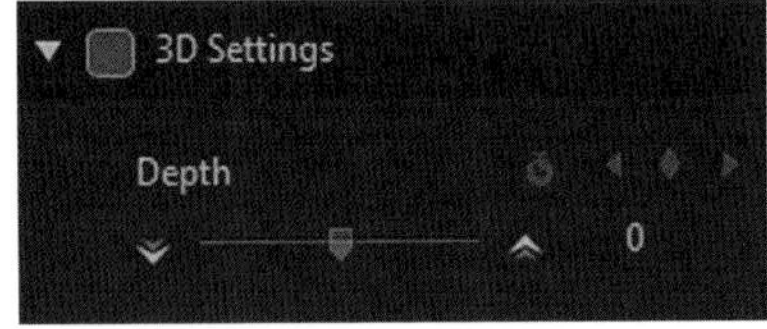

3D Depth is a setting for text or titles that are used in a stereoscopic 3D project.

Adjusting the **3D Depth** can make your text or a picture-in-picture appear closer in 3D space, as if your text or video clip is floating over the rest of your video.

What is Intelligent SVRT?

Intelligent SVRT stands for Intelligent Smart Video Rendering Technology, a tool that the program uses to analyze your source video and recommend the fastest and most efficient output format for your project.

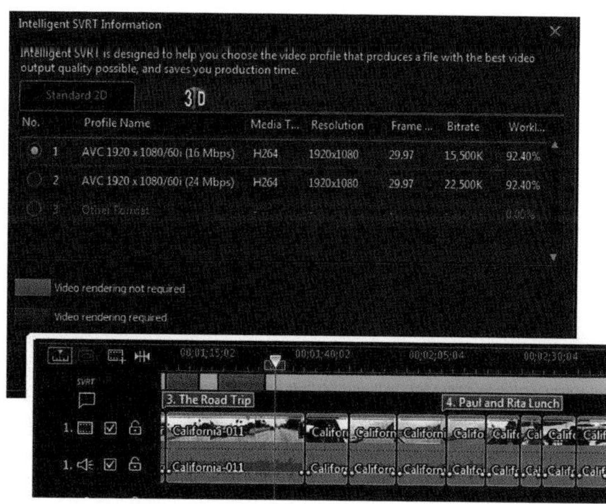

To view **Intelligent SRVT** information while you are editing, toggle on the **SVRT Track** on your timeline (**right-click** on the track headers and ensure that **Show SVRT Track** is checked).

The green line along the **SRVT Track** displays the segments of your video that will not need to be re-rendered if you use the SRVT-recommended output format.

To re-open this panel while you are editing, **double-click** on the green or red bar along the **SVRT Track.**

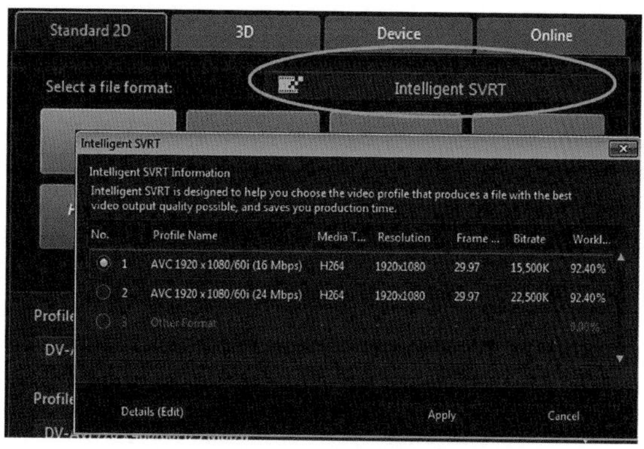

An **SRVT** analysis and recommendation can also be run in the **Produce** workspace by clicking on the **Intelligent SRVT** button a the top of the **Standard 2D** or **3D** panel. In the **Intelligent SRVT** pop-up panel, the program will recommend the most efficient output settings for your project's video.

To accept the **SRVT's** recommendation, click the panel's **Apply** button. The program will automatically set your output specs to this setting.

How can I add a time stamp to my videos?

The **Time Stamp** effect can be found in the **FX Room**, under the **Text Masking** category.

To display the **Time Stamp** over your movie, drag this effect to the **FX Track** and then stretch it to cover your entire movie.

To customize how and where the **Time Stamp** appears, select the **Time Stamp** effect and click the **Modify** function button along the top of the **Timeline.**

In the **Effects Settings** panel that opens, you'll be able to set the font, color and where in your video frame the **Time Stamp** appears.

What are Favorites?

Favorites, as you'd expect, are video effects or transitions that you especially like and you'd like easy access to.

To add an effect or transition to your **Favorites**, **right-click** on it in the **FX Room** or **Transition Room** and select **Add To/My Favorites**. The effect or transition can then be easily accessed by clicking that Room's **My Favorites** tag.

You'll also find the option to "favorite" **Character Presets** in the **Menu Designer** and the **Title Designer.** To save a **Character Preset** as a **Favorite**, select the preset you'd like to **Favorite** and then click the **Save Currently Selected Character as Preset** button to the right of the **Character Presets/Character Types** drop-down menu.

What is the CyberLink Cloud?

The **CyberLink Cloud** is a online storage bank (included free with most versions of PowerDirector) where you can save videos, effects and templates that you've created, and then access them from any computer anywhere in the world that is logged into your **Cloud** account. This includes devices, like phones and tablets, that are running the mobile version of PowerDirector.

Among the media you can save to the **CyberLink Cloud** are:

Program preferences and customized output profiles.

Produced videos or video segments.

Pip Objects, Particles, Transitions, Paint Animations, Title Effects and **Disc Menu Templates** that you've customized or created.

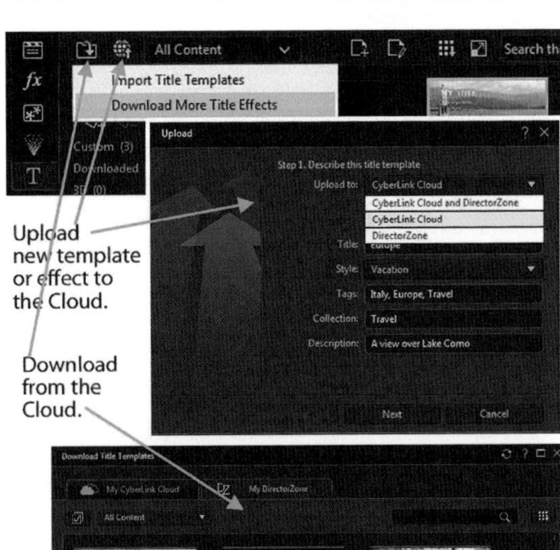

Unlike designs that you upload to the **DirectorZone**, templates and other media that you back up to the **Cloud** will only be available to a computer or mobile device that is logged into *your* personal **Cloud** account. In other words, the **Cloud** is your personal backup and storage area.

To back up or restore your program preferences, open the **Preferences** by clicking the **Cog** at the top center of the program and go to the **Cloud** page. Click the **Back up** or **Restore** button.

To upload effects or templates that you've created to your **Cloud** account (or to the **DirectorZone**), click the **Globe** icon in the upper left of the **Room** into which you've saved your custom effect or template, as illustrated to the right. (You can also click the **Share** button from many **Designer** workspaces.)

On the **Upload** panel, illustrated at the bottom of the facing page, you'll find options for naming and categorizing your design as well as for indicating whether your design will upload to your personal **Cloud**, be shared with your fellow videomakers on the **DirectorZone** site or both.

To access effects, media and templates you've uploaded to your **Cloud** account, click on the **Folder** icon in the upper left of an effect or template **Room** and select **Download More**, as illustrated on the bottom of the facing page.

How do I blur a face like on TV's COPS?

Occasionally you run into a scene that requires a little censorship.

Sometimes it's to hide something offensive in your movie. Sometimes there's someone in your movie who doesn't want to be in your movie.

The simplest way to salvage the footage is to blur the area of the video you want to censor beyond recognition – the way they blur or pixelate faces of people and license plate numbers on the TV show COPS.

This effect can be created using traditional keyframing, as described on the following pages, or by using the new **Motion Tracker**. For information on tracking an object or person in your video and then hiding this object or the person's face with a **Mosaic Effect**, see the discussion of the **Motion Tracker**, starting on page 98.

1 **Place your clip Video 1**

Ensure that the video clip you want to censor is on the **Video 1** track.

Move the playhead to the beginning of the clip, or to the point at which you'd like your blur to begin.

2 **Add the Mosaic effect to the FX Track**

Open the video effects library by clicking on the **FX Room** tab in the upper left of the program.

Locate the **Mosaic** effect and drag it to the **FX Track** on the **Timeline**, along the **Video 1** clip you want to censor.

Stretch or trim the length of this effect so that it begins where you'd like your blur to begin and ends where you'd like it to end.

The entire video segment covered by the **Mosaic** effect will the pixelated beyond recognition.

3 **Open the Mosaic Effects Settings**

Select **Mosaic** effect on the **FX Track** and then click the **Modify** function button along the top of the **Timeline**.

The **Effects Settings** panel will open. If you'd like, you can fine tune the **Mosaic** effect. A **Height** and **Width** of about 10 seems to work best for me.

4 **Open Keyframe Settings**

Click the **Keyframe** button on the **Effects Settings** panel.

The **Keyframe Settings** panel will open. A keyframe will already be created for the current position of the **Mask**, at the beginning of the effect's **Timeline**.

5 **Create an initial Mosaic Mask motion keyframe**

Without moving the playhead on the **Keyframe Settings** panel, click the **Mask** button, as illustrated at the bottom of the facing page.

6 **Size and position the Effects Mask**

Drag the corner handles on the **Mask** panel to size and position the **Effects Mask** so that the **Mosaic** effect is only over the person or object you're trying to censor.

Click **OK**.

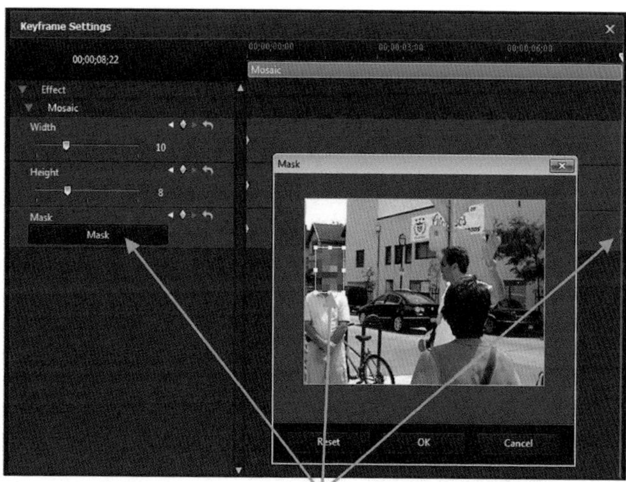

Move the playhead to the end of the effect's timeline and reposition the Mask as needed. A new keyframe will be automatically created.

7 **Create a closing Mosaic Mask motion keyframe**

Assuming the person or object you're trying to censor moves around the video frame over the course of the clip, you'll need to animate the **Mask's** position to follow him or it.

Drag the **Keyframe Settings** playhead or press the **End** button on your keyboard so that the playhead is moved to the end of the effect's **Timeline**.

Click the **Mask** button again and reposition the blurred area on the **Mask** panel so that it is again over the person or object you want to censor. Click **OK**.

A new keyframe will be created on the **Mask's** timeline.

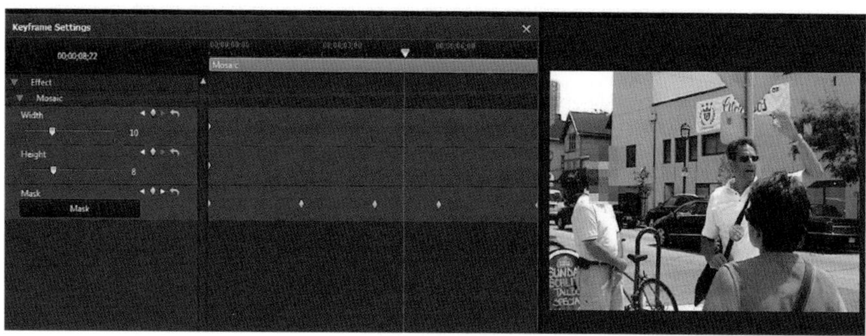

8 **Create additional keyframes**

Slowly drag the playhead from the beginning to the end of the **Keyframe's Settings Timeline**, watching the **Preview** window as you do.

Whenever the person or object you're trying to censor slips out from behind the **Mosaic** blur, click the **Mask** button and reposition the blur. When you click **OK**, a new keyframe will be created for that **Effects Mask** position.

When you've finished, the program will create an animation for your **Mosaic** area so that this pixelation follows the person or object you want to censor throughout your clip.

Symbols

A

B

C

17098493R00124

Printed in Great Britain
by Amazon